D1077225

Are We Nearly There?
A Complete Guide to Travelling With Babies, Toddlers and Children

Are We Nearly There?

A Complete Guide to Travelling With Babies,
Toddlers and Children

Samantha Gore-Lyons

First published in Great Britain in 2000 by
Virgin Publishing Ltd
Thames Wharf Studios
Rainville Road
London W6 9HA

Copyright © Samantha Gore-Lyons 2000

Figure 1 © Random Publishing
Figures 7–9 taken from *The ABC of Resuscitation*, edited by TR Evans, © BMJ
Publishing Group, 1986 (Third imprint of first edition).
Figure 10 taken from *The ABC of Resuscitation*, edited by TR Evans, © BMJ
Publishing Group, 1999 (Fourth edition).

The right of Samantha Gore-Lyons to be identified as the author of this work has
been asserted by her in accordance with the Copyright Designs and Patents Act
1988.

This book is sold subject to the condition that it shall not, by way of trade or
otherwise, be lent, resold, hired out or otherwise circulated without the publisher's
prior written consent in any form of binding or cover other than that in which it is
published and without a similar condition including this condition being imposed
upon the subsequent purchaser.

A catalogue record for this book is available from the British Library.

ISBN 0 7535 0399 9

Typeset by TW Typesetting, Plymouth, Devon

Printed and bound in Great Britain by Cox & Wyman Ltd, Reading, Berks

*To my accompanying adventurer
and perfect travelling companion,
my little boy Paris James*

Contents

PART TWO: PREPARATION

PART THREE: WHILE YOU ARE AWAY

List of Figures

Acknowledgements

With grateful thanks to my father Dr Peter Gore for his indispensable input and essential support of the facts.

To all the mothers I have quizzed about their own experiences and the mistakes they have made when travelling with children.

Many thanks to the National Meteorological Library and Archive for their assistance, and for taking the time and trouble to provide me with information about world weather conditions.

Pasteur Merieux MSD for their objective advice and supply of vital literature and information.

Random Publishing for kindly permitting us to reprint Figure 1, which simplifies humidity and temperature relative to comfort.

The Liverpool School of Tropical Medicine for the use of their library.

Author's Note

The information contained within this book is correct at the time of going to print. Malaria prophylaxis changes constantly and epidemics break out in every country of the world from time to time. Travel clinics will be able to advise you of current risks that develop.

Advice is not intended to be a substitute for skilled medical care if good care is available.

Introduction

The first time I travelled abroad with my son he was a stowaway. We had visited five countries together before I even knew he existed.

After an overnight coach journey from Manchester to London, I jumped on a train bound for Moscow on impulse and alone, and unaware that I was pregnant. During the five-day trip I was arrested, molested and deported with smugglers. I arrived in Warsaw in the middle of the night where, unable to find a hotel, I slept on a waiting-room floor in the railway station alongside 40 tramps before catching the next available homeward-bound train to sanctuary. It was six weeks after returning home that I discovered I had been seven weeks pregnant at the time of my adventure. My baby had been with me the whole time.

When I was a child myself, I dreamt of journeying to the four corners of the world. Travel was more than a passion; it was imperative for my future contentment and, before my baby arrived, it was an essential part of my life. Since leaving university, I had enjoyed ten years of independence and uninhibited roving. I spent every spare penny I had on foreign soil. By the time I became pregnant, I had visited over one third of the countries of the world. My hunger for travel should have been satisfied but I wasn't happy thinking that I wouldn't be able to travel again until my baby reached whatever age my friends and family deemed appropriate.

When I decided to book a holiday abroad soon after the birth of my baby son, whom I named Paris James, many of my friends and family advised me to wait until he was out of nappies. Others declared that I should wait until he was five or six before taking him travelling. Even my doctor was cautious about sanctioning my trip. 'There is no point in risking tragedy by going abroad. Have a holiday in England,' he told me. I was a very experienced traveller and couldn't imagine why travelling with a child should be so different from travelling alone or as a couple. I knew it would be a challenge for me but judged that, provided I picked my destination carefully, my son would be in no greater danger in many countries of the world than he would be at home. After all, statistically most accidents happen in the home.

I returned to work just a few weeks after the birth and became increasingly exhausted. I needed some sunshine and a break. My mum offered to look after the baby at home while my husband and I took a week's holiday, but it wasn't a break from my son I needed, it was escape from the telephone, the washing machine and a full-time job. I decided that a family trip abroad would be a tonic for us all. It would be the first time I had all day to relax and enjoy my baby since leaving the hospital with him when he was five days old.

I returned to my doctor. He advised me to choose a clean destination with good medical facilities. He also urged me to wait until my son had received the routine childhood immunisations. This advice I took. I booked a holiday in Tobago, an island in the Caribbean, to depart when my baby would be five months old. Despite a bout of mild heatstroke, this was one of our more relaxing and uneventful holidays. Our son was helpless and, although he could roll around, he was relatively immobile and easy to keep out of danger. This trip gave us the confidence to travel the world.

Suddenly I found that I had to learn how to travel all over again. My baby commanded more luggage, more expensive accommodation and a lot more preparation, but with him he brought fresh, increased pleasure to a walk on the beach, stroking a stingray, feeding a giant tortoise or picking mangoes straight from the tree.

Travelling with a child is never easy but what about parenting ever is? The little packages of our own genes enslave us to do their will. We suffer sleep deprivation with our babies, frustration with our toddlers, anxiety over what is best for our children, then worry about our teenagers, so why do we do it?

Travelling with them is just the same. Sometimes you will look at your partner or your screaming child and wish you had never left your cosy home but, on balance, the pleasures and the thrill of shared experience through innocent, wide eyes are worth every inconvenience and mishap.

We have made many mistakes and learnt how to travel with a child the tough and gritty way. Paris had visited sixteen countries before he was three years old and – regrettably – he has sometimes suffered along the way. Because of my extensive travel experience, I was able to pick safe, hygienic and child-friendly destinations easily but there are many things I would do differently a second time.

It may seem unbelievable that, despite completing a physiology and pharmacology degree, I had no idea how vulnerable a young child is to relatively mild extremes of temperature, and how quickly they can become at risk. In my final year at University, our practical sessions in the lab had included extrapolated studies on the body's temperature-controlling mechanisms. I cycled in a closed room hotter than the Sahara until I fainted, while thermometers measured my internal and external body temperature. My friend lay in a bath of iced water with a thermometer up her bottom while we timed her shivering fits and noted the colour changes in her black skin until her internal temperature dropped to a dangerous level or she could stand it no longer. We controversially reviewed the deadly experiments of the Dachau concentration camp, yet still, Paris has suffered mild degrees of both hypo- and hyperthermia. It didn't seem particularly cold when he caught his chill and he had been in the shade all afternoon when he got heatstroke. I reproached myself bitterly and set out to uncover why it had happened and note down the earlier signs so it would never happen again.

In this book I have discussed every situation I have encountered. I have researched every other eventuality. I hope that the book will be useful to all travellers with children, both in preparation for their holiday and whilst they are away. With advice to hand, most parents should be able to deal with minor traumas and health problems without jeopardy to the overall enjoyment of their holiday. Good packing, preparation and basic knowledge make travel safer, healthier and happier.

PART ONE: CHOOSING A HOLIDAY

1 When to Begin Travelling with Children

Every age group has different needs and difficulties but the toddler and the early teenager stages tend to be the hardest.

Provided that you plan, prepare and pack well, travelling with a very young baby is relatively straightforward, but as soon as they become mobile, they turn into a marauding hazard inclined to scurry into jeopardy at every opportunity. Once our babies start to crawl, we begin to childproof our houses. By the time they are toddling, we have baby gates and plug-socket protectors all over the house. It is virtually guaranteed that your holiday accommodation will be full of stone steps, slippery tiled floors, jagged furniture, self-locking doors and ancient electric points just at fiddling height. Outside your room there will be six-feet deep swimming pools, balconies, scabby stray dogs and crowds. Your senseless toddler could be lost in a minute. You should be ready for anything.

From about twenty months, travelling with children begins to get easier, until the age of around four or five, when travelling with them becomes a pleasure. We can then enjoy our holidays through their fresh and excited young eyes.

Holidaying with children of any age will be an entirely different experience. There will no languishing on the beach for hours or enjoying a quiet dinner and a bottle of wine watching the sunset. You will be up and down all day, checking their temperatures and sunscreen coverage. Then in the evening you will be fighting unfamiliar foods down them and falling into bed at ten o'clock, exhausted. They demand more expensive accommodation, more regular mealtimes and the relative proximity of a toilet at every minute, but if you are ready for this, you will share some of the most happy and memorable times in your child's life.

Normally swamped up in a world where we mothers often don't have time to peel our own vegetables, on holiday we can relax and devote the time to our children which, when the telephone is ringing and dozens of jobs need doing, we do not have. When so many women are forced to return to work for economic reasons, holidays are a time to indulge your children, discuss issues over dinner and expand their world.

I believe that travelling will enrich a child's life more than any other single factor. It will dispel the ignorance that contributes to racism, teach a love of different cultures and stimulate both the imagination and the memory. Whether it be a package holiday in Spain or a trek in Nepal, it will be something for your child to cherish. Even if he is too young to truly recall the trip, seeing the photos or watching the video will magic him back to a different time and place, then inspire him to imagine that he really does remember being there.

There will doubtless be minor illnesses and injuries on holiday, but a well informed and pre-prepared parent will be able to cope with most incidents without any major disruption.

BABIES ABROAD

Coping with a very young baby abroad is not much more difficult than coping at home. They still wake up at all hours and demand feeding at their convenience, then still want pampering, pandering, sterilising, feeding and changing.

It is advisable to wait until after the baby's first set of immunisations before holidaying independently. Visiting family and friends in a familiar country where you can guarantee hygiene levels should, in theory, be less of a risk but this is not necessarily the case. Even though you may have grown up safely in a particular environment, you will have lost your immunity, and your children will have none to local diseases. In effect your whole family will be just as susceptible to illness as any other travelling family, if not more so because of your extensive contact with local people. So even if visiting family, it will still be worth waiting that extra one or two months until the first set of jabs are completed.

The diseases that have provoked worldwide immunisation programmes for three-month-old babies are very serious, highly contagious, life-threatening illnesses, transmittable by sneezing and coughing. Due to the success of these programmes, a whole generation of mothers has never known the horrors of polio and diphtheria, but still today, with all modern facilities and antibiotics, the death rate from diphtheria is ten per cent (much higher in undeveloped countries).

Standard sterilising and feeding routines will protect against the common gastro-intestinal complaints but if travelling into a risk area with an unprotected baby, you will not be able to protect them against highly contagious airborne diseases. Once your baby has been immunised against pertussis (whooping cough), tuberculosis, tetanus, polio and diphtheria, he will doubtless contract all manner of coughs, colds and fevers, whether at home or abroad, but they will invariably be mild and are unlikely to be life threatening.

You probably won't feel much like a trek abroad yourself until your new baby is more than four months old anyway. It is hard enough breaking new ground and discovering new places without the added challenges of sleep deprivation, establishing solids and protecting a child when it is in its most vulnerable first few months of life. Holidaying with a four- or five-month-old can be a wholly pleasurable and relatively relaxing experience. There will doubtless be little hiccups. Even the most pre-prepared of mothers makes mistakes. Still, there are so many easy ways of averting problems which could devastate a trip abroad.

My son's first trip was when he was five months old. We took him to Tobago in the Caribbean. Apart from discomfort on landing in the aeroplane and a case of mild heatstroke, we had a relaxing and enjoyable time. I found him easier in Tobago than I found him at home where I had so many other tasks and responsibilities. I had stopped breast-feeding when Paris was five months old exactly, just before we left and, although it would have had its advantages at times, bottle-feeding was never a problem. The sterilising and feeding routine was exactly the same as at home. I bought bottled water and boiled it before adding the sterilising tablets. The hot water I used to mix with powdered feeds, I boiled twice. Other than that there was no extra effort. Take a travel kettle with you. In many modern hotels there will be a kettle in your room, but the risk of endless trips to the hotel kitchen for boiled water was enough to provoke me to prepare myself.

Breast-fed babies are even easier travelling companions and, unless you are really struggling, there are many advantages in continuing breast-feeding until you return home. Your baby will be easier to settle on long journeys and, as many babies will suckle for comfort even when not particularly hungry, you will be able to ease the pressure build-up in their ears on take-off and landing very simply.

Beyond about seven months, around the time babies begin to roll around and crawl, journeying becomes more difficult. They will scurry over unsanitary floors and find filthy corners to grub around in, then suck their thumbs. Your own home will, by this time, be crammed with all manner of things to make your life easier and you will have had to leave them all behind. The lounge carpet you recently had especially cleaned is swapped for one in your three-star hotel room which looks as if it has been in place for twenty years and has recently been smeared with a mixture of honey and diesel oil. Your baby will cheerfully crawl all over it then return to you with dirty, black hands, feet and knees. To combat this, request extra towels or bedding sheets and spread them all over any well-trodden, grubby sections of carpet or wherever your baby crawls over the most. If the floor is tiled, wipe over it with a cloth soaked in Milton or any other sterilising fluid suitable for use with babies. A good dousing all over the floor and surfaces with one of the domestic, antibacterial kitchen or bathroom sprays will keep the population of germs in your apartment or hotel room down to a minimum.

You will have to be tireless in your attempts to keep your baby's hands clean. Babies' hands are constantly in their mouths and upset stomachs can easily result. Even after a bath or a swim in the pool, I always cleansed my baby's hands with a wet wipe. President Franklin D. Roosevelt caught polio from his own swimming pool and was consequently paralysed. This virus and many others are waterborne. Even well-chlorinated pools can harbour germs and, for young babies with low levels of resistance, take extra care not to let them swallow any water or get it in their ears.

At around ten or eleven months, babies will pull themselves up on to their feet and then fall backwards and sideways on to table corners and hard, ceramic-tiled floors. You may have to do a full furniture removal job to make your room safe. If your baby develops a particular fascination for an unsteady table or keeps toppling off a chair, ask your maid to remove it or stick it outside on the balcony.

TODDLERS ABROAD

As your tot becomes even more mobile and steadier on his feet, he moves faster. Then the fun starts. Travelling becomes more challenging until about the time toddlers cease to be classed as infants and become fare-paying children at two years old.

We enjoyed a very pleasurable holiday to Margarita, Venezuela when our son was 23 months old. He had more confidence in the swimming pool and was more respectful of the sea. He was easier to feed and had a lot more sense generally. His jet lag combined with my own made sure we were all up at 5 a.m. every morning but we went to bed reasonably early so this wasn't an all-consuming problem.

On that occasion, we holidayed with my mum and dad. I noticed most of the other couples with under-twos who were staying in the hotel were doing the same. Travelling with an extra two helpers has many advantages and it may be worth considering for an easier and more relaxing time. My mum and dad helped us watch over and discipline Paris. They even let us have a couple of meals to ourselves while they babysat. It also meant that we could take turns to go off on trips without leaving each other to cope with the baby completely alone. Out of the four of us, there was always one who wasn't run ragged and was willing to get a drink or meet any other demand.

Travelling with friends with their own children might not be the best recipe for a relaxing holiday. Even short trips I have taken with good friends and well-behaved children have been hard work. They all seem to take it in turns to wake up at three in the morning, need feeding, injure themselves and have crying fits. You may battle with your own toddler for fifteen minutes every hour. In an apartment housing four others, there is always one who wants something. Provided that the children get on, they will enjoy the holiday far more and if you want to be self-sacrificing, try it but be ready to be very tolerant of other children's faults and demands.

Between ten and twenty months is probably the most challenging time to travel with a child. So be prepared.

At thirteen months they will totter unsteadily towards a lake or swimming pool and, if left unattended, will throw themselves in. Toddlers need watching every second of every day.

When our son was fourteen months old, a trip to the Seychelles ended with a life-threatening incident and a visit to the hospital. There were no high chairs in our hotel restaurant and he was constantly balancing on a chair and grabbing things off the table top. On the last day of our holiday he snatched up a glass ashtray and dropped it on to the floor where it smashed. He then fell off his chair on to the broken glass and slashed open his wrist. There was blood everywhere and it was one of the most terrifying experiences of my life. Somewhere at the back of our minds my husband and I knew to apply pressure around the wound and hold the arm up above his head to prevent excessive blood loss. A knowledge of basic first aid can be invaluable when travelling with a self-sabotaging toddler.

A trip we took to China when our son was eighteen months old was the hardest. Arguably, travelling with an infant is verging on masochism. The more mobile they are, the more danger and the more stress there will be, yet the challenge can be exhilarating and rewarding. We arrived in China to find our luggage had been lost and so without nappies, baby food, milk or clothes, we were in trouble. It arrived two days later.

We were all ill and suffered terribly from jet lag. It was absolutely exhausting. Yet because of our accompanying blond-haired boy we saw another side to China. Young men offered us help constantly and old women told us in broken English how beautiful our baby was. The tour guides saved us the best seats on the buses and even offered to look after him while we walked up the Great Wall of China. We returned to find a huge crowd gathered around him, more interested in his blond hair than the Great Wall itself. In Tiannanmen Square, students introduced themselves and asked if they could hold our son and have their photo taken with him. Parenthood is an international condition. It breaks down barriers and makes you far more welcome in many societies than you would be when travelling alone or as a couple.

YOUNG CHILDREN

Once a child has graduated from being an infant to a two-year-old, the fares increase dramatically. For most of us it is difficult to justify paying £700 for a holiday in the Caribbean for a 25-month-old child when, just four weeks before, their fare would have cost £49. An adjusted budget now becomes more of an issue.

As the nappies are shed, there is a period of increased difficulty when a nearby toilet is essential. I gazed on with frustration as we neared the front of a fifty-minute queue in Disneyland Paris and a little voice demanded, 'Toilet, mummy, toilet.' I didn't really have time to make a decision about whether or not to give up all our places in the queue before my son pulled down his shorts, thrust out his groin and sprinkled the air with his gesture. Thankfully we were surrounded by a group of Italians who always adore children. They laughed out loud and patted him on the head, so alleviating my acute embarrassment.

You have the battles next to the ice-cream stall. A two-year-old does not comprehend that a delicious-looking ice-cream cone in India may half kill him. He may demand ice for his coke and be inconsolable when you refuse. Still, what's the difference? At home he would be yelling down a supermarket aisle, demanding a ten-ton bag of sweets or shouting for chicken nuggets every time you pass the dreaded red and yellow sign. You will doubtless find that as you relax into your holiday, you will have more patience and so are better able to try and reason with your unmanageable monster. There will be all the time in the world to read together, gain confidence in the swimming pool and break bad habits in a relaxed environment without a guilty conscience clouded with nagging images of washing, cleaning and phone calls to be made.

A three- or four-year-old may remember very little but will have a sense of increasing enjoyment. They will appreciate being on the beach and digging sandcastles and delight in the family atmosphere, taking walks together and being with parents who are away from all the usual pressures of life. What could be better?

OLDER CHILDREN

For children over five, the family holiday will be as eagerly anticipated as birthdays and Christmas. Don't hesitate to book a trip with them; just concentrate on getting the most out of it for the whole family. A child's most vivid memories are usually the times spent relaxing on holiday and having both parents with them all day, every day.

Children of school age are infinitely easier travelling companions and, although more demanding in terms of where they want to go and what they want to eat, require far less effort to holiday with. You may want to choose your destination more carefully and pick a resort which caters well for children, or select a tour with visits to elephant orphanages rather than tea plantations.

Avoid a series of museums and long treks round hot cities or ancient monuments. One is much the same as another to a six-year-old and everyone will suffer. Opt for one or two at opposite ends of the holiday to achieve the most benefit.

A friend from university used to tell me on a regular basis that his family holidays were hell. His mum, dad and five children would tour all the major cities in Europe seeking out art galleries and national museums which they would creep around at a painstakingly slow pace. He assured me that it was a form of mental cruelty which had caused his brother to develop an obsessional disorder and himself to become depressed at exam time. I would not be quite so dramatic and suggested that his parents had just been a little unwise.

Don't let your children totally dominate your holiday. Negotiate a day in a theme park for a couple of hours' good behaviour while touring a vineyard, and go to the vineyard first.

Plan different things to do with your children before you go. Stimulate their imaginations. Harness their individual interests and ask them to look up what different birds, insects, shells, fish or plants they will see. If you are travelling to the southern hemisphere, explain the differences in the positions of the stars. Ask them to help you learn some of the history and culture of the children who live in the country you will visit: for example, what they wear and eat. Buy them a book or two on your destination. Often a work of fiction which is set where you will be going is a thrill. When you get there, find places they imagine are set in the book: quiet coves; pirates' dens; 'deep' forests. Promise to take them exploring either early morning on the beach, or through the wilds of the countryside hunting for – as yet – undiscovered species. Even a ten-minute walk across a field next to a car lay-by will become a memorable adventure.

If you prefer to rely on the resort for entertainment, spend time comparing the different facilities offered by the hotels.

As with all other ages, plan carefully, prepare for anything, pack well and you are destined to have a fantastic and unforgettable time.

2 Where to Go

Every country in the world has something to offer the traveller but sometimes the enjoyment and excitement of a holiday may be overshadowed by the likelihood of stress, danger, illness or war. As most illnesses are preventable, avoidable or curable, and most children's fatal accidents happen in the home, the only places in the world I would avoid when travelling with children are those which are politically unstable or subject to persistent terrorist activity and kidnappings. I have listed those countries in the following information so that you can do the same if you choose.

I have briefly cited every other country in the world in line with my own experience and that of friends who have lived, worked or were born in a particular country. There may be no surprises for the more expert traveller and others may disagree, but the real aim of this book is to open up the world to parents who think that they need to wait until their children have left home before they travel. Go now!

If you would like to visit a country with your family but don't have the experience to 'go it alone', consider joining a tour group. Package tours may not be quite so adventurous but the whole family will enjoy a much more stress-free trip. In countries with a poor infrastructure – for example, Burma, Vietnam and parts of India – this will totally change the experience you are likely to have in a short time. You will be able to cover much more terrain, and see a lot more, when everything, including where you eat, is organised for you.

In countries where very little English is spoken – for example, China and many countries of South America – a guide will be a great asset. A local guide will also be able to warn you about all the local tourist scams which vary dramatically from country to country. When travelling preoccupied with babies and toddlers, it is so much easier to fall prey to pickpockets. You will also feel more vulnerable. Con artists will sense this and take advantage.

The information on each country is intended to give an objective flavour and highlight anything which might be of major concern to most parents. It will hopefully give you ideas and help you to choose the destination without illusions.

AFRICA

Africa is certainly the most challenging continent to the traveller. Many countries suffer from a high incidence of parasitic disease and violent political unrest.

The greatest attraction Africa has to offer families is the abundance and variety of well-run wildlife safaris all over the eastern and southern regions of the vast continent. Children love animals, and what could be more spectacular and exciting for them than setting out to track lion, leopard, cheetah, elephant, rhino, zebra and giraffe?

Most of Africa would be tough going for the travelling family. Intense heat, disease and hostile locals are hard work but the untamed nature of Africa can be enjoyed in several countries which have settled their turbulent histories and now enjoy stability.

Countries in Africa to avoid or which have limited attractions or tourist infrastructure

Algeria Politically unstable. Tourists on desert safari are a target for militant Islamic groups. There are safer neighbouring countries, such as Morocco, in which to view the Atlas mountains and visit the Sahara.

Angola Angola has been in a state of constant civil war for the last twenty-five years. It is a war zone riddled with land mines.

Benin Benin has poorly developed tourism, poverty, malaria and high levels of fatal diarrhoeal illness, making it an unattractive choice for families.

Burkina-Faso Burkina-Faso is host to poor healthcare, political violence, high temperatures, arid land, dust, disease and extreme, widespread poverty.

Burundi The absence of a tourist infrastructure is an insignificant reason for not visiting Burundi when compared to its atrocities of Hutu massacres and appalling human rights records.

Cameroon Not much of a tourist destination but packages are on offer in the northern game parks. Health risks: malaria, diarrhoeal and respiratory disease.

Cape Verde There is tourist potential on the islands but this is, so far, underdeveloped. Mountain scenery and extensive beaches are the plusses. An active volcano is a mixed attraction, while scattered healthcare service and limited flight connections are the negatives.

Central African Republic There is little to attract the family on holiday.

Chad Poor tourist infrastructure.

Congo The Marxist-Leninist ruling regime does not seek to attract or develop tourism.

Djibouti There is little to attract the family on holiday.

Equatorial Guinea Poor tourist infrastructure.

Eritrea There are land mines on many beaches.

Ethiopia Worth a visit for those who love the rawest that Africa has to offer. However, the lack of tourist infrastructure and good accommodation increases the visitor's exposure to health risks and crime. Less than ideal for the family although there are five national parks in the country.

Gabon There is little to attract the family on holiday.

Guinea Poor tourist infrastructure.

Guinea Bissau Poor tourist infrastructure.

Ivory Coast A little more to offer the family than many African countries, such as a Club Med, but there are still health risks and a high incidence of violent crime to consider.

Liberia Liberia is a war zone.

Libya Libya is effectively closed to Western tourists.

Mali Timbuktu is in Mali which gives some idea of how hot, dry and inaccessible the country is. Mali's northern region is virtually uninhabited Saharan desert. There are safaris on offer but there are better destinations for a family desert safari.

Mauritania   Offers desert safaris but little else.

Mozambique   Tourism has been devastated by war. Even the beaches may be mined and the site of violence.

Niger   Politically unstable.

Nigeria   Politically unstable.

Rwanda   Politically unstable.

Sao Tome and Principe   Very limited tourist infrastructure.

Senegal   Day trips from the Gambia are available. The Slave Island of Gorce attracts African–Americans.

Sierra Leone   Politically unstable.

Somalia   Land mines are in use.

Sudan   There is political unrest and civil war.

Surinam   No tourist infrastructure.

Swaziland   Swaziland is safe and clean, and although it is not particularly cheap or easy to get to from the UK, if visiting South Africa, you might think about crossing the border to sample Swaziland's game reserves and mountain scenery where the crime rate is lower and there is less tension. Most of the tourists are from South Africa, travelling for the casinos and the relaxing temperate climate.

Togo   Politically unstable.

Uganda   The recent horrors in Uganda have destroyed Uganda's appeal.

Zaire   There are official restrictions on travelling within the country.

Countries in Africa that are at present suitable to travel to with a family

Botswana   Where wealthy South Africans head for on safari. Almost twenty per cent of Botswana's land is set aside as national parks or game reserves which is one of the highest percentages of protected land in the world. Environmentalists abound and the government is keen to attract tourists and trophy hunters. The Okavango swamps and delta are an inspiring taste of wild Africa. The largest collection of elephants remaining in Africa come to bathe alongside the mix of drinking and grazing animals – a sight that is unmatched anywhere else.

Feeding off the concentrated game are legions of predators including lions, cheetahs, leopards, hyenas and wild dogs. There are 80 species of fish, turtles, hundreds of hippos, crocodiles, fishing eagles and waterfowl. A family of wildlife lovers will be in clover. What child isn't fascinated by animals?

Much more costly for a family than Eastern Africa and without the beaches, Botswana has the benefits of political and economic stability which make for a more relaxing, refined and tout-free safari. Health risks: parasitic disease has been tackled aggressively. The tsetse fly and the associated problem of sleeping sickness have been virtually eliminated from Botswana, although this was more with protecting cattle in mind than humans.

Respiratory diseases are common and care must be taken with hygiene. Malaria tablets should be taken in the northern areas only between November and June.

Egypt   The terrorist attacks specifically aimed at tourists take the shine off the pyramids. Your children will have a lifetime to visit them and so there is no real point travelling in troubled times, although the giveaway holiday prices are attractive and it is highly unlikely that your family will be involved in any trouble. Mini-cruises from Cyprus which deposit you in Egypt for the day or two are a good option if you would really like to show your children the site of the most ancient of civilisations. If you do travel from Cyprus or opt to take advantage of the present bargain holiday prices to Egypt, you must visit the Egyptian museum in Cairo to see the contents of Tutankhamen's tomb, which are fascinating for both adults and children. The colours and detail are stunning.

Egypt's food hygiene standards are somewhat lacking and stomach bugs are common, even on the Nile cruises or in the best hotels. The chefs may do their best, but if the produce in the local markets is what finds its way to your table, you are likely to suffer. A trip to an Egyptian market may put you off feeding your children anything but crisps and chocolate.

As well as the amazing sightseeing that has attracted travellers for centuries, the Red Sea resorts offer excellent scuba-diving, luxury hotels, good water sports and great beaches.

There is a great deal to attract and entertain the family but this should be carefully considered on balance with the risk of stomach upset and terrorism. The time of year you visit should also be taken into account. The summer heat can be oppressive for children and the winters can be surprisingly chilly in the North. Spring or autumn would be the best time to take advantage of all the different aspects of the country with a family.

Combining time at the beach with a stay in Cairo and/or Luxor would be the best way of discovering Egypt.

Gambia Not an ideal destination for children due to the presence of drug-resistant malaria but it is well developed, with good hotels. If you have a passion to try Africa it is one of the safer options to head for but is perhaps a little characterless.

The beaches are broad and sandy. Every effort is made by the hotels to keep food hygiene standards high and there are trips along the river to break up your stay.

Ghana One of the more hospitable African countries. The government is keen to attract tourists and it views development of the tourist industry as a key to economic strength.

There are some good beaches but these are on the Atlantic ocean, which is cold. You will receive a warm welcome and be encouraged to travel to other regions of the country to visit rainforests. The horrifying evidence of the slave trade and places where they were held before transportation are still intact and a visit to them is offered as a tourist attraction.

The culture of true Africa is still undiminished and if you want to experience the 'dark continent', it may be somewhere to put on the list for when the children are older.

Kenya The well-publicised murder of several tourists has kept many others away. Bandits operating mostly in the north-east have meant that many safaris have been accompanied by armed guards. There are flare-ups from time to time. In spring 1998, many tour operators advised tourists to cancel their trips.

Kenya offers many short safaris combined with time relaxing at the beach. This is better for young children who may tire of the early morning awakenings and long days spent in a bumpy minibus, trekking miles looking for elusive game, elephants or big cats. A few days may be a great novelty, especially if they have the beach to look forward to. Older children are likely to enjoy the longer safaris but the combination of them with time spent on the beach is more fun for all the family.

Kenyan safaris are generally good value and considerably less expensive than in many other African countries. However, cheaper prices have brought the Kenyan safari within the price range of many tourists and so you may find yourself in a race with several other vehicles to be first to the kill.

Resistant malaria is a concern and tablets must be taken. Other health risks include respiratory and diarrhoeal illnesses.

Many hotels are of a high standard but service is generally very laid back. Take snacks such as cereals and raisins for your child to nibble on, just in case.

Lesotho Spectacular mountain scenery is the main attraction for tourists. In May, June and July the mountains are cold with snow fall. Much safer than South Africa, which surrounds Lesotho but is of limited accessibility.

Madagascar A huge island off the east coast of Africa. Its geographical isolation means it is home to many unique wildlife and plants. Protection programmes for lemurs and other animals are helped by the revenue of visiting tourists and are an interesting experience for young travellers.

There are thousands of miles of tropical beach and much to explore in Madagascar but malaria is endemic. There is a good, inexpensive domestic air network that compensates for the difficulties of getting around by road and rail over the long distances involved.

The country is relatively poor but the people are not hostile towards tourists and so a family of confident travellers could enjoy a nature-orientated trip.

Malawi A small country dominated by the eponymous Lake Malawi which attracts anglers and nature lovers. National parks, mountain lodges, good hotels and water sports are readily available but resistant malaria is a problem and young children are very vulnerable. My uncle contracted malaria in Malawi despite taking prophylactic medication.

Mauritius The main problem with Mauritius is the price tag. Eating, sleeping and babysitting in Mauritius costs a small fortune. The beaches are spectacular, and the wooded mountain peaks and turquoise waters make for a romantic and idyllic island for a couple, but as your child trips up the honeymooners who are too busy gazing into each other's eyes to watch where they were going, you may wish you had chosen somewhere cheaper and more geared towards family fun and relaxation. It is also important to remember that Mauritius has its winter during the children's summer school holidays. It can rain for days and be very chilly. Trying to entertain yourselves and your children on Mauritius is a costly business. Neighbouring Reunion is bigger, more affordable and arguably more naturally beautiful.

Morocco Child mortality is high, so if you do go and your child falls ill, get home.

Crime levels are low but be a little careful with blond children of both sexes in certain areas; they are very attractive to Moroccan men. The difference in culture makes Morocco a very popular destination for fair homosexual men, where they find they are much in demand.

The beaches are good, hotels standards are reasonably high and Morocco is cheap and nearby.

If you take care what you eat and avoid the water you should enjoy your family holiday. The bazaars and belly-dancers are interesting for even the youngest members of the family.

Marrakech offers culture and luxury.

Namibia Sand-dune skiing and desert ecology are the main attractions plus there are some good self-drive safaris on offer, but generally, Namibia is more expensive and there is less to entertain children than in other African countries. The western 'skeleton' coast is usually shrouded in cold, thick fog.

The Seychelles The Seychelles offer nature at her best and most beautiful. The islands support unique flora, fauna and wildlife. Thousands of spiders spin webs between the overhead telephone lines, hundreds of huge fruit bats weigh down the boughs of the mango trees and giant tortoises amble around hotel grounds. It is a nature lover's and children's paradise, the perfect place to teach them about the environment and stimulate their imagination by exploring deserted 'real' pirate coves.

The beaches are among the best in the world. They are quiet and the sand is soft and white. They are safe, the water is shallow and a real taste of paradise.

Prohibitive pricing and the distance from Europe, America or any other rich society are possibly what have kept the Seychelles more unspoilt and quieter than the Caribbean or the Mediterranean. Now prices have come down to relatively affordable levels it is a good time to visit. The Seychelles' attention to protecting the environment will hopefully mean that it can be enjoyed for the foreseeable future.

If you can afford luxury on the Seychelles, you will find it. At the other extreme, there is some budget accommodation available which is better value than some of the bigger, medium-class hotels which are expensive breeze block and concrete creations, rather than havens in which hibiscus and turtle doves abound.

The healthcare is good and free. We were unfortunate enough to end up in hospital on the main island of Mahe. At fourteen months old our son had slashed open his wrist deeply. He was treated faultlessly and well stitched up. The pharmacy shelf was a little sparse but the doctors were efficient and confident and the nurses were sensitive to our concerns. I was just grateful to have been staying on one of the main islands rather than on a more remote one.

South Africa   Times are still changing in South Africa and who knows how long it will be safe to visit. Crime is still escalating and Johannesburg is already the murder capital of the world. 'No go areas' have forced big international hotels in downtown Jo'burg simply to shut down. Capetown is less hostile and infinitely more interesting and so, if you want to see *the* South Africa, head there. There is plenty to do and see around Capetown for everyone. The Cape of Good Hope is a day trip worth taking. There are good hotels and beaches and pleasant sightseeing. Table Mountain towers over the city and you can take trips to the top by cable-car.

If you simply want beaches, Durban is an option. Northwest of Durban are Zululand and the Drakensburg mountains, both worth exploring. The excellent wildlife reserves in north-east South Africa are a good safari option. In the Kruger park there are 140 species of mammals and 450 species of birds. The lodges are of a high standard.

At the moment, South Africa is incredibly cheap. The whole family would be able to eat out constantly at bargain prices. The food standards and range of choice are high.

A 'fly drive' would mean you could take in much of what the country has to offer but be careful, many impoverished black South Africans drive without a licence or insurance and road deaths are common. A few days on safari, followed by a few days in the Drakensburg mountains, then a week on the beach would be perfect, but organised tours from the UK are relatively expensive when you consider the cost of living and how cheaply you could do it yourself.

The healthcare in the cities is good but in rural South Africa access to care is limited and black children suffer tragic twenty per cent death rates.

Political uncertainty is unlikely to resolve itself, at least for the time being, so if you want to sample what South Africa has to offer, avoid Johannesburg and go now.

Tanzania and Zanzibar Tanzania is a fantastic destination for a safari. One third of the country is national park or game reserve, offering amazing game-viewing opportunities. It is considerably more expensive than Kenya but the lodges and camps are first class. To bring down the price you could spend part of your safari in Kenya and part in Tanzania on an organised tour.

If you want to head for the beach for part of your holiday with the family, the beaches of Mombassa are a short flight away. Alternatively, the spice island of Zanzibar is an option. Zanzibar was built up on the slave trade and so has a strong history. It is undeveloped but offers good hotels, deserted beaches and warm, reef-protected waters.

Whatever you decide to do, be careful what you eat. The healthcare is good by African standards but in many areas is provincial. There is also a high incidence of malaria, diarrhoeal and respiratory diseases.

Tunisia One of the Mediterranean's cheapest holiday destinations. It is marketed as a winter sun destination but, as in Egypt and Morocco, it can be chilly in December, January and February. The summer is very hot.

The choice of hotels is wide and you are sure to get good value for money. Food hygiene levels seem to have improved over the years that Tunisia has been a popular tourist haunt but care still needs to be taken when feeding and watering a family.

Camel rides and tours into the desert are popular and enjoyable for all the family.

Although healthcare standards have improved, if your child falls ill enough to seek hospital treatment, get them home in good time.

Zambia Victoria Falls, the Zambezi river and safaris are the reasons to visit Zambia but all this and more can be found over the border in Zimbabwe. For a family, Zimbabwe is a better choice, with a better tourist infrastructure and standard of hotels. Corruption at the borders by officials is an issue.

Zimbabwe A beautiful country with some good game-viewing, the natural wonder of Victoria Falls and the Zambezi river. The hotels and game lodges are generally medium class, but the famous colonial-style Victoria Falls Hotel is fantastic.

Temperatures can soar in the summertime (December–January) but are still generally more bearable than on the plains of Tanzania and Kenya due to altitude.

Action holidays are being developed. Whitewater rafting has been developed on the Zambezi but is too dangerous for young children. Canoeing on the Zambezi is also available for older children but tell them that if they fall in, they must keep their mouths closed tight. Parasitic illnesses are common in Zimbabwe and as so many are water-borne, you don't want any member of the family with a tummy full of the Zambezi.

There are also cultural attractions and ruins. You won't get the bargain-priced safaris (so readily available in Kenya) or the beaches but you will get more peace and atmosphere.

ANTARCTICA

Great, if stepping off a cruise ship to view the penguins for half a day, but with ice, blizzards, fog and temperatures as low as −75°C, the Antarctica is not really the place to stay for a holiday with young children. It is too cold and windy with the risk of hypothermia, frostbite and possibly snow blindness. If visiting from a cruise ship, your family will almost certainly be supplied with suitable clothing to protect against the biting cold. December and January are the 'warmest' times of year with average temperatures around −25°C.

SOUTH ASIA

Bangladesh The climate can be catastrophic. Tropical monsoons from June to October create floods which can cover two-thirds of the country, devastating a whole season's crops, creating famine, disease and extreme hardship. Cyclones in April, May and after the monsoons can lead to huge death tolls.

The environment is harsh and the diseases take advantage when man is at his weakest. Despite this, Bangladesh is one of the most densely populated countries in the world. Clearly, in spite of the high incidence of parasitic, diarrhoeal and communicable diseases, millions of children still manage to survive. It would be an adventurous and extraordinary family trip if both parents felt they could cope with the untoward and the children were old enough to complain in the early stages of sickness. A baby or toddler can become very ill very quickly. An older child's complaints will give more warning, so that they are less likely to become seriously ill very suddenly, miles away from medical help.

It would be a tough holiday for families unfamiliar with Bangladesh. Even those brought up in the country must adhere to recommended immunisation and malaria prophylactic schedules.

Bhutan Tourism is not encouraged by the government but this country has only recently been open to visitors at all. For centuries this tiny kingdom remained tucked away in the Eastern Himalayas, secret from the outside world. It is possible that Bhutan gave rise to the myths of Shangri La.

The land is of outstanding natural beauty; 70 per cent of the country is forested and the bird life is exceptional. The treks are less well trodden than those in the more popular destination of Nepal. The people are deeply religious and gentle. Organised tours would be the best way of visiting Bhutan but as tourism and prices are strictly controlled by the government, you will not have the choice or flexibility you need with a family if you don't pre-arrange your visit.

Brunei Brunei's Sultan was once the richest man in the world. He lives in the world's biggest palace and still enjoys the ranking of third richest man.

Brunei's people enjoy one of the highest standards of living in the world due to the oil and gas reserves. The government of Brunei encourages tourism and there is a Western standard free health service. Brunei is a small country and 75 per cent of it is covered by rainforest. The beaches are good, crime levels are low and the standards of service are high. Perhaps visited in combination with Borneo, Brunei could be a good family travel destination with a difference.

Burma (Myanmar) Visiting Myanmar is like stepping back in time. It is one of the least developed countries in South-East Asia, rich in ancient customs and traditions.

Pagodas, temples, lakes and stunning scenery are commonplace. The road to Mandalay, Rangoon and the legendary Irrawaddy river are all major attractions. Five-star hotels and luxury cruises on the Irrawaddy are where tourists are encouraged to stay by the government. The prices paid in hard currency are in no way proportionate to the cost of living. As a result, visiting Burma is expensive.

If visiting the country with a family, it is a good idea to join a tour group. Travelling independently with children in Myanmar would be tough and tiring. Your guide would ensure that you are sensitive to the totalitarian regime still in place.

There is a lot to see, but getting around alone is difficult. Although the atmosphere and variety between boat trips and golden pagodas are likely to stimulate children, it would be a shame to arrive and stay in Rangoon.

Burmese people are gentle and remain constrained. Sadly,

human rights records are poor and they will be 'encouraged' to stay away from the tourists and may smile softly at you from a distance. Be respectful of the police and the military.

Avoid the tropical wet season in the summer, especially with children, when fevers can run riot. Take care to avoid diarrhoeal illnesses and be aware that malaria is on the increase. Leprosy in Burma is more common than in the rest of Asia.

Cambodia   A great destination for the adventurous, independent traveller although occasional tourist kidnappings and uncertain politics should direct most families to neighbouring Thailand or Vietnam. If you really want to visit Cambodia as a family, then join a tour group. You will see more and be able to relax and enjoy the trip instead of battling with transport, hoteliers and even the police.

India   Despite all that India has to offer, it remains in the mind of the tourist as an experience rather than a relaxing, enjoyable holiday. It is certain that you will never forget your time there, but concentrated attention to hygiene and careful choice of where in India you visit would ensure a happy – and not just a memorable – trip.

Whether or not to take your children for the real Indian experience is not an easy decision, especially when they are young. The roads are lethal and the terrible reputations for infestations such as 'Delhi belly' are all true. It may even be true that is not worth showing them the splendours of India when they are too young, because they could not truly appreciate them. There must be some corners of the world left for them to discover themselves when they are older. Seeing the Taj Mahal and the palaces of Jaipur when they are too young may take the wonder out of it.

If you do want to go and do not know India well, it is better to travel with a tour group with accompanying children. Journeying independently in India by road and rail is exhausting; even with a group it is tiring and the heat in India in the summer is insufferable. Your tour guide will usher you through crowds to the right train platform, take you to hotels and restaurants whose hygiene standards do not jeopardise the sensitive tourist stomach and protect you from scams and the multitude of overzealous touts.

The best family holidays in India would be in the north, where it is cooler, and more civilised colonialism is still strongly in evidence. New Delhi is surprisingly sophisticated with spacious boulevards, manicured gardens and 'gentlemen's' clubs where you can eat cucumber sandwiches watched over by a picture of the queen. Old Delhi is a mass of temples, mosques and bazaars. Sacred cows wander around in the main streets, unmoved by deafening beeping horns.

Alternatively, if you do want to relax on your holiday and have just a taste of India, choose a beach holiday in Goa. The influence of a Portuguese colony, golden beaches and welcoming local people ensure an enjoyable experience. You will get incredible value for money and the hotels do make every effort to ensure the tourists' stomachs are not upset. Be careful, take all the usual precautions, avoid salad, ice, ice cream and brush your teeth in bottled water and your family should have a cheap, trouble-free trip.

Indonesia Indonesia consists of 13,667 islands. The main islands are Java, Bali, Sumatra, Borneo and Sulawesi. The best of these islands to visit with a family is undoubtedly Bali.

Bali is beautiful, relaxed, safe and geared towards tourism. The five-star hotels in Nusa Dua are among the best in the world but are still affordable compared to the price you may pay for a room in an equivalent standard hotel in a European city. There are plenty of reasonable, lower budget options too.

Beaches are good and the island is easy to explore by car. As always, be careful on the roads but on Bali, they are not too crowded. The gentle Balinese temperament is reflected in their driving but be wary of mopeds and animals in the road.

Indonesian food is delicious and, in the tourist hotels and restaurants, it is quite safe. Even children usually eat the skewered meat or chicken satays and rice. American and Continental food is also widely available in the hotels.

Borneo is becoming more accessible, although tourism is developing more on the northerly Malaysian side of the island.

Java is more for the more independent traveller without a

family to worry about. The capital Jakarta is one of those cities where you step out of the airport and find that your passport has disappeared before you get to your hotel.

Laos Health is a concern. Sanitation is poor; dengue fever and malaria are an increasing problem. The infant mortality rate is more than ten per cent. One of the neighbouring countries would provide an easier option with children.

Malaysia Malaysia has many attractions, which is why it is South-East Asia's major tourist destination. It is civilised and easy to get around, so even with children, you could base yourselves in Kuala Lumpur or one of the beach resorts and still explore without a guide.

The beaches are stunning and many of the resorts are set in beautiful tropical gardens. The roads are good and car hire is reasonable enough to opt for a family fly drive.

Kuala Lumpur is safe and civilised, although a few days in the capital with a family would be enough. From Kuala Lumpur you could then visit Singapore, which is only a short train trip away and has attractions for the whole family.

The Malaysian islands of Penang and Langakwi, and the many beach resorts on the mainland, are stunning and the hotel standards are very high. Children are readily welcomed. The Cameron Highlands' cool climate is a break from the heat on the coast and offers a chance to see working tea plantations.

Health standards are high in the cities. Malaria is only a concern in certain areas and Western Malaysia is one of the few countries in the world that does not host the threat of rabies. Food hygiene standards are high but stay away from the street stalls.

Maldives The only concern I would have about taking a child to the Maldives is the question of what you would do if they had an accident on one of the outlying islands. It is unlikely, but I have experienced the panic of having to rush to a hospital with a bleeding baby. The thought of having to wait for a sea plane or a boat to take you to a hospital that is hours away freezes my blood. Aside from this unlikely event, a trip to the Maldives is total escapism. Good hotels on uninhabited islands offer white sands, clear waters and total relaxation.

The food standards are variable between resorts and the

choice is often repetitive. The water sports are better on some islands than others, which is worth considering. Older children could learn to water-ski or windsurf while you bury your nose in a book, happy that they are being entertained. The snorkelling and diving off the Maldives are also good.

Note that the weather during our summer school holidays can be rainy for weeks at a time.

Nepal Nepal's treks are becoming well trodden. Parents with a love of the mountains who know what to expect may opt for a gentler trek and travel in Nepal with confidence. Even for first-timers, there should be few problems. The guides will help you cater for your children's needs and even offer to carry them if they tire. However, basically a trek is a 'trek' with all its proverbial connotations and is likely to be easier with small children who are easily carried and happy to be wherever you are, or older, stronger children who can adapt to long walks and cold nights without being miserable. For a five- or six-year-old, the beautiful surroundings may not balance the gruel of a trek. Therefore if you want to witness the stunning scenery of the Himalayas with a young family, you are probably better to book a tour in an air-conditioned vehicle, especially between May and September.

Nepal is one of the most dangerous countries of the world to give birth in and in remote destinations, good healthcare is limited. Severe diarrhoeal illnesses are common and so be careful what you eat, particularly in Kathmandu.

Philippines Manila would be tough to tackle with accompanying children because it is a tough city. The poverty of the country is reflected in the capital, where armed guards are common as a result of high crime rates.

Outside the cities the country is poor but beautiful. The beaches are idyllic and the hotels are built to satisfy American standards. Tourism is underdeveloped relative to other regions of South-East Asia, possibly due to the image of corruption, poverty and American military bases.

Malaria has been eradicated in all but remote areas, but there is still a significant risk of respiratory or diarrhoeal illness.

Booking a package in one of the pleasant island resorts or

touring with a group would ensure that you enjoy your family trip. It is easy to be overwhelmed if you arrive in the bustle of Manila without preplanning where to go. The people are friendly, with a warm, genuine attitude to westerners, but there is a predatory side to the capital. Spend one or two days in Manila and then get out into the provinces.

Singapore Singapore is as safe as it gets. There are severe punishments for relatively minor crimes, including the sale of chewing gum and for not flushing the toilet, but this, and perhaps the fact that Singapore is so small and easily managed, makes this a very easy destination to enjoy without a hint of a worry or risk to your family.

The city doesn't really have an oriental feel and, when standing looking down Orchard Road, you could be excused for comparing it to any Western city. Even many of the department stores sell and advertise the same brands as the shops in London and New York.

The best place to stay in Singapore with a family, especially if staying for more than a couple of days, would be on Sentosa Island. It is linked with Singapore by causeway and cable-car and serviced by ferry. The island is one big, fun-packed resort with many attractions and activities such as theme- and water-parks.

Hotels are excellent and there are good – albeit manmade – beaches to relax on. It may not be an adult's ideal, but the children will really enjoy their time spent there. It is then easy to pop into Singapore for shopping or a barbecue at Raffles. Even at night you needn't worry about being out with your family.

Sri Lanka If it weren't for the civil war, Sri Lanka would be top on the list of many tourists' destinations. Sadly, terrorism is a threat and has been, on occasion, specifically targeted at tourists. Even children are involved and have been persuaded to become suicide bombs, often by their own families.

The war has had a serious impact on tourism which has resulted in many hotels becoming run down. However, the infrastructure is there and you can tour the country in your own private car very cheaply. There are magnificent caves, an elephant orphanage and beautiful, windswept beaches for the family to enjoy.

If you do decide to take advantage of the cheap offers and variety, get out of the capital, Colombo, as soon as you can and head for the beaches as a base or join a tour, preferably with a private driver who will be allocated by your tour company and can be trusted.

Healthcare is accessible and reasonable. Malaria is not of the resistant strain.

Thailand Thailand is a fascinating country but when you first arrive in the traffic and smog of Bangkok, in the heat, it is easy to be disenchanted. It takes a good few days to acclimatise and begin to relax and enjoy this city heaving with humanity. The traffic and noise never stop. If you look out of your hotel at 4.30 a.m. you will still witness a traffic jam as dense as it is in the London rush hour. As there is no underground system, Bangkok's rush hour never ceases.

Many of the hotels in Thailand, and particularly Bangkok, are among the best in the world. They are luxurious if not opulent, with abundant staff, excellent food and orchids for your pillow, yet they are cheaper per night than an English three-star hotel.

The Thai people are friendly and gentle but they drive a hard bargain and even in the grocery stores you will need to barter. Build up your children's confidence and let them barter for you. It is a wearying process you will soon tire of, but children seem to treat it as a huge game and thoroughly enjoy it. Don't buy any beach wear before you go. You will get better quality cotton goods in Thailand at cheaper prices for the entire family. Other good bargains are tapes and fake watches.

Couples are seeking out the less developed resorts and islands which are harder to reach but well worth the trip for their remote, tropical appeal.

The food in the hotels is excellent and standards of hygiene are high. Don't be tempted to feed your family from a street stall, however good the food looks and smells. The locals will have higher levels of resistance to the stomach bugs that could easily ruin your holiday.

The cooler season in Thailand is from November to March

which is a much better time to visit with children. It is also outside the monsoon season, when fevers are more common.

The sex districts in Bangkok around Patpong are safe during the day and some of the city's best market shopping is to be found in the surrounding streets. At night it is best avoided with your family. It is somehow more seedy, hostile and serious than Amsterdam. If you don't have much time, it is better to bypass Bangkok altogether unless you simply want to visit the Grand Palace which is stunning. If you are there for one or two nights, you won't have time to get your bearings and having two holiday centres will bump up the cost of your holiday for little extra enjoyment. It would be better heading straight for one of the beaches or islands.

Put Pattaya at the bottom of your list. It is dominated by the sex industry that has followed the single male tourists in search of prostitutes of both sexes and all ages.

NORTH ASIA

China   A fantastic place to visit. Most of China is now open to tourists and you can be assured of safe, free conduct in this fascinating country. Organised tours of China are available in abundance but even with a family in tow, you could safely explore alone. The only major problem travelling independently would be the language barrier and the fact that when you arrive in China, you will find yourself totally illiterate. Even train station names will be unreadable. Very few people in China speak English and so if you do intend to do it alone, you must at least take a phrase book and a list of common Chinese characters, for example, toilet.

You will also be likely to see less if you don't go with a group. Journeying alone will be tiring, but the cost savings are enormous. Many tourist activities and shops are run by the government and are very expensive. A tour from Beijing to the Great Wall of China is likely to cost more than £50. If you were to travel alone, it would be more likely to cost £5.

The water is unsafe to drink. Even the water put in your hotel room and labelled DRINKING WATER should not be used as such. Buy bottled water and always check the seal.

Many menus include mice, wasps, rats, dogs and cats, and,

sadly, even tiger. Diarrhoeal illnesses are very common and standards of hygiene differ dramatically between restaurants. If the rice doesn't have a fresh texture, don't eat it. It can give you food poisoning.

A visit to a Chinese acrobatic show is a must and a pleasure for the whole family. A Chinese opera may be an acquired taste but the screeching will certainly drown out any children who don't like it. The zoos are a little sad, with animals kept in fairly poor conditions.

You will see most families with only one child. However, each child is preened and cleaned and infinitely happy looking. Occasionally you will see two children in the same family but they are usually well dressed and appear wealthy.

Many of the sites are crowded and very tiring to visit but you should pace yourself and choose the time of year you visit carefully. On the Great Wall, the temperatures may vary from $-20°C$ to $+50°C$. June and October are the best times to go. The Forbidden City is a maze with thousands of steps and taking a pushchair around is exhausting, even in the spring. It would be impossible in $50°C$ heat. The Great Wall too is a challenging climb if you wish to walk beyond the crowds, but all the sites in China are well worth the effort.

Japan   Japan is as safe as it gets. Even in Tokyo, if you lose a purse or leave a camera on a train, there is a very good chance you will get it back. If you want to visit Japan with children, there is absolutely no need to join a tour. There are few families who could afford the price ticket for four on a guided tour around Japan but if you go alone, you could spend less than you would in the Caribbean or Europe.

Even language is no longer a barrier. The streets are crammed with Japanese youngsters anxious to practise their English and to help a disorientated family. In the main cities, there are now underground maps, train stations and even street names written in English, so you will comfortably be able to tackle the transport system. There is no need to fear anything other than the driving on the roads, which is confusing, dangerous and fraught with congested traffic.

A child in Japan is precious. They grow up without fear of

abduction or abuse. When you visit a famous site in Japan you will see as many as 100 schoolchildren with just two teachers. As young as four or five, they all hold hands obediently and practise calling out 'Hello' to foreigners without their minders looking at all concerned. Japan is also spotlessly clean. The health and hygiene standards are among the highest in the world. You need have no fear of visiting a hospital in Japan as you would be among some of the safest hands in the world.

As for the food, don't worry. I am blessed with a son who is so fussy that he will only eat certain brands of frozen sweetcorn, yet he adores Japanese food. You need to chose carefully. The best dishes for children are tempura in batter, sweet-chicken skewers called yakitori, rice and ramen or udon noodles. There are also Macdonalds and other fast-food restaurants everywhere. Look out for a big, red lantern hanging outside the restaurant which indicates that the restaurant is inexpensive.

Western-style hotel accommodation can be horribly expensive but there are many 'Ryokan', or Japanese inns, in which a family room is very reasonable. The etiquette is rather complicated but don't be put off. It is an adventure and a fantastic experience for all of you. Follow your children's uninhibited lead. They will doubtless adapt to your host's instruction with enthusiasm.

Train travel is the best way to get around Japan but it is very expensive unless you buy a rail pass, which you must buy before you travel to Japan.

The Japanese love theme parks and there is a genuine Disneyland outside Tokyo.

For children and adults, the best sites in Japan are in Kyoto. The Golden Palace is beautiful, and around all the gardens and shrines of Japan the ponds and massive Koi carp are fascinating for children. The deer parks and giant Buddha of Nara are worth a trip with the family.

The humidity in July and August in Japan is stifling. Springtime is the best time to go. Cherry blossom season is a time for celebration and picnicking under the trees.

There are also volcanic and hot spring areas, which are great fun, if not a little 'touristy'. Mount Fuji can be seen from the bullet train – and the aeroplane on descent into Tokyo, if you are lucky – but the Japanese say that 'she [Mount Fuji] is very shy'. I have been to the foot of the great mountain four times but have never seen her because she has always been shrouded in thick cloud. Japan is becoming more and more westernised but, thankfully, old traditions, respect for others and family values are very much intact.

Kazakhstan   There is little to attract a family on holiday.

Mongolia   There is little to attract the family on holiday.

North Korea   Tourism is banned by the government but you can travel from the South of Korea to the border where you can see the guns aimed rather disconcertingly at you.

South Korea   Like Japan, South Korea is spotlessly clean. This attracts many Japanese visitors who travel for golf, nightlife and excellent shopping in Seoul.

There are huge, safe children's theme parks outside the capital, making it attractive for families.

In the southern city of Pusan, which is easily reached by ferry from Japan, there are good beaches and shopping.

Crime rates are low but the country is under the constant threat of aggression from the north, which is, perhaps, why South Korea has remained off the list of many Western tourists, while any Korean will tell you that their country is clean, beautiful and safe for a family to travel in independently.

Taiwan   If you've done Japan and South Korea and love them, you may enjoy Taiwan. Health facilities are amongst the best in the world but manufacturing, the rise in sex tourism and the dense population on the coast have given the island the feel of being crowded, sprawling and slightly grimy.

In central Taiwan there is more opportunity to see quiet serenity, lakes, mountains and temples. The monsoon season falls between July and September.

WESTERN ASIA

Afghanistan   Political unrest, poor sanitation and extremes of temperature are what to expect.

Armenia   Armenia is at war with neighbouring Azerbaijan.

Azerbaijan   A long tradition of oil exploitation, the simmering war with Armenia and strong anti-Western feeling have kept all but a few business visitors away.

Bahrain   Tourism is important to Bahrain, particularly as its oil reserves are now almost depleted.

Between December and March is the best time of year to visit, when the weather is pleasantly warm. In the summer months, the temperatures are too high for children to be comfortable.

As a stopover, or as a short break in a Western-standard hotel with air-conditioning, the liberal lifestyle of the main island could be enjoyed by families who were respectful of the heat and intense sun, but there is basically just sea and sand and more sand to entertain you all.

Iran   Bazaars, mosques and history expand a child's mind, but there isn't much that Iran has to offer that will occupy each member of the family for a long stay.

Iran is not a place to go to relax. The strife of a highly religious and political populace repeats itself in the region. Antagonism with Iraq continues and although healthcare is adequate in cities, in rural areas conditions are basic.

Iraq   Iraq is effectively closed to Western tourists.

Israel   Jerusalem is important as a holy city for Jews, Christians and Muslims but even for those without a particular faith, Israel is deeply fascinating. You can visit the River Jordan where Jesus was baptised, see the stone where Jesus was sitting when he performed the miracle of the loaves and the fishes, then travel to Nazareth to visit a church built on the site where Mary was visited by the Angel Gabriel. Whether you leave believing that Jesus was the son of God or just a charismatic historical figure, Israel is thought-provoking.

The country is under constant threat from its neighbours, which is evident from the truck-loads of eighteen-year-old boys and girls in army uniforms with guns over their shoulders. Every Israeli is trained to protect their country. The political unrest is not reason enough to stay away from Israel. There is so much to see and do. Healthcare is good and health standards are high.

The road system is good and so hiring a car and driving east of Jerusalem to the Dead Sea and/or south to the Red Sea is easy. Snorkelling and diving in the Red Sea are amongst the best and safest in the world. As in many countries of the world, keep a keen eye on your blond children, boys and girls. There are some stories to be heard.

Jordan Jordan attracts as many tourists as Israel. Jordan, like Israel, borders the Red Sea and offers fine beaches, water sports and some of the best sub-aqua diving in the world without the political unrest. Travel agents describe the sightseeing as superb. One of the most spectacular sites is the ancient rose red city of Petra, carved into the mountains.   —

Follow in the footsteps of Lawrence of Arabia and visit the Wadi Rum where the famous film was shot. The tourist infrastructure is limited, so it may be better to join an organised tour. Travelling with children can be gruelling in the heat.

Kuwait Post-war Kuwait has little to offer the family on holiday.

Kyrgyzstan There is little to offer the family on holiday.

Lebanon In the past, Lebanon was known as the playground of the Middle East. Fine beaches, historical sights, superb cuisine and spectacular sightseeing attracted millions of tourists every year.

The civil war and the corresponding kidnapping of tourists made Beirut and Lebanon a 'no go' area for Western tourists.

Lebanon is beginning to re-establish itself as an exciting tourist destination but there is still the threat of terrorism.

Oman The home of the Arabian nights and alleged home of Sinbad the Sailor. Take the books with you and stimulate your children's imaginations.

Oman offers great beaches, a spotlessly clean environment and luxury hotels at affordable prices. Combine this with great weather and a rich cultural heritage for a good family holiday destination with a difference, although it will be too hot in the height of summer.

Pakistan The rich cultural heritage and unspoiled beauty are not enough to balance out the high levels of crime, including murder and rapes, appalling health standards and a high risk of fatal diarrhoeal infections.

Quatar   Quatar is all desert. Although there are some good beaches, the temperatures in the summer are scorching.

Saudi Arabia   Saudi Arabia does not encourage Western, non-Muslim tourists.

Syria   Syria can compete with many other Middle Eastern states for historical attractions.

Castles date back to the Crusades, and the capital Damascus is the oldest inhabited city in the world.

A small portion of the country borders the Mediterranean sea where good beaches can be found. However, hospitals lack modern equipment and services and human rights records are poor.

Most tourists to Syria are from neighbouring Middle Eastern countries, but for those attracted by the region the coast could make a good destination for a family holiday with a difference.

Tajikistan   Ther is nothing to offer the family on holiday.

Turkmenistan   There is the potential for tourist appeal. It is one of the politically more stable countries of the region with warm, dry springs and a border on the Caspian sea. Presently, highly polluted water is a major health hazard.

United Arab Emirates   For year-round sun, deluxe hotels and first-class service, the UAE is becoming an increasingly popular choice. Dubai is the first stop and probably the best choice for most tourists who are attracted by fantastic beaches, duty free shopping, water sports, good sightseeing, a fascinating culture and hotels which really are exceptional.

All the buildings in the UAE have a short life span and are constantly being knocked down. As a result, there is a succession of brand new hotels in which everything is sparkling, modern and luxurious to the extreme.

There is a safe, crime-free atmosphere, the healthcare is good and hygiene levels are generally very high. The only real enemy you will have when you visit with children is the intense heat.

Yemen   Threats of terrorism and tourist family kidnappings would reasonably deter all but the most determined and experienced traveller.

WESTERN EUROPE

Albania   Sadly, now is not the right point in history to visit Albania, despite its scenic beauty.

Andorra   Twelve million tourists flock to Andorra every year mainly from France and Spain for duty free shopping and, in the winter, 500,000 skiers descend on this tiny country. 180 square miles in area and populated by just 58,000, the impact of the tourist is evident everywhere.

There is a slightly tacky feel to the duty free shopping areas on each border and in the main town of Andorra, although this won't bother the children who are often attracted by garish signs and neon banners. Good, reasonably priced skiing in the winter, and hiking in the summer, are both enjoyable pursuits with older children. The negatives are that, in the summer, the ski runs blight the beautiful Pyrenean landscape and the mass of Day-Glo orange adverts stating the prices of duty free booze look unpleasant.

Another consideration, if driving to or through Andorra with children in the car, is that the roads often become heavily congested in peak season. Roads in the main town, Andorra La Vella, and in the border shopping areas, might be at a standstill. The open mountain roads need concentration.

On balance, there are plenty of reasons to visit Andorra. You and your children should be as safe as you would be at home. Interesting bird life, wildlife and unique mountain flowers are fun to discover, with the added advantage that the altitude ensures relatively mild weather in the spring and summer, making walking a pleasure and not a hot toil.

Austria   Austria is as beautiful and serene as its reputation suggests. In summer, the places to head for are the scenic Tyrol and the Austrian lakes.

Innsbruck is where you are more likely to find good value winter skiing but in the summer, Salzburg is the better destination. Salzburg is the birthplace of Mozart and home to the internationally famous summer music festival. It is also where the famous children's favourite *The Sound of Music* was filmed. You can tour and visit many of the sites featured in the film. Outside Salzburg, around the lakes you will find quiet, tranquil beauty in the surrounding mountains or water sports and sunbathing.

There is an unhurried feel about Austria and it is somewhere you can clean your lungs and relax. Healthcare is good and crime rates are low.

Hotel prices and eating out are reasonable, especially when compared to neighbouring Germany and Switzerland.

Vienna is a sophisticated city of dancing horses, palaces and interesting museums. The natural history museum is an excellent place for families to spend a rainy day. If you are in Vienna for a few days and feeling adventurous, Prague and Budapest are within reasonable distance by train. It will be an adventure which is interesting, enjoyable and affordable.

The disadvantages when travelling with young children in Austria would be that the dry cold in the winter can reach deceptively low temperatures and, as we have seen for the first time recently, although there is excellent skiing in the winter, it can be treacherous if snow falls too long and too deep.

Belgium   Bruges is an easy hop from England and is a city of canals, swans, horse-drawn carriages and chocolate shops. It is a pleasant stop or short break destination to relax in as a family.

Historic cities in the north and pretty countryside in the south are Belgium's main attractions. Good roads and a hospitable, tolerant population make Belgium an enjoyable part in the route of a European driving holiday. Unreliable weather and cool summers with a higher average rainfall in July than in the UK mean that booking a fortnight's holiday could be a gamble for those wanting to escape the British weather.

Cyprus   Cyprus was aggressively divided when Turkey invaded in 1974. It remains under Turkish control in the north and Greek control in the south.

The strangest thing about Cyprus is that it is promoted in all the winter sun brochures, yet temperatures in January and February can average 5°C. Good hotels cost next to nothing after Christmas but many of the resorts have an 'out-of-season' Blackpool feel about them and are more suitable for the retired than the family. In contrast, the summer temperatures can reach the high thirties, again, not ideal for children without air-conditioning and other cooling comforts.

50 per cent of Cyprus's tourists are British and so if you want British food, newspapers or English-speaking company for yourselves or your children, then you won't be disappointed. The friendly Cypriots welcome the British with refreshing hospitality. With a strong family culture themselves, they appear to be always willing to help make your family holiday more comfortable and relaxing.

Egypt and Israel are easily accessible if you take a mini-cruise from one of the ports in Southern Cyprus. The hotel standards are generally good. There are a number of deluxe tourist-class hotels and the three stars are generally run with care by local families. Everything in between should be acceptable as long as you make your choice carefully, as you would in any other tourist resort.

Healthcare is good and crime rates are low.

Denmark   Hans Christian Andersen's Copenhagen and Legoland may be the main destinations for a family trip, but Denmark offers plenty more for the family.

Summertime would be the best time to visit. Wintertime in Denmark is cold and grey and the days are short.

There is a great choice of affordable cottage accommodation in the Danish countryside which can be booked in combination with a ferry crossing at prices which would be within the budget of most families. Cheaper still would be the well kept, excellently situated campsites. There are also plenty of touring inns. Self-contained holiday centres are equipped with facilities such as indoor swimming pools and children's playgrounds, all the things which make a childhood paradise.

Denmark is perfect for touring in your own car. The country's small size means that anywhere is within a day's journey. The beaches are good, English is widely spoken and health service standards are high. Getting around locally is easy on a bicycle as Denmark is very flat.

You can book excellent deals with Scandinavian Seaways and get free child places for more than one child if you book early.

Finland   The most recently expanding reason to visit Finland is to see Santa at Christmas time. The trips are becoming increasingly popular and when you ask anyone who has been there with their children what it was like, they become a little hazy and a warm glow comes over them, as they recall the look on their children's faces. It is apparently in line with a trip to Disneyland on the scale of major events in a child's life.

It can be bitterly cold and to ensure a perfect day, you should travel prepared.

The best age to take most children is between six and seven years old. They are young enough to still believe, yet old enough to remember the trip for their lifetime.

France   Perfect for family holidays. It is a hop away and there are endless choices of the types of holiday on offer.

Touring France by car is the ultimate freedom holiday and the options for accommodation en route are endless, ranging from excellent camping facilities to luxury chateau hotels. All are flexible and welcoming. Combine a few nights' fun camping with the children as priority, then a few nights sophistication for yourselves.

Every region of France has something fascinating to explore. The north-west of France and its resorts are similar in many ways to the south coast of England. Even the architecture is familiar. So for those who enjoy Brighton or Bournemouth, why not pay a few extra pounds for the ferry fare and try Deauville.

Disneyland Paris is sheer torture for any sane adult but the pleasure it gives the children is worth it.

Paris holds many delights for every member of the family. You can ascend most things in Paris, including the Eiffel Tower, the Arc de Triomphe and Notre Dame. A short cruise along the Seine is a lazy pleasure but note that the lunch served on many of the Seine cruises is more like a school dinner than fine French cuisine, so don't think you have the cheap seats if you go for a simple boat ride without the meal. The Louvre is interesting for older children but the museum is huge and a trek around it with children may be a test of endurance for you all. Looking down over Paris from the steps of the Sacre Coeur is a memorable vista.

The best way of getting around Paris to see the sights with a family is by car and so, if you are on a driving holiday anyway, don't be put off by tales of traffic jams. If you want to avoid the traffic, pop in at night and see the wonders of Paris fully illuminated and stunning. It is much easier to find your way around without the traffic but even being stuck in long queues, you see the flavours and pace of one of the world's most fantastic cities.

The Palace of Versailles is a short distance from the centre but worth a visit. Its history is nice and macabre to keep the children entertained.

The countryside in France in the summertime is gorgeous, with fields full of sunflower and sweetcorn. More southerly, you will pass vineyards and cherry orchards between quaint villages and scattered farm houses.

In the south you will find a cosmopolitan style that the world over has tried to mimic, invariably without success. It comes with a price tag but there are excellent campsites and not-too-extortionate villas for rent just outside Nice and Monte Carlo. St Tropez is the place to people-watch and spot the yachts. It is much smaller than its other famous neighbours but with that, it has managed to retain a little more charm. Marseille is basically a port and host to many of France's racist clashes and criminals with little to attract the visitor.

The food markets in France are a delight, as are the bakeries. The French love their food.

In the summer, many campsites next to the lakes have water sports on offer, which is a far less expensive alternative to the south and the sea. The winter skiing in France is also excellent but expensive. Try to avoid French holidays because the ski slopes are so crowded.

Take a phrase book. The French are as reluctant to learn English as we are to learn French, and although there are more English-speaking Frenchmen than vice versa, you may struggle outside the cities or in an emergency without a word of French.

Germany   The reason we see so many Germans abroad around the Mediterranean is because, like us, their northern beaches are freezing for most of the year and they want a glimpse of sand and sunshine too. So if you want beaches, Germany is not the best place in Europe to aim for.

Germany is a good alternative destination for a driving holiday: the roadways are efficient and the Autobahns (motorways) are toll free. There are a number of holiday centres, such as centre parcs in Germany, which are always ideal for children. The Bavarian Alps and the Black Forest are beautiful and have an aura of rich folklore amid fairytale castles. The choice of affordable accommodation along the routes is good. You will find all the services, comforts and healthcare you have at home.

Greece Greece offers many choices of holiday destinations. There is the mainland and Athens with its history, whereas the islands offer a total contrast between remote subsistence with a small population and few visitors, to bigger islands whose economy centres around the tourist industry. Corfu, Crete, Rhodes and Kos are the most popular, and with that you can expect a mass of hotels, restaurants and night clubs. Many of the resorts are clusters of high-rises lacking air-conditioning and abundant balconies. The popular beaches are crowded and the hotel pools are rarely heated. On the positive side, Greece is cheap to get to, hot, sunny and relatively near by.

Although Greece is very cheap to get to, you should budget for the fact that in many places, it is expensive to eat out in. Parents may be surprised to learn that a meal for four in a popular tourist resort on the Greek Islands can cost more than it would in a restaurant in the Caribbean and certainly more than in America or Australia. The good points are that you are guaranteed beating sun and scorching heat even into the night.

Greece is not the cleanest destination in Europe and you are likely to see your restaurant chef with filthy overalls picking his teeth and smoking in a corner. Take care what you eat and drink.

If you plan to get to bed early and sleep, you really do need to check the situation of your hotel on a map of the town before booking. With children, try to book somewhere just outside the main shopping and disco area and, if possible, right next to a beach. The walk to the beach in the Greek summer is too long and too hot for children.

Healthcare is of a variable standard. A friend told me of an experience in Greece when a doctor (who was smoking at the time) stabbed a lance into her unanaesthetised groin and fished around in the wound while two nurses held her down. If you do need medical treatment, ask your hotel for an English-speaking doctor. If you can at least communicate, you have a good chance of getting decent care.

Greece is great if you are on a very tight budget but if you have a little more money to spend on your family holiday, look at offers in the Caribbean before you decide. You may be amazed to find that a fortnight in Tobago compares price-wise with Greece.

The safety, hygiene and general standards in Greece are lower than in many places, which is not ideal for children. Touring and sightseeing is hard in the intense heat and because the country is so arid, the scenery is limited to olive groves, vineyards and craggy mountain sides.

Although you may have had the time of your life in your teens, dancing all through hot, summer nights, I would avoid the summer in Greece with a young family. Spring is a better time to visit, when it is cooler and infinitely more pleasant.

Hungary Budapest is a pleasant, cosmopolitan city and I am certain that a family who based themselves in the capital would find plenty of cultural and enjoyable ways of passing their time. Cruise on the Blue Danube, explore the museums, or head out from the city towards Lake Balaton which is a popular summer destination for many Eastern Europeans. Your money will go a long way.

Iceland Nobody would travel to Iceland seeking sunshine but if you want snow, ice, fjords, hot springs and spectacular glaciers, Reykjavik will be keen to accommodate you. You can then settle in and travel to more adventurous regions at leisure. The winter wind is biting and even the babies' prams have real fur covers instead of woollen blankets, yet still, you will be enticed into bathing in hot, natural springs in the open air as Paris and I were. He was only very young and tried to catch the mist rising from the hot pool into the freezing air.

Civilised but expensive, Iceland offers an experience as far removed from the Mediterranean as is imaginable. The terrain in winter is evocative of images of the moon.

Ireland The only factor going against Ireland as a tourist destination is the weather. The climate is mild but wet. The average temperature, even in summer, is just 20°C. The beaches on the west of Ireland are among the best in the world. Sadly, it usually too cold to enjoy them.

It is one of the ultimate driving holiday destinations. Driving in Ireland is how it must have been in England twenty years ago when people went out for a Sunday drive to relax. The countryside is scenic and uncongested.

The lifestyle is incredibly relaxed and wherever you go to drink Guinness, no one looks at your children as if they should be in bed.

Ireland is a perfect destination for taking a caravan. There is also accommodation available in every price bracket, from a plenitude of bed-and-breakfasts to five-star hotels in converted castles.

Italy Italy is Europe at its best and most sophisticated. It is atmospheric, historic and romantic.

The camping in Italy is excellent and definitely the least expensive way of seeing the country where accommodation can be very expensive. Driving holidays in the summer are a very hot experience without air-conditioning in the car, and the Italian drivers are incredible. You will regularly come out of a blind corner to find some hot-head overtaking, and on your side of the road. The motorways are quiet and much safer, but the tolls are expensive.

The beach areas are built up and often unattractive, crime levels are high and holidaying in Italy with a family can be pricy. Many holidays to Sorrento are sold and it is therefore a big surprise to find that there are no beaches in that area. The better beaches are around Rimini and the Lido di Jesolo, which is very close to Venice, but both areas are very 'touristy'.

The cities are very hot and tiring in the summer. A better time for children to appreciate them would be the spring.

Liechtenstein A tiny country at the western tip of Austria where you and your children would be as safe as you are at home. The weather in the spring and summer is mild, with alpine scenery, but there is little to attract a family for a long stay.

Lithuania   Health and hygiene standards are OK but there are few attractions for a family.

Luxembourg   A small country of mountains, forests and castles. It is dominated by the capital city which is pleasant but not very memorable. It is nice to pass through on a driving holiday but differs little in terrain and atmosphere from its dominating, more charismatic neighbours.

Macedonia   War tensions make for a less than an ideal family holiday.

Malta   Well developed as a tourist resort but geared towards the older visitor. As over half the tourists who visit Malta are British, you often feel as if you are in Llandudno in a heat wave. English is widely spoken and the healthcare is of Western standards.

There are few beaches and the summers are very hot for children but it is very friendly, relaxing and excellent value for money. Neighbouring Gozo is quieter and prettier but, like Malta, can be very windy, especially early in the season.

Monaco   Monaco may be a little stuffy for a family trying to relax. It attracts the rich who travel for the James Bond-style casinos to wear their diamonds. The hotels are glamorous, probably too glamorous for sticky fingers and grubby faces.

It is great for a short break or a stop on a driving holiday through Europe but in terms of making it the main destination for your family holiday, when you should be having fun together, you are more likely to enjoy other destinations in Europe.

The Netherlands   The flat terrain here is ideal for family cycling holidays through tulip fields and windmills. For a city break, Amsterdam is certainly fascinating, with many aspects that make it appealing for a family. Anne Frank's house and Amsterdam's museums and art galleries provide the culture. The restaurants and accommodation are good and affordable. You can hire a boat by the hour and tour the canals alone or join an organised trip, then hire bikes and explore.

Amsterdam has a safe feel, even at night, but whether or not you choose to wander around the red light district with your children is something only you can decide. A friend of mine walked through the area with her parents when she was about eleven years old and commented on it briefly when she returned to school. It certainly didn't do her any harm. Stay clear of the sex-shop windows if you are with children; they have the power to shock even the most streetwise adult.

Outside Amsterdam, Holland is excellent for touring by car. Accommodation standards are high and reasonably priced.

Norway Skiing and fjord trips on cruise ships are the main attraction for visiting tourists. Norway's greatest attraction is its scenery which is so dramatic that even children may appreciate it.

The country is mountainous and some of the roads are challenging. You will need your concentration and if any of the children are likely to get motion sickness, travel prepared.

The history of the Vikings and folklore are fascinating for children. In Oslo you can visit Viking ships, and in south-east Norway you can find the home of the world's largest troll.

There is plenty of affordable country cottage accommodation which can be booked in combination with a ferry crossing at prices within the budget of most families. Good camping, holiday centres, touring hotels and resort hotels are also available.

Norway is also host to the midnight sun.

Portugal Holidaying in southern Portugal is as easy as it gets. Even someone who had never been abroad in their life and was travelling with ten children would be unlikely to get unstuck in the Algarve. The villas are perfect for families. Spotlessly clean, pretty, built to high standards, well equipped and tastefully furnished, they are the real lazy man's choice. There will be little adventure and a real sense of Portugal has been gradually nudged out of the south, but if you just want to relax in the sunshine then put the kids to bed and drink by the pool, the Algarve is perfect.

The other big bonus is that it is a stone's throw from the UK. Easy, cheap and abundant flights from all UK airports make Portugal accessible to everyone.

The only slight negatives are that the Atlantic is a little cold and rough and there are lots of large mosquitoes. It can get very hot in the summer, and from October onwards, the evenings can get very cold. There is little heating in the villas and so you will need to pack jumpers and warm clothing.

Be careful on the roads. The main road between Faro airport and the majority of the main tourist areas is allegedly the most dangerous road in Europe with the most fatalities. If you hire a car, get used to it before you get on the main highway, then go steadily. Don't let anyone hassle you into making a decision and if you get lost, what does it matter? You'll soon be on track again unless you try to veer off from the outside lane. Let someone map-read or stop the car to follow the route.

If you opt for a hotel, you will generally find high standards and good value for money.

Lisbon is more of a challenge and harder to find your way around than many other European capitals, but is invigorating and interesting with good seafood restaurants. Great for a short break or stopover. In Portugal the public health system is free and, although standards lag behind that of the UK, they are adequate.

Portugal still has lower crime rates and cheaper prices than Spain and Italy with good shopping and excellent golf courses.

San Marino A tiny republic in the centre of Italy, perched on the top of a mountain. You can see for miles from its fortresses, which is surely how it has managed to maintain its independence. It is pretty and worth a day trip or an overnight stay but there would not be enough to entertain a family for an entire holiday. You must also beware of the precipitous drops down sheer mountainside.

Spain The fact that British families flock to Spain in their millions is an indication of how easy it is to cope with family on holiday there. The tourist infrastructure is well developed and can cope with even the tiniest traveller.

Spain offers a huge choice of destinations virtually along the entire length of the southern coast. In addition, there are the Canary and the Balearic islands, each of which offers a choice of quiet and lively resorts. For culture, head for Madrid, Seville,

Granada and Barcelona, all of which are energetic and fascinating cities, but be aware that in the summer Seville can be the hottest place in Spain with temperatures over 45°C and children will be miserable.

Throughout the resorts there is accommodation on offer for every budget. Many resorts are a mass of apartment complexes and multi-storey hotels. Few are pretty and well planned to be in keeping with Spanish architecture, which is an indication of how quickly tourism swept over and dominated much of the Spanish coast. Some of the newer and more attractive hotels are set back a little from the main beaches because most of the prime coast was snapped up years ago and cluttered with grey towers. You can save a small fortune in the summer if you opt for an apartment or hotel a car's journey from the beach and town and hire a car for the duration of your stay. Car hire is very good value in Spain and will often cost you the same for one week as the return taxi fare from the airport. You will often find that you get prettier accommodation for your money as the nicer hotels on the beach front are very expensive in peak season, which unfortunately coincides with the children's school holidays. The bonus is that you will be able to sleep away from the noise of town nightlife which is unceasing in the height of the season.

The greatest attraction is that the sun; heat and lack of rain are guaranteed all over Spain in the summer. However, be aware that in the winter, and often in the spring and autumn, Spain and the Balearic Islands are cold. The Canary Islands remain generally warm but the weather can be terrible and very rainy, especially during January and February, despite the fact that it is heavily promoted for winter sun.

The down-side in the summer is the crowds and an abundance of childhood illnesses. Many children will pick up something in the height of summer, whether it be a mild tummy bug, a cold or an ear infection. The water and hygiene standards are a little unsanitary which has led to the much publicised outbreaks of food poisoning. In the heat, bacteria multiply at an alarming rate, so be wary of the hotel buffet and drink only bottled water.

The other concern is that building regulations and safety

standards vary from those in the UK. Balconies can be positively dangerous.

Sweden   Children may enjoy a Scandinavian driving holiday more than one in the southerly parts of Europe because you won't be battling to keep them cool in the car. The roads in Sweden are toll free and uncrowded, which relieves the anxiety faced on some French and Spanish roads.

The choice of affordable accommodation is extensive and can be booked in combination with a ferry crossing at prices within the budget of most families. Choose from country cottages, well-situated campsites, or touring inns and hotels. You can book excellent deals with Scandinavian Seaways and get free child places for more than one child if you book early enough.

Switzerland   Switzerland offers excellent skiing but it is expensive compared to many other European resorts. The plus is that it isn't as crowded and overrun by snow boarders as some of the cheaper destinations.

Switzerland in the summer has a sleepy beauty. Even the cities are relatively quiet, all except Zurich, which is lively but has a drug problem. In Zurich, the authorities are fighting a constant battle to clean used needles out of the parks. Watch where your children are playing. Berne and Geneva are a peaceful contrast.

Switzerland suffers from the stiff competition and cheaper prices in Austria, but if on a driving holiday, why not visit them both?

EASTERN EUROPE

Belorussia   After being under arrest at the border and deported with a train load anxious to flee the country, I feel confident in claiming that there is little to attract the family.

Bosnia and Herzegovina   Many roads, railways, bridges and historic sites have been destroyed. Little infrastructure remains.

Bulgaria   Most tourists arrive from Eastern Europe but many family resorts are now trying to attract Western visitors. At present, families will benefit from cheap sea and sun on the Black Sea, but be prepared for very basic standards and do not go out of season where you may find frogs in the swimming pool and cows eating the parsley off your meal.

The skiing in Bulgaria is acceptable for families though may be lacking in challenge for many more experienced skiers. Once again, the benefit is that it is cheap.

Be wary; food standards are variable and hotel food can be inedible, although a family of six can apparantly enjoy a fantastic meal, with wine, for around £20 in local restaurants.

Unfortunately tourists in the major resorts are targets for muggings but to no greater extent than in Spain or Italy.

Croatia Croatia has acquired much of former Yugoslavia's Adriatic coastline which has encouraged a creeping recovery of the tourist industry. Sadly, beautiful cities such as Dubrovnik were shelled during the country's break-up.

Czech Republic Prague is the main reason most tourists choose to visit. The capital is one of the most enchanting cities in the world. It is well worth a visit in itself, but overnight sleeper trains run between Prague and Budapest if you prefer to pick a two-centre holiday.

If your family are music lovers, Vienna is a tolerable distance by train (five–six hours), which will give you the chance to view the Czech countryside and experience the more expensive Austrian capital from your less expensive hotel room in Prague.

Due to the fact that Prague escaped being bombed during the wars, the evolution of architecture through the centuries is still intact on an impressive scale. Prague has a fairy-tale feel. The tiny dwellings built into the castle fortifications on Golden Lane look as if they should be inhabited by Thumbelina and Tom Thumb. The central squares in Prague ring with horses' hooves and bring to life notions of the Emperor parading through the street naked in his imaginary new clothes. Even Wenceslas Square was named after a real life 'Good King Wenceslas'.

Food is variable but cheap. Western tastes are catered for.

Health service standards lag behind those in Western Europe and infant mortality is high in some of the outlying polluted towns. The benefit is that the Czech Republic is close enough to home to whip straight back if you suspect your child is becoming seriously ill.

Prague gets very cold in the winter. Even in late April, the easterly winds can be icy, so travel prepared with thick socks, coats and mittens.

Beware of pickpockets.

Estonia Estonia offers a gentle introduction to Eastern European life. The capital Tallinn is the main attraction, whose architectural beauty with its perfectly preserved buildings, spires and twisting lanes has been compared by some to Prague. Like Prague, Tallinn escaped being bombed in the wars, and has remained virtually unchanged over the centuries.

Georgia Political strife is a deterrent.

Latvia The capital Riga is the destination of a number of cruise ships attracted by its medieval centre.

Moldavia Crime is low and there is a relatively well-developed infrastructure in the country but healthcare is rudimentary and doctors are poorly trained.

Poland In the winter Poland is grey and bleak. Even the historic areas of Warsaw have a dreary feel.

The summer is good for hiking but the food and hotel standards are perhaps more Russian than Western, which make it difficult when travelling with children.

Romania Romania would be worth a visit to explore *Dracula* country. The Carpathian mountains and Transylvania are steeped in historical heritage.

Other attractions in Romania are the Black Sea and the mouth of the River Danube.

The negatives are that the availability of hotel accommodation is limited and the standards of healthcare are among the lowest in Europe.

Russian Federatian Tourist trips to Moscow and St Petersburg are on the increase again. Both offer overwhelming history. A short break in either city would be a fantastic cultural opportunity for an older child of either sex. There is the ballet and the palaces, or they can take a tour in a MiG jet and drive a Russian tank!

Crime is a huge problem. Muggings are commonplace.

Slovakia Slovakia was half of the former Czechoslovakia, which split in 1993 into the Czech Republic and Slovakia.

Slovakia is the less developed of the two, and has a poorer health service. The main attraction is the Tatra mountains, which attract families for skiing, caving and hiking.

Snowfall is heavy in the winter, and the summer temperatures are warm.

Slovenia   Slovenia is trying to attract village tourism to the farms as well as mountains and beaches.

Ukraine   The warm resorts in the south are the main potential attractions. Crime rates are rising and foreigners are targeted by muggers. The Mafia, corruption and a poor economy do not make for a cheerful holiday.

Uzbekistan   Uzbekistan was on the silk route and is famous worldwide for its architecture. However, culture in isolation is often dreary to children.

Yugoslavia (Serbia and Montenegro)   Sadly the provocation and political unrest are ongoing and tourists should avoid the country.

THE CARIBBEAN

Most of the Caribbean islands rate quite highly in their suitability for travelling with children. There are a few exceptions but generally the only disadvantage when travelling from the UK would be the long journey.

Shop around and you will be able to get a week or two in the Caribbean in the school holidays for around the same price or less than in the Mediterranean. In summertime, while the Mediterranean is peak season, the Caribbean is low season. The hotels offer all sorts of incentives for the family. There are hefty child discounts and free child places available on most islands between June and September.

Varying between the individual islands, June through to November is the hottest, rainiest time. Still, the temperature and humidity are child's play when compared to the intense sweaty heat of the Greek summer. The rainfall on many Caribbean islands is brief and refreshing, so when you might be considering paying double the rates in the sweltering Mediterranean, research the options across the Atlantic.

Caribbean women love children. When we travelled to Tobago with our five-month-old son, the waitresses would often squeal with delight when we entered a restaurant and our chambermaid spent more time talking and playing with him than she did cleaning our room. The hotel staff would laugh and fuss at our table. Nothing was too much trouble. Few restaurants have highchairs but we were welcome to help ourselves to as many chairs as we needed to pin the baby carrier, complete with baby, in a safe place.

The Caribbean environment is safe and free from tropical diseases. The abundance of white, sandy beaches with warm, shallow seas are a delight for even the tiniest baby sitting and watching the gentle waves tickle his toes. You can relax while watching your unstable toddler gaining the confidence to take successive steps into the water. Even the mosquitoes are less prolific than in Spain, Portugal or Italy.

The hotels and restaurants are accustomed to dealing with the sensitive American stomach which is suitably intolerant of upset. Standards of hygiene and cleanliness are well above those in many Mediterranean destinations, where we Brits seem to accept falling ill as part and package of our holiday. Throughout the Caribbean you can get presentable American and continental food and you will always find something in the majority of restaurants to feed to your children.

On most of the islands it is better to secure your accommodation before you arrive, as the package deals negotiated by tour operators are invariably good value and, with the added incentives of cheap child places offered by many of them, the prices in the summer are hard to beat. Pick the accommodation you are comfortable with. If it would stress you out dressing three children and yourself for dinner, don't bother with a deluxe hotel. Opt instead for a motel style or less elaborate hotel where you can walk through reception with sandy feet if you wish.

All the islands are easy to get around by hire car. They are mostly small enough to tour in a day or two and so it is doubtful that you will need a car for longer. The roads are good, uncrowded and many of the systems are similar to that of the British, that is, driving on the left. Jamaica is the most challenging and dangerous destination to drive around independently and so be careful.

Hurricanes may occur between July to October but they are usually nothing to write home about and because they come with good warnings, there are few fatalities. The most important thing is to follow advice. The winds can whip up suddenly and so if you are instructed to stay in your hotel for the day, do so.

For stimulating a child's imagination, the strong history of pirates, sugar plantations and slaves is too powerful to go unmentioned.

Antigua and Barbuda The disadvantages relative to some of the other islands are that it can be expensive to stay and eat on Antigua and Barbuda, plus there is a little hostility towards tourists, but the standard of living on the islands is high which keeps most of the locals free from animosity.

The advantages are that typically, Caribbean Antigua is safe, clean, hygienic and disease free. The medical facilities are good and as the island is English speaking, so are the doctors. The hotels and restaurants are to the highest standards. A bonus is that Antigua is less humid than other Caribbean islands and so if you are travelling to the Caribbean in the children's summer holidays you are likely to be treated to less heat, less rainfall and milder hurricanes if they do hit!

Bahamas There are six tourists who visit the Bahamas per inhabitant per year and the consequence of this is inevitable. The main islands of the Bahamas serviced by major airports are a mass of casinos, hotels and tourist trips and there is some animosity between the local population and the trippers. To add fuel to the fire, the Bahamas are in the path of the main narcotic drug routes between South and North America, and so on some of the islands, there is the associated crime, tourist muggings and occasional tourist shootings, possibly the accidental result of a bungled mugging. As a result, the Bahamas can be disappointing.

For the average family, Paradise Island is the best place to stay. The island is separated from Nassau by a large bridge, which is an effective barrier to the spillover of crime from downtown areas. There is a wide choice of accommodation from villas, apartments, budget and luxury hotels. Its relative detachment from the capital brings security and safety. There are plenty of water sports on offer and safe, shallow beaches. Most of the hotels have a number of good swimming pools, too. Orientation towards American short, casino-bound, budget trips ensures the prices are reasonable and the service is to a good standard.

There are high standards of health and hygiene in the resorts. The locals and the doctors are all English speaking. Typical American-orientated menus feature all the foods children love.

The Bahamas may not be the ideal of the Caribbean you imagined and the Caribbean culture seems a little watered down by the strong American influence, yet on balance they offer a comfortable, child-friendly environment with reasonable value for money if you are careful and choose the right spot.

Sailing to the outlying islands is out of the reach of most pockets but if you have your own yacht it would be a perfect destination. Just avoid hurricane season from July to December and prepare for high temperatures and uncomfortable humidity in the summer.

Barbados For the British visitor there is not a drastic culture change in many of the resorts. The lovers of Barbados tend to be those who like their very British, pampered home comforts, or children who can revel in luxurious familiarity. Expensive hotels, exclusive members' clubs and elitist control of business have resulted in a disparity between the local Bajans and the more affluent residents of the island. This has led to some resentment and so not every local welcomes the tourists with open arms. Attacks on tourists are on the increase. There is an intrusive degree of local hawking and touting all over the beaches and tourist spots of Barbados.

The real beauty of Barbados is its serenity and natural exquisiteness. Just inland, behind the busy public beaches and multitude of hotels, huge ginger lilies, hibiscus and sugarcane fields decorate a tidy, pretty island. Ask a local to cut a piece a sugarcane from the field for your children to taste.

The tropical gardens of Barbados are memorable, as is Harrison's Cave, which is Barbados's number one tourist resort. Aboard an electric tram you can view a beautiful, natural underground world of stalactites and stalagmites, fantastic for even the youngest children. The Barbados wildlife reserve would be another enjoyable family day out as a change from the miles of pink and white beaches.

Magnificent beaches, hotels and facilities ensure that your holiday will be easy and relaxing but it is wise to choose your hotel whilst considering that, with accompanying children, you may find a budget class hotel far more restful than a more exclusive one where pretensions can run high. Your children just want to have fun and run around screaming, not dress for dinner and mind their manners so that you can avoid condescending stares.

There are an increasing number of very good value holidays to Barbados on offer, especially during our summertime. Many hotels, faced with the downturn in trade at the end of the high season, and increased competition, offer free child places and it usually follows that those hotels offering free child places are the most likely to be child-friendly.

Healthcare and hygiene standards are good. English is the official language of Barbados.

Beware of swimming on the east coast. The white-capped rolling sea would not be safe for children.

The Cayman Islands The Cayman Islands are pleasant but more barren than many of their lush neighbours.

There is not a great deal to do with children other than relax in pleasant hotels and enjoy the sea. The diving is good in deeper waters but this is of little use to children under twelve years old. The snorkelling is good by Caribbean standards.

Seven Mile Beach is an expanse of gleaming white sand which is, in parts, totally deserted. Instead of being clumped together, the hotels are spread out along the beach, giving relative seclusion between them. The sea is gentle and crystal clear.

Service is excellent and the choice of restaurants close to Seven Mile Beach is perfect for families. There are fast-food restaurants which rather blight the landscape but are a sure, cheap meal for the children. Slightly upmarket American style diners are also a good option for a clean plate. In Georgetown there are patisseries and big American supermarkets which sell everything you are likely to need. Gourmet cuisine is easily found, too.

Sightseeing on the island is limited to a long day trip. You can travel to picturesque 'Rum Point', with its shallow turquoise waters and silver-white sand, then turn around and drive to the other side of the island to visit the turtle farm in one day. Car hire is good value and Jeeps are a cool option with older children.

Health and hygiene standards are excellent.

Families can get some very reasonable deals for British summertime, but it can be very rainy in June and, as life in the Caymans revolves around the sea, there is little else to do.

Cuba   The image of Cuba as a military regime or communist stronghold is still in the minds of many would-be tourists but it is now, largely, an untrue impression. Cuba is completely unique with an intriguing history, culture and a spectacular mix of scenery and excellent beaches. The hotels are very good and the all-inclusive deals are good value. There are some very cheap child offers available with major tour operators.

The islands off the north coast are reputed to be for tourists 'with more money than sense' although this appears to no longer be true, with deals on offer to match any of the more popular islands. The beaches both on the islands and on the mainland are lovely.

Healthcare is good and crime rates are low.

Dominica (do not confuse with the Dominican Republic)   The airports on Dominica can only take small propeller planes and not commercial aircraft. This, and possibly the lack of easily accessible beaches, has kept many tourists away. There are flight connections from a number of surrounding islands, including Martinique, Guadeloupe, Barbados and Antigua.

Dominica is the most unspoilt, untamed and rugged of all the Caribbean islands. There are waterfalls, green grottos, clear rivers and hot springs to bathe in, instead of the sea.

Nature-lovers and child explorers will relish trekking up mountain sides and through safe, tropical rainforests.

Accommodation can be secured at bargain prices. Food is more traditionally Caribbean than American or continental. The local delicacy is mountain chicken, more commonly known as frog!

For the more earnest searcher of paradise, the inaccessibility would be worth the trouble.

Dominican Republic and Haiti   Haiti is the poorest country in the Americas. The political instability has sent most tourists east of the border to the neighbouring Dominican Republic.

The Dominican Republic has received a lot of bad press recently, with claims that the hygiene standards are very low. Foods tested in even the best hotels in the resorts were found to contain levels of food-poisoning bacteria which would certainly cause illness.

The positives are good beaches and cheap prices. If you are vigilant, there should be no problem. Ask other hotel guests who arrived before you if they have been OK. If not, ask them what they think caused the problem. Ice? Salad? Sea food? The swimming pool?

For families seeking out reminders of Spain in the Caribbean (including the tummy bugs), the Dominican Republic is perfect.

Grenada   The spice island of Grenada is as tranquil and pretty as it gets. The beaches are good and healthcare has improved since the restoration of democracy.

Tourism is still lagging behind that of other Caribbean Islands, but in a positive way. Food is good and the locals are friendly, if not a little money wise. It may turn out a more expensive holiday than a similar one taken on a more developed neighbouring island.

Jamaica   Jamaica is a tough place.

Inside the all-inclusive resorts you may find the paradise you seek, but outside the gates you will get constant, persistent hassle. The Jamaicans rely heavily on their tourists but they don't treat them well. They target you most before you get a tan. They know that the whiter you are, the greener you are.

My own experiences in Jamaica, thankfully before any

children, amounted to a holiday from hell. I left smiling but my husband spent the last week of our holiday wishing the time away. In the first week, we were robbed twice. My passport then disappeared and we were forced to travel to the British embassy in Kingston before I could get home. When I did get home, I received reverse-charge calls telling me that if I sent some money, I could get my passport back. My husband and I went on a horse-riding tour but the horses were so poorly kept that mine collapsed and fell on top of me. Luckily he started to get up before he crushed me. In addition, a motel owner tried to trick me into signing a credit card slip that stated two nights' stay would be US $600 instead of Jamaican $600. If I hadn't noticed, two nights in a dingy motel would have cost £400 instead of £60.

We had headed for Jamaica with images of a colonial Caribbean no longer in existence. Life in the slums around Kingston is as tough as it gets. There are dons, gangs, guns, drugs and violence. Jamaica is basically a Third World country. If you decide to go, book carefully. Go into an enclosed beach resort if you have the budget. You will still be able to venture out on trips and see some of the beauty of the island if you choose, but you will have the security and protection for your family at night and when you want to relax without constant harassment.

St Kitts and St Nevis A little off the traditional Caribbean beaten track, St Kitts is historically and scenically fascinating. The beaches are stunning and prices are more reasonable than on some of the other islands. St Nevis is just a ferry ride away. Between them, the two islands have everything typically Caribbean to offer, except the crowds.

St Lucia St Lucia is lush, green and beautiful. It is a volcanic island which ensures that its botanics and fertility are spectacular, but it also means that you won't find the powder-white beaches to be found in many other parts of the Caribbean. It is also pricy when compared to many of the other islands, although an increasing number of good value packages and unbelievable child holiday offers are making St Lucia more accessible.

There is some hostility towards tourists but the local people are generally welcoming. Ruled by the British and the French at different times, St Lucia retains some of the character and cuisine of both.

Hotels are good and many are positively luxurious. Getting around is relatively easy and there are many sites and coves to explore. There is plenty to see, including a 'drive-in' volcano and some of the finest tropical gardens in the Caribbean.

The Grenadines The Grenadines offer the finest yachting areas in the Caribbean sea and have an atmosphere of sleepy beauty, but there is little to do and see on the tiny islands.

St Vincent Has more to offer a family but still is more orientated towards the jet set, so prices are higher than in other parts of the Caribbean and there are few child reductions available. Most of the islands are too small to do anything other than escape from the real world. Other Caribbean islands with more variety may be a better option with children.

Trinidad and Tobago Tobago is purported to be the legendary Robinson Crusoe island and it certainly lives up to the image. Life in Tobago is quiet, simple and very relaxing. The beaches are lovely, the seas are warm and the countryside is rich in tropical flora and fauna. Both Trinidad and Tobago have rainforests. Crime is a problem in Trinidad and this is sadly spilling over on to sleepy Tobago but the major targets are the bigger, more popular hotels. The smaller, cheaper, family hotels without much beach front remain unsullied.

Tobago is a lovely destination. You won't find the crowds which you do on the other islands, and the island is excellent for families. The people are friendly and welcoming and the beaches are soft, safe and clean.

The food is good and hygienic. The healthcare is to a high standard and, if there are any huge mishaps, Trinidad is host to a major teaching hospital, ensuring that some of the best medical facilities in the Caribbean are available. It is an island you will want to go back to if you just want to enjoy the laid-back image and shoeless lifestyle of the Caribbean seas.

CENTRAL AMERICA

Belize   If you want to visit a Central American country with a family, Belize should be your first choice. It has everything to offer, from jaguar sanctuaries where big cats roam free, to pristine rain forest, Caribbean beaches, excellent diving and tiny cays off shore, where there are no tarmac roads and few people wear shoes.

Travelling around Belize is a challenging task and is very hard by road. Car hire is unbelievably expensive and a journey that will cost you $3 by bone-jerking bus will cost you up to $150 by dilapidated taxi. It is incredible. There is no rail system and so a network of short, reasonably priced flights has built up between the cays on the reef, the resorts on the south-east coast and the interior of the country. There are few reductions for children on tours and the flights offer a nominal discount.

Packages to Belize are very expensive but if you go it alone, you will save a fortune. Flights are relatively cheap and so is the accommodation if you pick well. On the quieter Cayes, a cabana on the beach which can host a family would cost just US $20–$30 per night. On Ambergris Caye, by far the most expensive, there are cheap rooms in the main street motels, and if you wander around or hire a golf cart, then drive around the sand streets, you may pick up a condo for a bargain.

Everyone speaks English and everyone appears to live a comfortable enough lifestyle to sustain themselves honestly. Belize is an unspoilt, refreshing haven.

El Salvador   Offers unspoilt beach resorts in the region of the Costa Del Sol and now the civil war is ended, you will enjoy safe transit in the country. Sadly, most of the rainforest has been cut down and the healthcare system is lacking. As a result, Costa Rica, which is near by and claims to be the safest Central American country, or Belize, would be better choices for the family.

Costa Rica   Offers the family cable-car journeys through spectacular rainforest, rich and varied countryside, volcanic mountain ranges and delightful beaches. The government is keen to attract tourists and secure their safety. Crime in the country is mostly limited to petty theft and Costa Rica is considered the safest country in Central America. The health system is one of the best in Latin America and the country is a good introduction to the atmosphere and land of the tropics for a family. Rainfall is least in January and February.

Guatemala   There is a problem with terrorists and aggressive muggings in Guatemala. Tours to the fantastic Mayan ruins of Tikal are accompanied from Belize by armed guard. With a family Guatemala is best visited from a base in neighbouring Belize.

Honduras   The devastation caused by the last hurricane to hit central America will take a long time to recover from. The whole infrastructure of Honduras was hit hard and there are many priorities to be fulfilled before the people plan to focus on drawing tourists back into the region.

Nicaragua   As for Honduras.

Panama   Panama is purported to be the most under-rated tourist destination in the world but perhaps not when travelling with accompanying children.

The north coast of Panama is known as the Mosquito Coast!

Mexico   Has recently become much more accessible and affordable from the UK and has much to attract visitors.

It offers powder-white sands on fabulous Caribbean beaches, mixed with a rich, colourful culture. It is a lively place of fun and excitement for each member of the family.

Mayan and Aztec archaeological sites, if introduced with enthusiasm, can be fascinating for older children. There are many luxurious hotels and good restaurants and there is excellent shopping.

A stay on the mainland at Cancun or Playa Del Carman is preferable to Cozumel when travelling with a family as the mainland offers a much greater variety of activities and sightseeing.

Private healthcare is good and you only need to take malaria tablets if travelling inland to certain areas.

SOUTH AMERICA

Argentina   Buenos Aires is one of the safest cities in South America and there are more doctors per capita in Argentina than there are in the USA. Older children may appreciate the history and atmosphere of city life in Buenos Aires, which is arguably one of the most chic cities in the world.

Children can enjoy horseback riding in the pampas, a stay on a cattle ranch and the good skiing available in the highlands.

Outside the capital, head for the Iguassu Falls; they are spectacular but you should aim to see them in the wet season because otherwise they might be no more than a trickle.

Bolivia One of the poorest countries in South America and geographically one of most inhospitable places on earth. You must not drink the water. Diseases such as Chagas' infest the population. Once the most politically unstable country in the world, Bolivia is now a country of elected governments and growing economic stability.

Despite the negatives and the poverty, the capital of La Paz is one of the safest cities in South America and tourists do not have to be constantly on guard as they do in the cities of Peru or Brazil. Plaits, bowler hats and ponchos are not just for the tourists. Colourful markets and well fed bootshine boys with toothy grins are all around.

Music is a big part of life in Bolivia and an enjoyable memory for the visitor. The country has a very rich folk culture and some of its festivals are among South America's finest. Carnival time in February and March would be a fantastic experience for children and infinitely safer and more relaxing for you all than the infamous Rio Carnival.

Lake Titicaca is well worth the trouble it takes to get there. It is the highest navigable lake in the world, surrounded by distant, snowy peaks, and a site of serene history and legend. There is plenty here to stretch a child's imagination, from frog men in the lake, to the island's birthplace of the sun, according to Inca mythology.

Jungle trips into the Amazon basin reportedly knock spots off those in Brazil, but may be more challenging with children. The well trodden paths around Manaus or Iquitos in Peru are probably safer for little legs than waist-high jungle flora.

Brazil Life is cheap in Brazil. The grinding poverty in the cities is horrific. The dramatic splendour and natural beauty of Rio and its Statue of Christ are thrilling but you can't even carry a handbag in the streets because of the risk of theft.

There are stories of women being forced to strip in the streets. Rape isn't the objective; the money they may have hidden in their underwear is. This constitutes the type of hassle you can do without when travelling with a family.

The world-renowned Rio Carnival can be viewed inside the sambodromo for a price. Here you can sit in grandstands in relative safety and comfort and watch the thousands involved parade all through the night. Even aloof from the clamour of the streets, the carnival is still an exhausting, repetitive and claustrophobic business. Any child could be excused for falling asleep in the seat you have paid a fortune for. A visit to the carnivals of neighbouring Bolivia offers a greater and safer opportunity to join in and have more family fun.

The rainforest region around the massive Amazon River covers one third of Brazil which covers half of South America. Manaus is the best place to head for with children. The tourist-class jungle lodges are exciting, hospitable and pleasant. The treks around them are safe and well trodden.

Chile Perhaps not the destination you would choose if you were to put your children first but it is a country which can be enjoyed by the family whose objective is to spend time together and relax, surrounded by diverse and breathtaking scenery.

Chile is an untamed country with a clean and tidy European-ness about it. There are fjords which even the Norwegians admire, turquoise lakes, stunning Andean mountain vistas, glaciers, geysers and desert. Rich Argentines flock there for a taste of its wild nature.

Skiing, hiking, biking, canoeing and general delights of the outdoors can be fun for all the family.

Colombia Many tour groups have pulled out of Colombia, which begs the question, why?

Political instability, narcotic-related crime, kidnappings, violence and killing of street children are five good reasons. Colombia is the most violent society in Latin America and one of the most violent in the world. Murder is one of the major causes of death, alongside cancer and heart disease.

The resorts on the Caribbean coast of Colombia offer some appeal for the family but there are so many safe and beautiful beaches in less dangerous surroundings and more accessible parts of the Amazon rainforests that it is probably pointless to risk Colombia if you are not familiar with the country.

Ecuador   Ecuador is one of those places, like Nepal, where the serenity-seekers go to find themselves amidst soul-enriching mountains. Malaria is a problem, but resistant malaria is not. When compared to other countries around the Amazon basin, this is a distinct advantage.

Tourism is well developed and accommodation is easy to find and incredibly cheap.

If you intend to go trekking in the mountains where healthcare services are sparse or nonexistent, read up about first aid and carry a basic medical kit, complete with drugs to combat any intestinal infections you might pick up.

Guyana   Guyana has no significant tourism because it is generally the most dangerous place to visit in South America.

Paraguay   Iguassu Falls would be a good enough reason to visit Paraguay but as this breathtaking spectacle also borders on Brazil and Argentina, you must take your choice as to which country you approach it from.

The border town of Cuidad Del Este is where South Americans from the bordering countries go to buy cheap electrical goods and designer copies.

Peru   As stunning and inspiring as Peru is, it is not the best place for a young family. Infant mortality is a horrifying 25 per cent, and parasitic disease, especially all manner of stomach upsets, is a huge problem. Outbreaks of resistant cholera, endemic malaria and dysentery are all hazards for the tourist as well as the locals. However, the countryside is stunning, the mysterious Inca history is fascinating and the impoverished people – except for the guerrillas and those outside the bustle of Lima – appear serenely happy.

Despite the high infant mortality the rural areas are full of children keen to earn coins by doing anything from bringing you a llama to stroke and dancing, to just looking cute. They will all demand money for having their photo taken.

Unless you speak Spanish, travelling around Peru without a tour group is tough, and with children in tow it would be extremely tough. The country's infrastructure is poor and thieves in the cities work in teams. However, with a tour group and organised local guide, older children/young teenagers would be OK and the memories of Macchu Picchu and Cuzco worth the hassle.

Uruguay A safe, hassle-free country, particularly by South American standards. It has good beaches, mainly occupied by Argentineans who flock from Buenos Aires, which is only a ferry or short plane ride away. The small capital of Montevideo has a quiet, colonial feel but the charm is in the countryside virtually devoid of people, being home to nine times more cattle and sheep than humans.

It is easy to get around the country but driving is treacherous. Two out of three accidents are caused by drunken drivers. The health services are good, ensuring that the Uruguayans enjoy a high life expectancy. Malaria is not a concern, and crime rates are low.

AUSTRALASIA

Australia Australia has something to attract the majority of travellers. It is a vast country, as diverse as any other, and is now very accessible from most parts of the world. There are impressive, well-managed national parks, mountain ranges, tropical rainforests, incredible coral reefs, desert, wilderness and exotic white beaches. With good sailing, swimming, snorkelling, diving, trekking, camping and skiing, the diversity is incredible.

Unique wildlife is clearly visible all over, from kangaroos racing your car, koala, possums and flocks of wild budgerigars in the trees, to giant clams and brilliantly coloured fish in the turquoise seas, everything children love. Then there are aquariums, zoos, water parks and fast-food take aways amidst colourful city life. Add in a splash of Aboriginal culture and a host of stories about runaway convicts, and there is little more a child could wish for.

Australia always seemed tame to me as an independent traveller but with a family it would be an exciting destination. The standards of aircraft and service on the flights between

Europe and Australia via Asia are excellent and good value for money. The country's abundant attractions offer enjoyment for every member of the family.

There is a wide choice of accommodation to suit every budget. Good camping facilities with municipal barbecues on most sites can offer a family a taste of adventure. Clean, well-run motels and deluxe hotels by even the highest international standards are all better value than in many places of the world.

Eating with children will never be a problem and healthcare standards are as high as any in the world.

There are, however, disadvantages. Australia is home to ten of the most dangerous creatures known to man. There are poisonous toads, deadly snakes, jellyfish whose sting is so painful it can kill, dangerous spiders who live under toilet seats in the cities, sharks and crocodiles. Still, most Australians manage to survive and so it is more than likely that you will too, especially if you warn your children and prepare yourself.

The sun is very strong and, inland, the central desert temperatures can reach 50°C which is uncomfortable and dangerous for babies and young children.

Be respectful of the roads. The Pacific highway on the east coast witnesses many fatalities. In more rural areas, collisions with wild animals, including kangaroos, can cause serious accidents on the road, particularly when driving at night.

It is a long, arduous journey. The jet lag is horrendous. It is said that it takes one day to adjust per hour of time difference and so, after a fortnight in Australia, you will have enjoyed only a few good nights' sleep before it is time to come home and you will need to adjust all over again.

The distances between cities within Australia are huge. Internal flights are preferable and, if booked at the same time as an international, air tickets can be bought cheaply. Often one or two internal flights may be included free. Cars are quite expensive to hire and, with days on the hot road and children complaining, you have to make careful, well prepared decisions.

New Zealand New Zealand has the feel of 1950s England. It is one of the safest and most peaceful countries in the world.

Roads are quiet and the countryside is unspoilt. You can travel for miles without seeing another car.

There are a number of popular attractions scattered over the country but they are not close together and so you will need to make choices. If you travel from Auckland with the children in mind, head for the Waitomo caves. Travelling through the illuminated stalactites and stalagmites in a little boat is a joy. Inside the roof of the caves is a mass of glow bugs which look like tiny stars covering the ceiling. You can also try river-rafting in the area. Rotorua is a popular destination. The children will wrinkle their noses at the smell of sulphur but enjoy the boiling mudpoles and geysers.

There is also skiing and bungee-jumping. Lake Taupo is the place to bungee but there is a minimum height for children. There are many water sports available at the lake, too. Whale and wildlife watching is an attraction in the more remote south.

Health and hygiene are of the highest standards.

SOUTH PACIFIC

The sun in the South Pacific is very aggressive and can burn viciously. Check the weather. Tropical storms, hurricanes and cyclones occur between November and March.

Cook Islands Raratonga is one of the main destinations in the South Pacific for round-the-world ticket holders.

It is pleasant, safe, but not very good value for money. The price you will pay for a hotel room will suggest deluxe facilities but in reality it will be medium class. It doesn't have the South Pacific atmosphere of Tonga and French Polynesia. It is a popular honeymoon destination for Antipodeans and caters for their taste.

Fiji Fiji has more attraction for the family than many of the other South Pacific islands. This is possibly a function of cost. It is generally less expensive to stay and eat on than other South Pacific islands. The food, healthcare and accommodation standards are good.

French Polynesia Tahiti and Bora Bora are everything you would imagine. The islands are surrounded by coral reefs which act as a barrier to the ocean, giving shallow, safe seas. The beaches are literally palm fringed and stunningly beautiful. The only blights on the islands are as a result of tourism. Papeete is safe but unattractive.

The major negatives are the high prices (you will need a budget of at least US $150 per day just for food and drink in the hotels for a family of four) and the distance. It takes you 48 hours' solid travelling from Bora Bora to the UK.

Kiribati Kiribati is being developed to attract tourists but is still fairly inaccessible with a limited flight service from Honolulu. The expense and the time it takes to travel to this part of the Pacific outweigh the attractions when compared with other islands in the region, such as those of French Polynesia and the Cook Islands.

Marshall Islands The attraction would be the unspoilt beaches but there are few hotels or attractions for the family other than total escapism.

Nauru Nauru has little to attract the family on holiday.

Solomon Islands Distance, cost and sparse healthcare would be deterrents. Malaria is on the island.

Tonga Tonga is still a little less commercialised and orientated towards tourism than some of the other South Pacific islands. It is beautiful and a mass of tropical beaches with over 170 islands. There are some modern healthcare facilities available on the islands.

Tuvulu Tuvulu is isolated and has only one 'real' hotel. Parasitic illnesses are common.

Vanuatu Vanuatu is appearing on more South Pacific travel itineraries recently and tourism is definitely growing. However, with children, especially when travelling from the UK, there are more accessible islands with the same to offer, which, unlike Vanuatu, are malaria free.

Western Samoa Tourists are more often directed to American Samoa by accessibility, levels of healthcare and an overall better-developed tourist infrastructure.

There is concern about the impact of tourism but somehow the Samoan people have retained their true Polynesian way of life, centred around the family and chiefs.

Unspoilt, lush and traditional, with very little to threaten the family, it would make for a relaxed holiday with tales of cannibals and pirates.

NORTH AMERICA

Canada and the USA   Too vast and varied to attempt to cover in a few sentences.

If your children are good travellers by car, a fly drive in the USA or Canada offers freedom, flexibility and variety. Petrol is unbelievably cheap, as are many other things when compared to Europe.

Accommodation, eating out, clothing, videos, CDs and books are all much cheaper. Service everywhere is excellent.

Theme parks are major attractions for families. National parks offer natural beauty and there are no difficulties with getting around. There is more for those who want to relax and amble rather than search for culture or adventure.

It is very important that you get well insured. Healthcare is excellent but if, for example, the entire family needed hospital treatment after a car accident, the bill would run into tens of thousands of dollars.

SPECIAL INTEREST HOLIDAYS

The major factor which will help you to decide which country you choose to visit is likely to be the type of holiday you seek out. You may simply want a sunbed round a clean pool which you will find virtually anywhere in the world. The more discerning you are, and the lower your budget, the more you will have to work to get the ideal holiday. The more you read and research before you go, then the more likely you are to know what to expect, to find what you are looking for and so enjoy the positive aspects of your destination.

Adventure holidays and the great outdoors: where in the world to find them?

The wilderness is exciting for most of us. Horse-back riding, caving, camping, climbing, cycling, rambling and canoeing can all invigorate. These activities are wonderful for children, too, but you must avoid energetic recreation in high temperatures, especially in seasons of high humidity, because heatstroke will be a serious risk.

High altitudes are always cooler, but walking in high mountain ranges can seem like much more effort because the air is thin, and so our lungs and hearts need to work much harder to get enough oxygen to all of our working muscles. Too high or too cold are dangerous for children.

The best areas in the world to head for the great outdoors are Southern New Zealand and Northern UK. It rarely gets too hot and, as long as you avoid snowy seasons, the temperatures should not be too cold for children either. Something we British tend to take for granted is that Scotland is one of the last great wildernesses on Earth. The wilds of Scotland still actually exist. On a sunny day, the Lake District is one of the world's most beautiful places. The rivers are free from parasites and the woods free from snakes, bears, wild pigs or other dangerous, potentially rabid animals. We can dress for our sport instead of dressing to fend off ticks and insects.

Other good options would be Canada, the USA, Scandinavia and, for somewhere with a difference, Southern Chile, although you will be within the realms of tick-borne disease and other parasites in these countries.

Before booking an activity holiday:

- Check which parasites and creatures are in the area. A canoeing holiday with children who are likely to fall into the water would be no fun in a region riddled with Bilharzia. Caving amidst rabid bats is dangerous. There have been cases of rabies being contracted from bats in caves without the victim having been bitten.
- Check your travel insurance carefully. Many policies exclude sporting activities, even those considered relatively safe.

Where in the world to go camping with children?
Many countries of the world offer excellent camping facilities for tents or caravans, but camping in France is hard to beat. The choice of campsites is huge and in the summer it is hot without you being roasted in your tent. The only negative is that the French toilets are usually just holes in the ground and are nasty places.

Most of the countries of Western Europe offer good facilities for campers in the summer, either travelling with your own tent, or on organised sites where you can rent a tent.

Northern Europe generally offers perfect temperatures and woodland environments for peaceful country relaxation. Across Scandinavia, Belgium, Holland, Germany, Austria, and Switzerland, beautiful countryside is matched by warm welcomes and comfortable sites.

As you get into Southern Europe, including Spain, Southern Italy and Greece, camping makes it difficult to escape the heat and mosquitoes and you will be forced out of your tent by the sun at 7.30 a.m. to avoid being baked. Tenting in these countries with children would be more bearable in the spring. If you do go in the summer, try to find a pitch with some shade, rather than just an open field.

Camping in Northern Italy is preferable to further south and there is a good selection of excellent sites a short boat ride outside Venice in Lido di Jesolo. You can reasonably drive to Venice from the UK and the northern Italian drivers are nowhere near as crazy as those around Rome and in the south. If you want to fly, the Lido is well serviced by buses from Venice airport.

Camping in summer on the southern Spanish coast is crowded and hot. It is far more pleasant further north in the Pyrenees. Greece is even hotter and can be unbearable.

The national parks of the USA offer fantastic camping, although those at altitude, including Yosemite in California, are freezing cold at night.

The campsites in the USA and Canada are often huge and rarely get as crowded as those in Europe. The scale of everything, including the trees and rivers, is much bigger.

At night you will often be able to hear bears, but beware, they are dangerous and will rip into your tent on the hunt for food if you don't dispose of your rubbish properly.

Also important to remember is that raccoons and other fluffy indigenous American mammals can be vicious and carry rabies. You must warn your children to leave all wild animals well alone. All US campsites will ensure that you will be well informed about any precautions you need to take in the area.

One of the great things about camping is cooking in the open. This is something you can enjoy in the USA. Camping shops will sell firewood, barbecues and beef steaks with marshmallows for toasting.

Paradoxically, cooking in the open air is something that is banned in many southern European campsites, although there is good reason. The foliage and grass in the summer become very dry and there is a real fire risk from sparks or discarded coals.

Camping in New Zealand and Australia is excellent. Scattered around all the campsites in Australia are fixed barbecues for everyone's use. The sports facilities are often good and many sites are near to the beach or have swimming pools. Camping is comfortable and the nights do generally cool down more than in southern Europe, making sleep more comfortable, too.

Central and northern parts of Europe are host to ticks which spread a form of viral encephalitis. However, there is a vaccination which should be considered if you are spending time camping and walking in the countryside. Watch out for ticks while camping in Australia and Northern USA, too. They spread disease and are also responsible for some deaths in children due to the fact that they pass on a lethal toxin as they feed.

Totally independent camping with a family in many other parts of the world, although possible, is more difficult. You will find sites from Zimbabwe to St Lucia but the availability of sites and their facilities differ drastically. It is difficult to escape insects, which is very important when travelling in areas where the malaria is drug resistant. No matter how hard you try to rid your tent of mosquitoes, there always seems to be one inside in the morning. If that one is a disease carrier, you may all suffer.

Camping with guides and porters on treks or on fixed sites in national parks is totally different. The accommodation, although canvas, can be quite luxurious. Mosquito nets will be provided and every effort will have been made to deter and diminish resident insect, arachnid and parasitic populations.

For the intrepid, it is possible to camp virtually anywhere in the world, but you should carefully check what the temperatures, rainfall and humidity are likely to be when you intend to visit. You are more at the mercy of the elements in a tent than when you have four walls and a hotel lobby to retire to.

Nature and the environment
The most unique flora, fauna and wildlife are usually found on isolated islands such as Madagascar, the Seychelles and the Galapagos Islands.

If you want natural beauty and rich, lush foliage aim for larger volcanic islands in hot climates where the soil is fantastically rich in nutrients and minerals. The peaks of the volcano attract clouds and rainfall so that the trees, plants and flowers grow to awe-inspiring sizes. The negative is that the beaches are mostly black sand. Such paradise islands include Tahiti, Reunion, St Lucia and Hawaii.

Where in the world to safari?
A safari is an adventure and one that your children will remember for a lifetime. The places you will stay will be as memorable as the wildlife. The comfortable lodges or camping safaris all have appeal.

Kenya, Tanzania, Zimbabwe, Botswana, South Africa and Namibia are certainly the better safari options when travelling with children. Many other countries in Africa do have national parks and game reserves but those named above all have a good tourist infrastructure and high standards of accommodation and do cater for families.

Kenya is generally the least expensive and has the added appeal of the white, sandy beaches so that the two aspects can be combined. The range of safaris on offer in Kenya is extensive and you can pick one which will not be too long or arduous. In Kenya there will be every opportunity to book a safari when you arrive and so if you are unsure whether or not the heat will tire your children too much, wait until you arrive at your beach resort then decide when, for how long, and how far to go.

A safari in Tanzania is more expensive but probably a little more luxurious and less crowded than one in Kenya. From the game parks of Tanzania, the spice island of Zanzibar is just a short flight away. Alternatively, splitting the holiday between the beaches of Mombassa in Kenya and a safari in Tanzania will bring the price down and is more likely to have child discounts on offer.

The Kruger Park in South Africa offers good game viewing.

The uncertain economy in South Africa means that at present you will get exceptionally good value for money and the country has much more to offer besides, including beach resorts, mountains, vineyards and fantastic restaurants.

Zimbabwe offers the wonder of Victoria Falls and good, high-class safaris. It can be pricy but the infrastructure is in place to allow you to book a basic deal to get out there and then arrange suitable trips and journeys to different lodges once you arrive.

Botswana has excellent game viewing. The largest population of elephants left in Africa, big cats, hippos, grazing animals and many species of birds are protected in the country's well-kept National Parks. Significantly more costly for a family than East Africa, and without the beaches, Botswana has the benefits of political and economic stability which make for a more relaxing, refined and tout-free safari. When travelling with a younger family, it may be worthwhile opting for your own safari vehicle. This gives you more flexibility and is easily and affordably arranged through most tour operators. It will also ensure that any squabbling over the window seats will not cause you acute embarrassment, although many good tour operators do guarantee one to every passenger travelling in a minibus or four-wheel drive vehicle.

Check for minimum age limits which usually apply for good reasons, such as long night walks or accommodation sited next to a precipitous drop.

Theme and water parks

The greatest concentration of theme parks is in northern Europe and USA. Wealthier Asian countries, including Japan and South Korea, also have huge, clean, safe children's theme parks. Florida has the highest concentration of parks and is the perfect environment, unless you go in the peak of summer when it can be unbearably hot and humid. Children soon grow out of the Magic Kingdom and, even as young as eight years old, can come away untouched. It is important to try to get the balance between them being so young that they trudge round totally bewildered, or too old when they skulk round, their hands in their pockets, refusing to be impressed. In Florida the range of parks ensures that you will find something to suit most ages. Sea

World has broad appeal and Universal Studios and Epcot are more stimulating for older children.

Disneyland Paris is OK. The accommodation is good and reasonably priced but the food and novelties are very expensive.

Diving and snorkelling

Your children will not be able to tank dive until they are twelve years old but you will often see as much, if not more, snorkelling because many of the more colourful corals and fishes live nearer to the surface. A child who can hold his breath and is willing to put his face into the water can at least have a look under the sea. It may be around eight – or possibly seven – years old that a child can get to grips with snorkelling.

If you want to introduce your child to the wonder under the seas, the best snorkelling (and tank diving) close to the UK is in the Red Sea off Egypt or Israel.

The best way to increase a child's confidence is for them to be able to wade out waist deep, put on their mask and fins and see plenty of sea life a stone's throw from shore. Don't try to teach your child to dive yourself. Leave it to the experts.

WHAT WILL THE WEATHER BE LIKE?

Checking the weather

Reference and geography books are the most reliable means of judging what the weather will be like in your destination at the time of year you intend to travel. Travel agents may be unsure and holiday brochures may give biased information.

Temperature

Note that while text books will usually give the average daily temperature, many holiday brochures will give the average daily *maximum* temperature. This makes a huge difference. For example, the average maximum daily temperature in June in Mauritius is 75°F but the average daily temperature is 64°F. In Mauritius in June the temperature may reach 75°F for 30 minutes a day, but for the rest of the day it is much cooler and often windy.

It is also important to realise that temperature in isolation is a poor indicator of how comfortable a climate will be. How hot or cold we will feel is a precise combination of temperature, humidity and wind.

Hours of sunshine and average rainfall will also affect your holiday enjoyment.

Humidity

Humidity is a measure of the moisture content of the air. We can stand dry heat much better than damp heat which makes us feel listless and lacking in energy. At 80°F with low humidity we may feel comfortable, but if the humidity is high, we will feel hot and sticky. It is more difficult for our bodies to lose heat by sweating in high humidity. A breeze greatly lessens discomfort in hot, humid conditions.

Before booking your destination, think carefully about which season it will be when you intend to arrive. Will it be especially rainy, hot and humid or cold and windy?

Avoid monsoon seasons when there is high rainfall. Mosquitoes proliferate in the rainy season and there are more contagious fevers around.

Children are more at risk from the cold than they are from the heat. Be prepared for chilly nights, especially in desert and mountain areas. Wherever and whenever you go, take at least one thick, warm jumper, a coat and a blanket.

The other important thing to consider is how high you will be. Irrespective of the level of latitude, the temperature falls by approximately 1°C for every 150 m rise above sea level.

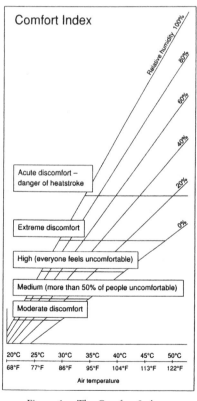

Figure 1. The Comfort Index.

Weather information can be obtained from the Meteorological office (overseas enquiry bureau). Telephone 01344 420242.

CHOOSING YOUR DESTINATION: A SUMMARY

- When your children are very young, choose a destination in line with your own experience, somewhere you will feel comfortable and safe. It can be hard work breaking new ground, although for others, it is part of the fun.
- Consider any vaccinations you may need and whether or not they are indicated for your child's age group (see chapter 5).
- Is malaria a risk? If so, is the malaria in the area you intend to visit resistant to drug prophylaxis? If yes, and your children are very small, can you seek out a similar holiday in a different country without resistant malaria? Will you be able to cope with administering the tablets to your family? (see chapter 5).
- Be aware of any other illness common to the area you will be visiting. Recognise their signs and symptoms. Be conscious of how to avoid them (see chapter 5).
- Check which season it will be when you arrive and what the weather is likely to be doing. Travel agents may steer away from advising you on the weather. You need to look this up in reference and geography books, not just tourist brochures. What the weather will be like is the last thing many people consider checking. When travelling with children, it is particularly important to do so (see page 80).
- Avoid a country's peak season if possible. This is usually related to demand and is a result of school holidays rather than ideal weather conditions. The Mediterranean is much more pleasant in spring than in the intense heat of August.
- If your children are under school age, you will have the option to travel outside school holidays which is strongly advisable. The most popular resorts will be less expensive and less crowded and the flights will be less cramped.

  Also worth considering is the fact that, when there are fewer children around, there are fewer childhood bugs and contagious ailments around too.
- If you must holiday in the school holidays, broaden your horizons. The Caribbean has its low season when the

Mediterranean has its peak. Prices are often comparable for a family, especially when you add up items such as car hire, tour prices, taxis and dining out, all of which are more expensive when the crowds descend.

- Don't rely totally on travel agents for advice. They will inevitably try their best but can't always guarantee your seat on the plane, or the room you will be assigned to in your hotel on arrival. They may relay your preferences, but a message to the airline may get lost in translation and a facsimile to your accommodation months before arrival can easily be over-looked. Do the follow up yourself. A facsimile to your hotel and a phonecall to the airline carrier to confirm your seats is worth the effort when travelling with babies and small children.

The following conditions would make for the ideal destination when travelling with children. Although no country in the world will satisfy all the criteria, think about what is most important to you.

1. Safe and unthreatening environment. Low crime rates.
2. Clean and hygienic environment.
3. Free or low risks from parasitic diseases.
4. Insect, spider, snake and scorpion free.
5. A child-friendly population which doesn't impose.
6. Good medical facilities and emergency hospitals.
7. English-speaking doctors.
8. Western-standard hotels with patient service and reliable hot water and electricity supplies.
9. Entertainment or trips available suitable for your child's age group.
10. Not too intolerable a journey or too many time zones away from home (although it is often worth it).
11. Moderate temperatures and humidity.
12. Low rainfall when you will be travelling. Insects and diseases proliferate in the rainy seasons.
13. Good, clean restaurants.
14. Safe seas without venomous creatures or predators.
15. Low risk of rabies and attack by dangerous mammals.
16. Low risk of road traffic accidents.
17. Good transport infrastructure.

3 Where to Stay

When travelling with children, it is important to upgrade as much as you can and stay in the best hotel you can reasonably afford. The rooms need to be free of cockroaches and the mattresses free of blood-sucking parasites, especially with an accompanying young baby.

The younger the baby, the more essential it is to have a reliable electricity supply to boil water for milk and sterilising. If you are on a very low budget, it may be better to consider tackling the wild and going camping than trying to cope with the risk of disease in a flea-ridden one- or two-star hotel.

CAMPING AND CARAVANNING

For years, whenever Simon and I went away, we would pack a tent. We would always travel 'flight only' and usually on a shoestring. The tent was security so that, if we ran out of money, we would always have somewhere to sleep.

This habit developed after a trip to Paris, France when I was a student and we had no money at all between us. It was my twenty-first birthday, which unfortunately fell on Easter Sunday of that year. Simon saved up to buy us the overnight coach fare, which meant that we then had virtually no money to live off for the three days we were there. We even took our own sandwiches from the UK.

We arrived in Paris at 5 o'clock on Saturday morning and began to try to find somewhere to stay. Because it was Easter, Paris was bustling and all the places we could afford were fully booked. There were deluxe hotel rooms available, but a two-night stay would have cost us more than £350. At the time, my grant, after paying for university accommodation, was £900. It would have cost over a third of what I had to live off for the year.

Early afternoon we gave up on finding a room in the centre of Paris and decided to hire a car. We had hoped that we would find one cheap enough which would then give us the freedom to drive to the outskirts of the city to find some budget accommodation. But the prices of car hire in Paris didn't allow our budget to stretch to a hotel room too.

We finished up sleeping in the car in a campsite car park in Versailles. We sneaked in to use the campsite washrooms late at night to freshen up. It wasn't the most comfortable two nights sleep we ever had, but it was infinitely better than being on a coach or sleeping on a station somewhere. Despite the discomfort we made the best of it and enjoyed a very special weekend. However, we then got into the routine of packing a tent when on a driving holiday or a fly drive, just in case.

We camped with Paris for the first time when he was two-and-a-half. He loved it. He scuttled around excitedly as we erected the tent and cooked our evening meal on a camping stove. As the sun set, we snuggled up together for the night. I awakened several times in the early hours, freezing cold, while he slept like a log throughout. I cuddled up to him to keep myself warm.

Most children love camping. It is adventurous and challenging, and they can help. There is the warm joy of sleeping with mummy and daddy, plus the fun of nighttime open-air cooking and the midnight trek to the toilets. Camping isn't for every adult, but children will be kept content.

Camping on a site with fixed tents is straightforward and much the same as booking self catering accommodation, without the air-conditioning.

Camping independently offers variety and freedom but it is more difficult. If you don't like your neighbours, you can repitch your tent. If you don't like the site, you can move. But if you are camping with a family, you might struggle moving between sites without a car. Camping equipment on public transport is hard enough without children.

The other bonus of a car is that you don't have to neatly repack your tent and deflate your airbeds each time you move on. You can bundle it all into the boot and worry about it later.

The best campsites are usually fairly inaccessible and situated in beauty spots with poor transport links. However, if you all enjoy camping, it is often cheaper to hire a car and camp in the countryside than pay for a hotel in a resort or city centre.

If you find campsites in travel guides, you can check that they are still in existence and reserve your spot by fax anywhere in the world. If you don't speak the language, booking by telephone is an expensive nightmare, but by fax, it is both efficient and cheap, and you can request a reply back in English. Better still, if you can get an email address for a campsite, you can correspond easily and confirm details of site fees, accessibility by public transport and facilities.

In the summer, sites in the South of France are often full. Space is limited and rather than open fields, you will be assigned a numbered pitch. Campsites in or just outside major cities fill up too, so it is a good idea to confirm availability.

In the heat of southern Europe, the igloo tents with reflective silver flysheets are the best. They do stop the tent from absorbing the early morning sunrays and don't get too hot inside until slightly later in the morning when the outside air temperature rises, allowing you to sleep in longer.

One of the negative aspects of a holiday in the open air is the toilets, especially in France. A potty or 'special' bucket may be more hygienic for their sensitive little bottoms.

Caravanning or travel by motor-home gives the fun, flexibility and variety of a camping holiday without the bugs, extremes of temperature or grubby toilets. It may not have a very glamorous image but those who do it invariably enjoy it and do it again. Campervan deals to America offer good value. The van parks are of the highest standard and easy to find and are great for kids.

For those with a budget, a spirit and a sense of adventure, camping with children is ideal. Even young babies will sleep well next to you and you can sterilise all the necessary equipment by boiling. (See page 75, Where to go Camping.)

HOTELS

If you can upgrade a little when travelling with a baby or young child, particularly a child under four years old, do so. A low-class hotel with shoddy structure, dodgy electrics and a dangerous swimming pool is no place for a toddler. You would be better camping.

There are certain precautions you can take when choosing and booking a hotel, but there will always be something you could not have accounted for. In the Seychelles, a thirty-foot drop to the road from the hotel breakfast restaurant was an ongoing concern for us. In China, half of the bars were missing from the cot provided. We had to position it against the wall in such a way that Paris could not slip or fall out between them. You will be lucky to find the perfect destination but certain facilities will ensure a more comfortable holiday.

In Europe, many tour companies have children's reps on site who run children's clubs, games, children's discos and other attractions. However, don't rely on the clubs to entertain your children. Some are little more than a babysitting service and many only operate for an hour or two a day. Levels of stimulation and the variety of activities on offer vary between hotels, tour companies and even the reps, who vary widely in their enthusiasm.

For children to sleep well, you really will need air-conditioning, but if your budget dictates that you either stay in Greece in a one-star hotel without air-conditioning or not go at all, you should go every time.

Try to pick your accommodation as carefully as you can from the brochures. Alternatively, just book a flight with a civilised arrival time and you will always be able to find something when you arrive and then shop around to find a hotel that is suitable at a reasonable price.

Don't forget that if you arrive at a hotel's front desk and they have rooms free, even five-star hotels will negotiate on price. Often the price first quoted will halve if you push and request a budget room.

You will often find that many good hotels allocate the more spacious rooms to young families. Whenever we travel with my parents, my dad always skulks around our room grumbling that it is bigger and better than his own. I always suggest that he is welcome to swap if he would like to have Paris sleeping with him.

Book into the best hotel you can afford and, when requesting your room, consider the following:

- In a small hotel in a safe environment, the ground-floor room is arguably the best, with fewer stairs to fall down and no treacherous balconies. The best spot in a hotel with an accompanying infant is a ground-floor room which backs out on to the pool. You can leave your child sleeping peacefully in the cool while you laze by the pool a few feet away.
- With older children, or in malarial regions, the third floor and above may be preferable. There will be fewer insects and fewer threats from intruders or thieves than at ground level.
- If your child is unlikely to settle in a strange cot alone and likely to end up nuzzled next to you, request a king size bed. If there is one available, the hotel will usually oblige.

Booking half board (HB)

My dad once made the mistake of paying half board in a hotel on Jersey for my seven-year-old sister. She was a terribly fussy eater but he was absolutely determined she should eat whatever was put in front of her as he had already paid for it.

Every meal time became a battle, with my sister ending up in tears and my mum in despair. Thankfully I wasn't there, but mum claimed that dad 'trying to get his money's worth' ruined the entire trip.

If your children are fussy, unless you know the hotel or can guarantee that it will serve food they like and will actually eat, be very careful about booking half- or full board for them. You don't want to experience meal time frustrations on your holidays. It all comes down to cost. If it is an extra £2–3 for half board per child per day, it is probably worth it. Anything more, in my opinion, is a risk.

Most hotels around the world will do a portion of chips, spaghetti or omelette for a child for a few pounds and, done to order, your children's meals will be much fresher and safer than if they have been sitting on a hotel buffet for an hour.

Booking fully inclusive holidays with children

If you are planning on staying at an isolated resort or island which only caters for fully inclusive guests, then you often have no choice. The nearest restaurant may be a ten-pound taxi- or boat-ride away, and so feeding your children will prove very costly and tedious if you try to opt out.

In these instances, try to book a hotel with more than one restaurant. Even in destinations as luxurious as the Maldives or Mauritius, menus are often repetitive if there is only one place to dine. Many all-inclusive deal hotels offer a 'varied choice of bars and restaurants'; this is very important.

If the hotel will let you book all-inclusive for yourself, and just bed and breakfast for your children with a significant cost saving, then do it. Booking fully inclusive for children, especially between the ages of two to ten years, is usually poor value for money. Their appetites will decrease in the heat and they will probably want to live off chips and cola anyway. If you have paid an extra £200 for the week so they can appreciate the fantastically elaborate hotel buffet, you'll be driven mad.

Under-twos are always virtually free. This is great. They need plentiful supplies of soft drinks (half of which they knock over), and it is a godsend having food available all day which your child can pick at whenever they are hungry, instead of having to worry about every meal time.

For the over-twos, if, having compared the holiday prices for bed and breakfast and all-inclusive, you find that you can get the all-inclusive deal for between five and ten pounds extra per child per day, it is good value. Anything more will probably end up more costly than feeding them from the menu, unless they are very good eaters. Note: All inclusive hotels rarely have kettles in the rooms, so take your own.

Facilities to check for before booking a hotel

1. Are a kettle and a fridge provided in the room? If there is no fridge available, the minibar is a useful substitute. Squash up the whisky miniatures and squeeze in the ready-prepared bottles, open baby foods, or your own canned drinks. (NB: Some hotels may charge you for this.)
2. Are cots available?
3. Are babysitters available at a reasonable cost? If you are relying on the hotel babysitter promised in the brochure, check the rates. A friend who recently married in Mauritius and took her toddler along found out on arrival that the babysitter was ten pounds per hour. The £300 babysitting bill she and her husband received was quite a shock.

4. Can you get an early supper in your hotel? Will the kitchen provide children's meals outside hours?
5. Are highchairs available in the dining rooms?
6. Are a crèche, playroom or children's activities available?
7. Are the beaches near enough to the hotel? Children hate walking far in the heat. If so, are they safe, clean and free from dangerous sea life such as jellyfish, sea urchins or stonefish?
8. Is there a children's swimming pool or a shallow end to the main pool?
9. Are the grounds enclosed and, in more hostile African or Caribbean countries, are they protected by guards?
10. Will your child be the only one in the hotel and a constant source of irritation to all the other guests?
11. How close is the hotel to attractions?
12. Is there a courtesy bus into town and to and from the airport?
13. How well is the hotel serviced by public transport?
14. If there is no transfer from the airport included, what is the hotel's proximity to and accessibility from the airport?
15. If your flight times are late at night and checkout is at midday, will you be able to have the use of a room either for free or a nominal cost? You don't want to be hanging around the hotel grounds for twelve hours with a young baby and toddler in tow, without access to a shower or air-conditioning.

SELF-CATERING HOLIDAYS

A holiday in a self-catering villa, cottage, *gite* or apartment is probably one of the easiest, cheapest and least risky options when travelling with children.

You will have total control over what your child eats and drinks. You will be relatively free to rearrange furniture and juggle sleeping arrangements. There is more space for the children to amble around, spread out their toys and make themselves at home without worrying about the wrath of the chambermaid. They can scatter food all over the floor and you have the tools to clean up. Many times I have skulked out of a hotel room with lentils, crisps and dry noodles scattered all over the carpet and melted chocolate among the crisp, white bedsheets.

Washing facilities will cut down on the packing considerably and are essential if you aren't using disposable nappies. You can also wash all your clothes before you go home which will ensure that your suitcase isn't packed with sicky bibs, pants and accidents, or clothing caked in sand and sea salt.

Individual apartments have far superior soundproofing between them than hotel rooms. I have often found myself responding to crocodile tears at 4.30 a.m. in a hotel room to save the neighbours from being awakened. Thus self-catering offers more independence and privacy than hotels.

The only real disadvantages are that someone still has to clean, tidy and wash up, and furthermore, it will probably be you. Also, self-catering apartments are usually rented by the week and generally don't offer the flexibility of hotels if you are planning to move around. However, they are often so cheap you can book them for the week and just use them as a base. It is not uncommon for a package with an apartment to cost less than a flight only to many European destinations. Therefore, even if you were only to stay for one night in the apartment, it would still be a bargain, and you can take off and book into hotel or camp, knowing that you have something to fall back on.

Facilities to check for before booking self-catering

1. Check washing, kitchen and bedroom facilities.
2. Are cots available?
3. Are babysitters or maid service available at a reasonable cost?
4. Where are the nearest shops, supermarkets and restaurants? Can you walk there?
5. Are towels and bedding provided?
6. Will you need a hire car? In countries such as Spain, Portugal and the US, the cost of your taxi fare to and from the airport could be more than an entire week's car hire. Couple this with having to buy all your provisions in the expensive resort shop instead of whizzing into town to the local markets or supermarket, and you could actually save a fortune by renting a car.

If you do decide to rent a car, is there secure parking?

7. Are the beaches close by? Children hate walking far in the heat. If so, are they safe, clean and free from dangerous sea life such as jellyfish, sea urchins or stonefish?

8. Is there a children's swimming pool or a shallow end to the main pool?

9. Is there adequate security? Are the grounds enclosed and, in more hostile African or Caribbean countries, are they protected by guards?

10. How close is the accommodation to attractions?

11. How well is the accommodation serviced by public transport?

12. What is its proximity to the airport?

13. Self-catering checkout times are more likely to be compatible with flight times than those in hotels which are more standard. It is still worth confirming that you will not be requested to leave mid-morning and sit on the street with your cases and children until midnight.

4 How to Get There

TRAVELLING BY AIR

The risk of cot death

There was some speculation that flying can contribute to the tragedy of cot death but the evidence is inconclusive. The research, which has only recently been published, was carried out in 1992. It noted that babies placed in a room with a reduced oxygen supply might have a reduced oxygen content in their blood. However, it is thought that provided we remain vigilant and take all the usual precautions, babies are at no greater risk from cot death after flying than they would be on the ground.

It is important to avoid flying in, or near, the smoking section of the aircraft and to keep the baby cool during the flight. After landing, *always* place your baby on his back to sleep. Don't smoke around your baby and avoid smoky places. Keep your baby cool but don't let paranoia ruin your holiday. Don't forget that millions of babies born in the tropics survive.

When my son was first born, I was very anxious about the risks of cot death. An Indian midwife tucked my baby against me one night when he was just three days old. It was 4.30 a.m. and he refused to go to sleep. I was close to tears. She tenderly assured me he would be fine.

'You will never roll on to him,' she promised. 'You are his mother.'

I must have looked doubtful.

'We don't have cot death in India,' she told me. 'A new baby always sleeps next to its mother, where it belongs.'

That night I enjoyed a good night's sleep.

An Indian doctor reiterated the same advice. Provided that she has not drunk too much alcohol or taken any sedative drugs, a mother will not roll on to her baby. I found this wonderfully reassuring and my son slept in my arms for the first five months of his life. After this he seemed much stronger. He could kick off his blankets if he was too hot and I began to sleep easier.

If you are travelling in very high temperatures with a very young baby, consider sleeping next to him. You will be much more aware of his temperature, breathing levels and any threatening mosquitoes.

Pre-booking seats
Many airlines will pre-book your seats for you but it is a matter of deciding where you will be most comfortable.

The bulk head seats, in my opinion, are not as ideal as most people imagine when travelling with an infant. These are the seats right next to the emergency exits and have a partition directly in front of them. The in-flight movie screen is attached to the partition and there are fixings to secure a kind of suspended travel cot just below the screen. This has the disadvantage that you might be constantly fighting your child to stop them from standing up in the cot to touch the flickering lights above. You will make enemies up and down the length of the plane, as they want to watch the movie, and not your child doing a balancing act. With a very young baby, the cot could be an advantage, but if you manage instead to get other seats with a little more leg room, your baby might be more comfortable in his familiar car-carrying seat on the floor.

On a jumbo there is an added problem with the middle row of bulk head seats. There are five seats in the middle row, so if you book as a couple with an infant, there are three occupied seats next to you. Unfortunately, the wall fixings for the travel cot are over the middle seat and so your baby will be in someone else's lap. This is awkward for you and them.

The final big disadvantage of the bulk head seats is that the arm rests are fixed. This means that if you are travelling with an older child who might not be able to sleep upright, you cannot lift up the arm rests and allow them to lie flat across you and/or your partner. The key to pre-booking is to ask for seats with extra leg room. Then there is room for bags, books, toys and sleeping arrangements.

A few airlines provide 'cots' which fit on the floor in between the seats under your feet. They are little more than human-shaped cardboard boxes with a thin mattress but they keep your child off the floor and I have seen many infants settle in one, then sleep for an entire eight- or ten-hour flight curled up with an airline blanket and pillow. Older and longer children will often sleep well on the floor, too, at your feet on a mattress of several airline pillows.

If you decide to take your chances or aren't able to pre-book your seats, when you arrive at the airport find out how busy your flight is. If it is quiet, ask check-in to reserve you the seats at either end of a row. It is a slight gamble but if you are only paying for two seats and you request the window and the aisle seat in the same row, it is very unlikely that the check-in will land a lone passenger between you.

On a jumbo, if you book the two aisle seats at either end of a row of five, you are likely to find that the middle three will be left empty. Even if you find this is not the case, you can virtually guarantee that one of the three people sandwiched between the two of you and your infants will be more than happy to swap their place for one of the aisle seats and you will still end up sitting together. I have tried this a number of times, twice while pregnant, and then a few times since on very long flights. It has worked on every occasion. Obviously if the flight is heavily or fully booked, this strategy won't work.

Pre-booking a travel cot
This is tricky. No matter how firmly your travel agent promises you a travel cot, check with the airline. Many aircraft don't carry cardboard 'cots' and some airlines do not allow infants in the bulk head seats because they may obstruct the emergency exits. These airlines do not carry wall-mounted cots either. Up until your baby is nine months old it is likely that he will sleep more comfortably in his car-carrying seat or on your knee anyway. At twelve months old you can arrange him on the floor with airline pillows and blankets.

Relaxation and aiding sleep

You will be amazed at how comfortably and long your baby sleeps on an aircraft. On night flights, children will invariably sleep through the entire journey. Even in the day, the gentle hum of the engines seems to lull babies and children in the same way as a car journey.

Take it for granted that your child will sleep and they will. It is only if you get anxious and expect trouble that they absorb your weakness and so deliver. If they do start to create, I have always found that, even from a young age, I could persuade Paris to wear his seat belt and sit down, by convincing him that I was on his side, but that the stewardess would be really cross if he didn't do as he was told. He couldn't care less if I went purple with rage but a few mock stern words or a frown from the stewardess usually do the trick.

It isn't always easy to pick the timings of your flights but for long haul, given the choice, I would depart early evening and fly overnight every time. Night flights are ideal for a child of any age. Ten hours in daylight is much harder but still, the positive aspect is that the ten hours seems to pass in a blur when I am preoccupied trying to feed, entertain and cope with Paris. Yet when I am alone and free to do as I please, I often find such long journeys torturous. Short haul is probably better tackled in daylight. You arrive at your destination relatively fresh and organised and so able to negotiate which room you are about to be checked into, to get a meal and to deal with all the hazards in your room. Others may disagree, but when I am checking in for a two-hour flight, exhausted, in the early hours of the morning, I can't even find which pocket my passport is in.

If you are a nervous flyer, try as hard as you can not to let your child sense it. Statistics state that if you flew every day for the next 26,000 years you would still never be involved in an air crash, so never forget that you are far more likely to be killed driving to the airport than on a plane.

Babies and toddlers will often fall asleep more readily on a plane than they do at home. Slightly older children may be excited and need time to settle. Once this has passed, brush their teeth, change them into their night clothes and read them their favourite story. They will soon be snoozing for hours.

If your baby is slightly unwell, a dose of Calpol or Disprol can be relied upon for a good night's sleep. For children over two years of age, a dose of an antihistamine, such as promethazine (Phenergan), will calm down excitement, protect from motion sickness and act as a sedative.

If your child is attached to a soother or comforter, don't forget it. When my son was eight months old, I took my dad on a trip on Concorde. As infants are free, I thought it would be nice to take my baby along, too. In years to come, I would be able to show him the photos and tell him about our adventure at Mach 2.

Somehow, when we were all busy taking photographs of each other under Concorde's nose, the pushchair was whisked away, along with a precious satin-edged comfort blanket. By the time I realised, it was too late. The hold was closed and boarding had started. Soon after take-off, Paris noticed that it was missing and the trouble started. Before long he was screaming inconsolably and this continued for most of the flight. He threw a bread roll in my champagne and bellowed with fury. It certainly didn't turn out to be my trip of a lifetime.

In-flight feeding

Don't rely on in-flight meals, especially with young children. They are often served at irregular times, particularly on long-distance flights, and when travelling through time zones. The chances are that your child won't eat the meal anyway. It is amazing how, no matter how hungry a child is, they won't let a grain of food past their lips if they don't like the look of it.

There is also the concern regarding differing levels of hygiene. Most airlines adhere to strict guidelines, but when flying between Third World countries, the meal and ice or water served may not be safe. A friend of mine contracted dysentery actually on a flight to Pakistan. Take back-up snacks such as bananas, raisins, bread rolls and crisps, and if you are in any doubt about the water available on the plane, take plenty of bottled water to prevent dehydration. On most flights there are safe drinking-water dispensers around the toilet areas. If you prefer, ask the stewardess for bottled water or fruit juice. Don't be embarrassed when she frowns at you as you ask for your tenth soft drink. It is important for your own and your children's comfort.

For babies, take on board jars of baby food and ask your stewardess to heat them for you. They will happily provide boiling water for warming bottles and food, but it isn't such a good idea juggling with it in your seat. Plan your baby's meals carefully and have a few extra at hand. A packet or two of powdered baby rice or chicken casserole in your hand luggage will be very light and provide several back-up meals in the event of your flight or the rest of your luggage being delayed. For bottle-fed babies, pack extra formula milk too, for the same reasons.

In-flight entertainment
For babies and younger children, you are it.

Invariably the film will not be particularly suitable for children. Few airlines, such as Virgin, have the fantastic advantage of a mini-screen for every passenger with changeable channels. You can watch *Titanic* while the children watch *Cinderella*. Unfortunately there are only a few airlines with this benefit. Older children, to a large degree, will entertain themselves. They will read or play with the headsets or hand-held computer games. These games are not to be used during take-off and landing but are often sold on the aircraft reasonably cheaply and are permissible once the flight is underway.

On a long journey, it may be a good time for you to catch up on listening to them read. Choose a book you wished you had read as a child or one you enjoyed and which will bring back memories. There will be little or no distractions and your child will benefit from your input and interest. It may also be an opportunity to find out mathematics principles or any other topics they are struggling with. If you can't help them there and then, write it down and look it up when you get home. Babies, too, love to be read to. From the age of five months old, books entranced my son. The only time he would keep still was when sitting on my knee and gazing at the brightly coloured pages. On a trip to Iceland when he was twelve months old, he sat on my knee for the entire two-and-a-half hour daytime flights, there and back, reading book after book and pleading with me,

'Again, again.' My husband and I took turns and it was a very enjoyable, stress-free journey. It was a bit repetitive and boring, but when everyone around commented on what a perfectly behaved child he was, I smiled with relief.

You will be given a few puzzles and crayons on board which will occupy young children for a short time. Take extra paper, pencils and possibly a colouring book. On my first trips, I brought small jigsaws, games, plastic animals and all manner of tiny toys which I spent most of the flight clambering around on the floor to retrieve. The only things I will pack into hand luggage now are books, comics, paper, pencils and one new little surprise.

Nappies
Don't forget nappies as the airlines will not provide them. Change your baby's nappy last thing before getting on the plane. Take a handful in your hand luggage and then a reserve stock just in case your luggage is delayed. We arrived in China with our eighteen-month-old to find that all our cases were still in Heathrow and we were down to our last nappy.

Discomfort during take-off and landing
Your baby may be subject to an inconsolable crying fit during take-off or landing. The reason is a pressure build-up in the ear which can cause acute pain.

On my first ever plane journey from London to Tobago with a young baby, he was as good as gold for eight hours. We had to land in Barbados en route and he woke up and began to cry. We took off again and he became hysterical. The Caribbean stewardesses barked at me, instructing me that he was hungry and that I must feed him. Although I knew he wasn't, I tried to persuade him to take a bottle of milk. The stewardesses watched me with irritation and finally confiscated him to try and console him between them. As we began to descend again in to Tobago, they brought him back still screaming, and shrugged. A toddler in the next row looked on with amusement, sucking gently at her dummy. I was helpless; there was nothing I could do to soothe him. Then I saw the toddler drop her dummy and begin to cry and tug at her ears. It was only then that it dawned on me that my poor child was screaming in pain.

From then on I would always save some of his feed, or give him a lolly at take off and landing. Sucking equalises the pressure in the ear and relieves the discomfort. If your baby is breast-feeding or has a comforter, there will be no problem. If not, save a bit of their bottle or give them a treat to avoid their pain and you being deafened. An alternative is a product called 'Children's ear planes'. There are ridged, disposable ear plugs that are said to regulate the rate of change in ear pressure and so ease the discomfort and pain often experienced while flying. They are suitable for children aged one to eleven and cost around £3.99. I am quite sure my child would totally refuse to have anything placed in his ears, but if you can persuade yours to keep them in place, they might prove worthwhile.

TRAVELLING BY CAR

Travelling in your own car – either around Great Britain and Ireland, or into Europe – I consider to be one of the ultimate freedom holidays. You can stuff your boot with things you might just need, stop where and when you want, and even follow the weather. If you arrive in Normandy and it is pouring down, you could be basking in the sunshine on the South of France in the same day. Fly drives, too, are incredibly flexible and so relaxing. You are free to stop and tend to your children's needs whenever you chose, you can go as near or as far as you decide on the day and need not stop until you find somewhere which satisfies the whole family.

Fly drives are very popular in the US but many countries as far flung as Costa Rica and Malaysia offer similar holiday packages. Often in such countries the roads are good and the cars are of a comfortable standard with air-conditioning. However, with or without children, it is important to remember that the roads abroad are a very real, potentially fatal danger. There are more tourists and expatriates killed on the roads than by any of the diseases we protect ourselves against with such care.

Driving in a strange country, with strange road etiquette, not to mention the signs in a foreign language and driving on the wrong side of the road, all amount to a recipe for disaster. Foreign roads must be treated with the greatest of respect.

Teenagers are at very real risk, especially if they have the means to hire a car. I lost a school friend to the roads in Spain. Some years later, a friend's son was killed at the tender age of eighteen in Majorca. It happens all summer.

The most deathly road in Europe is reputed to be that between Faro airport and the Algarve. This wouldn't surprise me. Tourists jump off a plane into an unfamiliar hire car, often driving on the wrong side of the road. They are trying to find their way, switch gears with the wrong hand and make sense of the Portuguese road signs in the heat. This, combined with tourist-hating, hot-blooded locals in a hurry, spells trouble.

Naturally, some countries are far worse than others. You can usually judge by the state of the local cars how bad the local people are at driving them. Italy has one of the highest death rates on the roads in Europe. A walk round Rome counting the number of dented cars gives you a good idea of this. Another hint is the cost of local insurance. In some places, for example, Jamaica, you have to put a US $1,000 deposit down which is non refundable if you have an accident, whether it is your fault or not. Portugal and Spain are very dangerous places to drive. France, too, has many more deaths per 1,000 of the population per year than the UK. Countries where drink-driving laws are strict are much safer places to travel by road.

If you do decide to hire a car, check that it has seat belts in the back. Take your own children's car seats. They may be bulky, but if you are planning to travel any distance on foreign roads they will be an invaluable asset. Check what petrol the car takes and find your lights, horn and hazard lights before you set off.

If the children start fighting or screaming, stop the car. There is enough to cope with on strange roads without the added stress and confusion coming from the back.

Drive defensively at all times and avoid getting lost at night in strange cities. A few years ago, driving through Naples at night, we were forced to stop at traffic lights where we were accosted by a window washer. It was an oppressive area and we were too frightened to wind down the window even if we had wanted to give the washer some money. As the lights changed we sped off and the guy tried to smash our windscreen with his metal-backed sponge.

Always take the greatest care and adapt to the country you are driving in. Decide where and by which route you will travel when you arrive. Judge the quantity of traffic, the local driving ability and the weather. Motorways may not be so scenic but they are often a country's safest road system.

It is a good idea to avoid the roads altogether in hot countries during very heavy rains. Often the road drainage systems are very poor, or non-existent, and they can quickly become flooded.

Despite all this, I have covered tens of thousands of miles on foreign roads in complete safety. Be careful and be lucky.

Making your journey easier
If you take a trip by car with young babies, don't forget a window blind. We spent an entire week driving around France with a towel trapped in the window. It was November but it was warm and sunny and our son squawked until we assembled a makeshift screen to shield him.

If the weather is hot, a blind will be essential. Even then, beware of heatstroke. Stop the car regularly to try to cool your baby by taking him into an air-conditioned room. If this is impossible, buy chilled mineral water, even if only to put the bottle against his forehead and the back of his neck (not too cold!). Fan your baby too, again, particularly around his face and the back of his neck.

In intolerably hot weather, make sure you have an air-conditioned car or travel out of the heat of the day, otherwise your journey will be a totally miserable and potentially dangerous experience.

If you can stand them, children's tapes always keep things quiet in the back. The repetition sends my husband mad but it is far more tolerable than a protesting, bored toddler.

Have the essentials ever ready, including nappies, baby wipes, tissues, snacks and drinks.

If your child suffers from motion sickness, avoid positioning them facing backwards. You will usually know whether or not your child suffers on car journeys before you go and, depending on severity, it is a good idea to give your child an anti motion-sickness drug which will also help your child to relax and sleep. Remember to give the drug well before you intend to set off, so it has time to take effect (see page 106). Don't allow older children to read on the twisty roads and avoid giving them greasy meals. On long straight roads, such as motorways, most children will be fine reading, but warn them of the symptoms and tell them if they feel queasy to put down their book immediately.

Reassure them that if they need you to stop at any time, they must tell you. With younger children, keep an eye on them and, if they go pale and quiet, stop anyway for a runaround.

Talk to your children and sing with them. Encourage them to invent their own games and distract them by suggesting car games you played yourself as a child. Ask them to watch out for car registration letters or numbers. Counting in this way from 1 to 99 will keep them quiet for hours. You may find 'I-spy' crushingly boring but the children will be far more enthusiastic about a game which you join in with. If travelling in a foreign country, guess what the words on road signs and adverts mean, or let your child test you from a phrase book. Encourage them to give you clues which will make them think about it themselves, and sow the first seeds of a new language in their little brains.

TRAVELLING BY LOCAL TRANSPORT

Short treks are no problem, but travelling across country in many parts of the world unfamiliar to you is destined to be hard work. It is hard enough without children, so planning a huge journey across mountain and savannah should not be taken lightly.

Buses can be smoky, sweltering and stinking of diesel with unpredictable drivers. We were once on a bus from the South of Turkey to Istanbul when our driver got off and had a fight in the street with another road user. He re-embarked, covered with blood, and just carried on driving.

Getting pushchairs, children and luggage on trains is also hard work, especially when you find out that the kind old man who helped you board so concernedly has picked your pocket and the whole family are now without passport, tickets or money.

Organised tours are sometimes expensive and can make you feel that you are missing out on a real travel experience. The balance is that they will often be more relaxing and a much, much easier means of exploring and seeing the sights with children in tow.

If you do decide to go it alone in many countries of the world, by the time you have been cheated, you don't save that much money. After being hassled and confused into getting on to the wrong local bus crammed with chickens and a driver with a death wish, you may wish you had paid up for the tour, whatever the cost.

Tour guides usually have a grasp of local politics and geography and can save you from being duped by the most popular local frauds. In Rome, the guide warned us that crooks were rushing up to confused tourists, flashing badges and shouting, 'Police! We need to see your passports and your currency', then disappearing with the lot. In the US Virgin Islands, we were warned not to let ourselves be photographed with one of the local's donkeys. The owners would encourage the snap and then charge you US $15. In South American countries it is important to check that any change you are given is still legal tender. Many vendors will try to give you currency which is no longer in circulation and so useless.

A good intermediate between tour bus and local transport is to hire a private taxi. This will often be a much more relaxing way of exploring a foreign country for the whole family than hiring a car and driving yourself, but don't forget that swindling is the international inclination of almost every taxi driver on earth. Negotiate the price hard and fast before you set off for the day and refuse to pay a penny more when you return at night. Often a tip is deserved but if, having been your best friend all day, your driver turns around and tries to fleece you, with children or without, don't be a bit surprised.

One worldwide favourite con is agreeing a price with you, then, when you come to settle up, telling you that they didn't mean 60 lire, kroners or sols, they meant 60 US dollars. Don't give in. The driver of a cycle-powered taxi in Beijing became quite hostile when I firmly dismissed his claim that the price he quoted me in local currency equating to £8 had suddenly jumped up to £50. He argued that he had quoted me in US dollars, not yuan. I got more annoyed than him and threatened to call the police. With this, he disappeared with my change. As the average wage in China is £250 per month, there was no way to justify a £50 fare for a 45-minute bike ride, plus, because of the strictly controlled one-child policy, he would only have had one mouth to feed.

TRAVELLING BY BOAT

The experiences I have had on short ferry rides with a rowdy toddler put me off cruising too soon.

My little monster refused to be contained and I trailed after him, hot on his heels. I was petrified that any second he would lurch overboard and disappear down among the waves forever. The fact that a child of any age can fall off a boat means that you can never really relax with them out of sight.

If you are considering a cruise, choose a ship that sails mostly at night and docks most days. It is then just like any other holiday with plenty of variety and activities on shore. Being confined on a ship for days at sea with a toddler or young child for me is hell. I don't even particularly enjoy the days at sea myself. On some ships, the pool gets steadily more filthy as the days wear on. Aside from golf lessons and afternoon tea, there is nothing to do but get drunk! This is not a good idea when in charge of children on the open sea.

Older children enjoy cruises more, but prepare for sea sickness. When we were on a cruise around the Indian Ocean, every child except Paris (who was probably too young) suffered from sea sickness. Also, remember that long, elaborate dinners will be boring for them, so book the early sitting. Children love the shows, but they are usually on late. When Paris was three, he would get up every morning on ship, and the first thing he would say was, 'Mummy, when is the show starting?' I then had to take him to the stage, so he could see that he wasn't missing anything.

One major advantage that cruise ships offer is that you are never far away from a well-trained doctor with a well-stocked and sterile medicine cabinet. This is a huge reassurance if you are travelling around more adventurous regions with young ones. If your child becomes very sea sick take a trip to the doctor's straight away. The doctor can administer strong anti-sickness drugs that bring considerable relief. Remember that it is too late to give anti-histamine drugs once your child is feeling sick on ship, as these must be taken at least two hours before sailing.

In contrast, ferry rides are often only a short part of a holiday. As such, they are fine with a toddler and pleasant with older children. Hiring your own boat or an organised day trip out to sea will be great fun. On the whole, children seem more likely to keep still in smaller boats.

Beware of sunburn which can be much more severe on a boat due to the sun's rays being reflected off the water's surface. You will all burn much quicker and deeper, so hats and factor 30 sunscreen are imperative.

TRAVEL SICKNESS

The terms 'motion sickness' or 'travel sickness' apply to sea, car, air or swing sickness. It is a thoroughly miserable condition which has ruined many expensive cruise holidays, when those prone to sea sickness may find themselves bedridden for days.

Aircraft can fly above adverse weather conditions. The only problems that usually arise are when air traffic control insist that planes are held in areas of high turbulence for operational reasons. I once spent an hour circling above Lisbon in a violent storm. I very rarely suffer from motion sickness but other people vomiting all around me was torture.

You will usually be aware whether or not your child suffers from car sickness and, if they do, you can almost guarantee they will suffer if you hit turbulence, so prepare yourself.

Symptoms
The condition is characterised by headache, nausea followed by vomiting, pallor, and cold sweating with excessive sweating of face and hands. Increased salivation and light-headedness occur. They will also feel apathetic, miserable, depressed and be unable to get up from their seat or bunk. Motion sickness can be life threatening because, in some cases, the sufferer becomes so dejected they can lose their will to live and make uncalculated decisions. Small children will be very quiet and pale with sweaty palms. If they complain of a tummy ache, get ready.

Avoiding travel sickness

The exact cause of sea sickness is still unclear but it is known to be linked to the balancing system in the ear. Because the condition can last for several days, it needs to be carefully considered and prepared for before travel. Thankfully, many safe and effective medicines are available as preventative measures against the problem but they must be taken at least two hours before travel. Once you are on board and feeling sick, it is too late.

The eyes also play a definite role in easing or worsening the feelings of sickness. This can be manipulated by asking a child to focus their eyes on a fixed point such as the horizon, or the seat in front, so that the brain has something to concentrate on. Ballet dancers can pirouette indefinitely without getting dizzy by fixing their eyes on something in front until the last moment, when they whip around their head in line with their body. Deter children from watching any oncoming traffic, or waves if at sea. Also worth considering is that a few people suffer more if travelling backwards on a train or by car.

Make a child aware that if they read or play computer games, it can make symptoms worse, and that they must stop as soon as they start to feel any nausea or they are very likely to be sick.

Although occupying the mind decreases travel sickness, and psychological factors can exacerbate the feelings, it is a physiological condition. Like many things, it seems to run in families. Each of the most susceptible people I know has a parent who suffers just as easily. I am glad to say that, akin to my father, I am usually the last person on ship to be ill while my husband, Simon, is always the first. I wasn't therefore surprised to find that Simon's mum suffers badly too.

Sleep eliminates sickness and if you have left it too late to take the tablet, encourage your child to close their eyes and relax while you tell them a story to take their mind off their stomach. It may also be abated if you give your child a sweet to suck.

There are several medicines available to prevent motion sickness which you can purchase over the counter. Your pharmacist will only too willing to advise you. When Simon and I first started to travel, he would even feel bad on short ferry journeys. A pharmaceutical collegue told me that Cinnarizine was the drug of choice for the British Navy and had solved all his travelling problems. I now always dose Simon up. On a sea-crossing to Egypt, which was so rough that the dancers had to abandon the show after falling off the dancefloor, and the buffet had to be cleared as it was all toppling off the table, to our amazement, Simon felt fine throughout.

For children between five and twelve years, the dosage is half that of the adult. It should be detailed on the pack but if you are buying the drug abroad and cannot read the instructions, you should give children one (15 mg) tablet, one to two hours before travel, and then half a tablet every eight hours. The recommended adult dose is double. Cinnarizine should not be given to children under five years old.

Babies do not suffer from motion sickness but a few toddlers do. For them, the choice of drug is fairly limited. However, those available are safe and very effective, although they have a significant sedative effect.

- Dramamine (dimenhydinate) can be given to children over one year. The recommended dose is a quarter to half (50 mg) tablet for one- to six-year-olds. For seven- to twelve-year-olds, half to one tablet. Both two or three times daily.
- Phenergan (promethazine hydrochloride) can be given to children over two years. The advantage of this medicine is that it comes as an elixir and is also of benefit if your child is badly bitten by insects or develops an allergic reaction while away. Phenergan is useful on a plane journey as it will send your child into a deep sleep, giving you plenty of peace. This drug has been around for a long time and is considered very safe. My doctor dad would always dose us up with phenergan on Christmas Eve if we couldn't sleep with the excitement. However, it does wear off after five to six hours and repeated dosing is necessary. The recommended dose is 5 mg for children aged two to five years; 10 mg for children aged five to ten years; 25 mg over ten years. To be taken the night before a journey and repeated after six to eight hours if necessary. Higher doses are needed for allergic reaction. 10–15 mg for children aged two to five years; 10–25 mg for children over five years. To be given once daily.

You must pay careful attention to not overdose your child.

Other ways of ensuring you have a sick-free journey are by limiting the amount you feed your child beforehand. Only allow them to eat light, fat-free meals.

Choose your seats carefully. Seats between the wings are the most stable on an airplane. The front of a car or bus gives good visibility and less likelihood of travel sickness. On a boat, stay on deck if possible and if not, make sure you choose a seat near a window so you can all see the horizon and you are away from the engine and the diesel fumes. Midship is usually the best place to be, but on some small craft, the back may buffet around least. Ask the crew where it is best for your child to sit.

5 Judging the Health Risks of Your Destination: Immunisations, Malaria Tablets and Planning How to Avoid Illness Before You Travel

It is important to know which immunisations and malaria prophylaxis are necessary for the area you will be travelling to. In some instances, this may affect your choice of destination, especially as certain age groups are more susceptible to certain illnesses.

There are two million deaths from malaria every year, most of the victims being infants or pregnant women. With very young children, therefore, it is probably wiser to avoid those areas of the world where malaria is commonly resistant to all available drug treatment. Most of the vaccines are safe for use with children. The malaria tablets you and your children will need to take in countries where malaria has not developed drug resistance have been used by children and pregnant woman for 40 years without any associated problems.

Experienced travellers and those who are visiting the country of their birth should be aware that even though they may have developed some resistance to tropical diseases, their children will be susceptible to all local illnesses and care should be taken to protect them.

You will be able to obtain the necessary immunisations via your GP surgery or a specialist travel vaccination centre. It is important that you arrange your first appointment well in advance, at least five weeks prior to departure. The usual immunisations required for travel will normally be given over four weeks. If your child is not up-to-date with the full complement of normal childhood vaccinations (diphtheria, measles etc), you will need longer.

The order of immunisations will be tailored to your needs

and the time you have left before travel. Even if you have booked a last-minute trip, or have left it later than four weeks before departure, you will still be able to get cover for most of the illnesses which would be a threat.

Many health clinics held in GP surgeries do not charge for children's vaccinations (except yellow fever). If you visit a private clinic there will be a charge for each vaccine.

Figure 2 is a guide to which vaccines and anti-malarial drugs you are likely to require when travelling in each country of the world but you should contact your GP or local travel clinic to confirm. The data is updated continuously and the guidelines, particularly for anti-malarial regimes, change constantly. The table also indicates the other illnesses that could be a danger to you and your children. The information below was correct at time of going to press. For up-to-date information, telephone your local travel clinic or ask your GP.

Key to Figure 2
Malaria Regimes:
P   Proguanil
C   Chloroquine
PC   Proguanil plus Chloroquine
ME   Mefloquine (Larium). For children under one year or 15 kg, the alternative regime would be Proguanil plus Chloroquine, which would not be as effective in areas of drug resistance.

Yellow fever vaccinations and certificates:
A   Yellow fever vaccination certificate might be required if travellers pass through a country where yellow fever is present.
B   Yellow fever vaccination certificate might be required if travellers pass through a country where yellow fever is present, except children under six months old.
C   Yellow Fever vaccination certificate might be required if travellers pass through a country where yellow fever is present, except children under one year old.
D   Vaccination is essential and requires a certificate.
E   Vaccination is essential and requires a certificate, except children under six months old.

F	Vaccination is essential and requires a certificate, except children under nine months old.
G	Vaccination is essential and requires a certificate, except children under one year old.
H	Vaccination is recommended.
I	Vaccination is compulsory if transitting an area within six days.
J	Vaccination is compulsory if transitting an area within six days, unless under six months old.
K	Certificate might be required on leaving.

Other illnesses

Leish	Leishmaniasis
Schist	Schistosomiasis (bilharzia)
Tryp	Trypanosomiasis (sleeping sickness – Africa, Chagas' disease – Central and South America)

THE SAFETY OF MODERN IMMUNISATIONS

You might be deterred from visiting a country because of the injections that are needed before you travel. You might have doubts or feelings of guilt about subjecting your child to the needle and possible consequences of any complications or side effects caused by a vaccination. However, you must be aware and remember that all those available under licence in the UK are extensively researched, very well tolerated and extremely safe.

Side effects are very, very rare. A child who is healthy and well nourished will skip out of the health clinic after a few pinpricks, primed to fight unseen enemies and enjoy their trip to the full. There are still minor illnesses to be encountered abroad, and diseases such as dengue fever for which no vaccine is available. However they are generally rare and do not have the same severity, likelihood of occuring or risk of fatality as those for which there are vaccines on offer.

It is important to note that children who are already ill or feverish should not be vaccinated until they have recovered. Their immune defences will be concentrating on fighting the bug causing the illness and should not be compromised by loading more bugs into the body.

Figure 2. Vaccines and anti-malarial drugs required, by country.

Country	Hepatitis A	Recommended malaria regime	Typhoid	Polio	Yellow fever	Meningitis A+C	Other illnesses
AFGHANISTAN	YES	PC	YES	YES	A	—	Dysentery, TB, rabies, leish, worms
ALBANIA	YES	—	YES	YES	C	—	—
ALGERIA	YES	—	YES	YES	C	—	—
ANGOLA	YES	ME	YES	YES	A	—	Cholera, dysentery, plague, rabies, schist, filariasis, sleeping sickness
ANTIGUA	YES	—	YES	YES	—	—	Dengue, schist, worms
ARGENTINA	YES	C (in north-west)	YES	YES	—	—	Chagas, dysentery, rabies, worms, leish on NE
AUSTRALIA	—	—	—	—	G	—	Dengue in the north-west, dangerous sea and land animals (snakes and spiders)
AUSTRIA	—	—	—	—	—	—	Tick encephalitis
AZERBAIJAN	—	C (in south)	—	YES	—	—	—
AZORES	—	—	—	—	C	—	—
BAHAMAS	YES	—	YES	YES	C	—	Dysentery, dengue
BAHRAIN	YES	—	YES	YES	C	—	Dysentery, rabies, leish
BANGLADESH	YES	PC OR ME (no risk Dhaka)	YES	YES	I	—	Cholera, dysentery, dengue, rabies, typhus, filariasis, worms, leish

Country	Hepatitis A	Recommended malaria regime	Typhoid	Polio	Yellow fever	Meningitis A+C	Other illnesses
BARBADOS	YES	—	YES	YES	C	—	Dysentery, dengue
BELGIUM	—	—	—	—	—	—	—
BELIZE	YES	C (rural areas)	YES	YES	A	—	Dysentery, dengue, leish, filariasis, worms, Chagas
BELORUSSIA	—	—	—	—	—	—	Dysentery
BENIN	YES	ME	YES	YES	G	YES	Cholera, dysentery, rabies, schist
BERMUDA	—	—	—	—	—	—	—
BHUTAN	YES	PC (in south)	YES	YES	A	—	Dysentery, worms, rabies, TB
BOLIVIA	YES	PC OR ME	YES	YES	H+A	—	Cholera, leish, worms, Chagas
BOSNIA AND HERZ	—	—	—	—	—	—	Dysentery
BOTSWANA	YES	PC (in north, Nov–June)	YES	YES	G+B	—	Dysentery, rabies, cholera, worms
BRAZIL	YES	ME	YES	YES	B+H	—	Cholera, amoebic dysentery, plague, leish, schist, worms, Chagas
BRUNEI	YES	—	YES	YES	C	—	Typhus, worms
BULGARIA	—	—	—	—	—	—	Dysentery
BURKINA-FASO	YES	ME	YES	YES	G	YES	Dysentery, cholera, rabies, sleeping sickness, worms
BURMA	YES	ME	YES	YES	A	—	Cholera, dysentery, dengue, rabies, worms, filariasis, plague

Country							
BURUNDI	YES	ME	YES	YES	C	YES	Cholera, dysentery, typhus, sleeping sickness
CAMBODIA	YES	ME	YES	YES	A	—	Cholera, dysentery, rabies, worms
CAMEROON	YES	ME	YES	YES	G	YES	Cholera, dysentery, rabies, sleeping sickness, worms
CANADA	—	—	—	—	—	—	—
CANARY ISLANDS	—	—	—	—	—	—	—
CAPE VERDE ISLANDS	YES	—	YES	YES	C	—	Cholera, TB, rabies, typhus, schist, worms
CAYMAN ISLANDS	YES	—	YES	YES	—	—	—
CENTRAL AFRICAN REP.	YES	ME	YES	YES	G	YES	Cholera, TB, rabies, typhus, worms, sleeping sickness
CHAD	YES	ME	YES	YES	G	YES	Cholera, TB, rabies, typhus, worms, sleeping sickness
CHILE	YES	—	YES	YES	—	—	Cholera, worms, filariasis
CHINA	YES	ME OR C	YES	YES	A	—	Bact dysentery, rabies, schist, filariasis, leish, plague
COLOMBIA	YES	ME	YES	YES	H + C	—	Cholera, dysentery, dengue, leish, worms, Chagas
COMOROS	YES	ME	YES	YES	—	—	—
CONGO	YES	ME	YES	YES	G	—	Cholera, TB, rabies, typhus, schist, worms, sleeping sickness
COOK ISLANDS	YES	—	YES	YES	—	—	—

Country	Hepatitis A	Recommended malaria regime	Typhoid	Polio	Yellow fever	Meningitis A+C	Other illnesses
COSTA RICA	YES	C	YES	YES	—	—	Dysentery, rabies, leish, filariasis, worms
CROATIA	—	—	—	—	—	—	Dysentery
CUBA	YES	—	YES	YES	—	—	Dysentery, dengue
CYPRUS	—	—	—	—	—	—	Typhus
CZECHOSLOVAKIA	—	—	—	—	—	—	Dysentery, worms
DENMARK	—	—	—	—	—	—	—
DJIBOUTI	YES	ME	YES	YES	C	—	Cholera, dysentery, rabies, typhus, sleeping sickness, schist, worms
DOMINICA	YES	—	YES	YES	C	—	—
DOMINICAN REP	YES	C	YES	YES	—	—	Dysentery, dengue, rabies, leish, schist
ECUADOR	YES	PC	YES	YES	H+A	—	Cholera, amoebic dysentery, leish, schist, worms, filariasis
EGYPT	YES	C	YES	YES	A	—	Schist
EL SALVADOR	YES	C	YES	YES	B	—	Dysentery, rabies, typhus, leish
EQUATORIAL GUINEA	YES	ME	YES	YES	H+A	—	Cholera, dysentery, rabies, sleeping sickness
ESTONIA	—	ME	—	—	—	—	—
ETHIOPIA	YES	ME	YES	YES	H+C	YES	Cholera, dysentery, rabies, typhus, sleeping sickness, schist, worms

Country							Diseases
FIJI	YES	—	YES	YES	C	—	Dengue, filariasis, dysentery
FINLAND	—	—	—	—	—	—	Dysentery, Tick encephalitis
FRANCE	—	—	—	—	—	—	—
GABON	YES	ME	YES	YES	G	—	Cholera, dysentery, rabies, typhus, leish, sleeping sickness
GAMBIA	YES	ME	YES	YES	H+C	YES	Sleeping sickness, cholera, dysentery, TB, rabies, schist
GEORGIA	—	—	—	—	—	—	—
GERMANY	—	—	—	—	—	—	—
GHANA	YES	ME	YES	YES	D	—	Dysentery, cholera, rabies, typhus, sleeping sickness, schist, worms, TB
GIBRALTAR	—	—	—	—	—	—	—
GREECE	—	—	—	—	—	—	Leish
GREENLAND	—	—	—	—	—	—	—
GRENADA	YES	—	YES	YES	C	—	—
GUADELOUPE	YES	—	YES	YES	C	—	Schist
GUAM	YES	—	YES	YES	—	—	Dysentery, dengue, leish, worms, filariasis
GUATEMALE	YES	C	YES	YES	C	—	Dysentery, rabies, leish, worms, filariasis
GUIANA, FRENCH	YES	ME	YES	YES	G	—	Cholera, dysentery, typhoid, leish
GUINEA	YES	ME	YES	YES	H+C	YES	Cholera, dysentery, filariasis, schist

Country	Hepatitis A	Recommended malaria regime	Typhoid	Polio	Yellow fever	Meningitis A + C	Other illnesses
GUINEA BISSAU	YES	ME	YES	YES	H + C	—	Cholera, dysentery, filariasis
GUYANA	YES	ME	YES	YES	H + A	—	Cholera, bacterial dysentery, rabies, leish, tryp, schist, flukes
HAITI	YES	C	YES	YES	A	—	Dysentery, dengue, filariasis
HONDURAS	YES	C	YES	YES	A	—	Dysentery, dengue, rabies, leish, Chagas
HONG KONG	YES	—	YES	YES	—	—	Rabies
HUNGARY	—	—	—	—	—	—	Dysentery
ICELAND	—	—	—	—	—	—	—
INDIA	YES	PC	YES	YES	B	YES	Cholera, dysentery, rabies, leish, filariasis
INDONESIA	YES	PC (not nec in Bali)	YES	YES	A	—	Dysentery, dengue, rabies, filariasis
IRAN	YES	PC (March–Nov)	YES	YES	C	—	Dysentery, leish
IRELAND	—	—	—	—	—	—	—
ISRAEL	YES	—	YES	YES	—	—	Dysentery, rabies, leish
ITALY	—	—	—	—	—	—	—
IVORY COAST	YES	ME	YES	YES	G	YES	Cholera, dysentery, sleeping sickness, schist
JAMAICA	YES	—	YES	YES	C	—	Amoebic dysentery, dengue, worms

Country							Notes
JAPAN	—	—	—	—	—	—	—
JORDAN	YES	—	YES	YES	—	—	Dysentery
KAZAKHSTAN	—	—	—	—	C	—	—
KENYA	YES	ME	YES	YES	H+C	YES	Cholera, typhus, leish, sleeping sickness
KOREA	YES	—	YES	YES	—	—	Typhus
KRYGYSTAN	—	—	—	—	—	—	—
LAOS	YES	ME	YES	YES	A	—	Amoebic dysentery, dengue, rabies
LATVIA	—	—	—	—	—	—	—
LEBANON	YES	—	YES	YES	A	—	Cholera
LESOTHO	YES	—	YES	YES	A	—	Cholera, TB, rabies
LIBERIA	YES	ME	YES	YES	G	YES	Cholera, dysentery, rabies
LIBYA	YES	—	YES	YES	C	—	Dysentery, rabies, TB, schist
LITHUANIA	—	—	—	—	—	—	—
LUXEMBOURG	—	—	—	—	—	—	—
MADAGASCAR	YES	ME	YES	YES	A	—	Cholera, dysentery, plague, rabies, typhus, sleeping sickness, filariasis
MADEIRA	—	—	—	—	C	—	—
MALAWI	YES	ME	YES	YES	A	—	Cholera, dysentery, rabies, schist, filariasis
MALAYSIA	YES	(PC)	YES	YES	C	—	Dengue, dysentery
MALDIVES	YES	—	YES	YES	A	—	—

Country	Hepatitis A	Recommended malaria regime	Typhoid	Polio	Yellow fever	Meningitis A + C	Other illnesses
MALI	YES	ME	YES	YES	G	YES	Cholera, dysentery, rabies, schist, filariasis
MALTA	—	—	—	—	E	—	—
MAURITIUS	YES	C (rural area)	YES	YES	C	—	Schist
MEXICO	YES	C (rural area)	YES	YES	B	—	Dysentery, dengue, rabies, leish, scorpions
MOLDAVIA	—	—	—	—	—	—	Dysentery
MONACO	—	—	—	—	—	—	—
MONGOLIA	YES	—	YES	YES	—	—	—
MOROCCO	YES	—	YES	YES	—	—	Dysentery, TB, rabies
MOZAMBIQUE	YES	ME	YES	YES	C	—	Cholera, dysentery, dengue, rabies, tryp, filariasis, plague
NAMIBIA	YES	PC (in north, Nov–June)	YES	YES	C	—	Rabies, schist, dysentery, sleeping sickness
NAURU	YES	—	YES	YES	C	—	—
NEPAL	YES	PC (no risk Kathmandu)	YES	YES	E + A	YES	Cholera, dysentery, rabies, worms, leish
NETHERLANDS	—	—	—	—	—	—	—
NEW CALEDONIA	YES	—	YES	YES	C	—	Dysentery, worms
NEW ZEALAND	—	—	—	—	—	—	—

NICARAGUA	YES	C	YES	YES	C	—	Dysentery, dengue, rabies, leish, worms
NIGER	YES	ME	YES	YES	G	YES	Cholera, dysentery, rabies, sleeping sickness, schist, filariasis
NIGERIA	YES	ME	YES	YES	H + C	YES	Cholera, dysentery, rabies, sleeping sickness, schist, filariasis
NIUE	YES	—	YES	YES	C	—	Dysentery, filariasis
NORWAY	—	—	—	—	—	—	—
OMAN	YES	PC	YES	YES	A	—	Rabies, cyphus, leish, schist
PAKISTAN	YES	PC	YES	YES	B	—	Cholera, dysentery, rabies, typhus, leish, filariasis, dengue
PANAMA	YES	PC	YES	YES	H + C	—	Dysentery, dengue, rabies, leish, tryp, filariasis
PAPUA NEW GUINEA	YES	Resistance is a problem	YES	YES	C	—	Dysentery, dengue, worms, filariasis
PARAGUAY	YES	C	YES	YES	K (rural areas)	—	Cholera, dysentery, rabies, leish, schist, worms
PERU	YES	PC	YES	YES	H + B (rural areas)	—	Cholera, dysentery, rabies, leish, flukes, worms
PHILIPPINES	YES	PC (rural areas)	YES	YES	J (rural areas)	—	Dysentery, rabies, schist, flukes, worms
PITCAIRN ISLAND	YES	—	YES	YES	C	—	—
POLAND	—	—	—	—	—	—	—
POLYNESIA, FRENCH	YES	—	YES	YES	C	—	Dengue, dysentery, filariasis, worms

Country	Hepatitis A	Recommended malaria regime	Typhoid	Polio	Yellow fever	Meningitis A+C	Other illnesses
PORTUGAL	—	—	—	—	—	—	—
QATAR	YES	—	YES	YES	C	—	Schist
ROMANIA	—	—	—	—	—	—	Dysentery (bact), rabies
RUSSIAN FED.	—	—	—	—	—	—	Tick encephalitis, TB, dysentery
RWANDA	YES	ME	YES	YES	G	—	—
SAINT HELENA	YES	—	YES	YES	—	—	—
SAINT LUCIA	YES	—	YES	YES	C	—	Dengue, schist
SAINT VINCENT AND GRENADINES	YES	—	YES	YES	C	—	—
SAMOA	YES	—	YES	YES	C	—	Dengue, worms
SAO TOME & PRIN	YES	ME	YES	YES	H+C	—	Cholera, dysentery, sleeping sickness, filariasis
SAUDI ARABIA	YES	PC (rural areas)	YES	YES	A	YES	Amoebic dysentery, leish, schist
SENEGAL	YES	ME	YES	YES	G	YES	Cholera, dysentery, TB
SEYCHELLES	YES	—	YES	YES	A	—	Dengue, filariasis
SIERRA LEONE	YES	ME	YES	YES	H+C	YES	Cholera, dysentery, TB, rabies, schist, filariasis
SINGAPORE	YES	—	YES	YES	C	—	—
SLOVENIA	—	—	—	—	—	—	Dysentery

Country		Resistance is a problem				
SOLOMON ISLANDS	YES		YES	A	—	Dengue, worms
SOMALIA	YES	ME	YES	H+C	—	Dysentery, cholera, rabies, TB
SOUTH AFRICA	YES	PC (rural areas and safari)	YES	C	—	TB, schist, worms
SPAIN	—	—	—	—	—	Dysentery
SRI LANKA	YES	PC (except Colombo)	YES	C	—	Amoebic dysentery, dengue, rabies, worms, filariasis
SUDAN	YES	ME	YES	—	YES	Cholera, dysentery, rabies, schist, filariasis, TB, leish
SURINAM	YES	ME	YES	H+C	—	Cholera, dysentery, leish, tryp, schist, worms, filariasis
SWAZILAND	YES	ME	YES	A	—	Dysentery, dengue, rabies, schist
SWEDEN	—	—	—	—	—	Tick encephalitis
SWITZERLAND	—	—	—	A	—	—
SYRIA	YES	C (In north, May–Oct)	YES	—	—	Rabies, typhus, leish, schist
TAIWAN	YES	—	YES	—	—	Dysentery
TAJISTAN	—	C (South border area)	—	—	—	Dysentery
TANZANIA	YES	ME	YES	H+C	YES	Cholera, dysentery, rabies, sleeping sickness, plague
THAILAND	YES	Cam, Burm border	YES	C	—	Cholera, dysentery, rabies, leish, dengue

Country	Hepatitis A	Recommended malaria regime	Typhoid	Polio	Yellow fever	Meningitis A+C	Other illnesses
TOGO	YES	ME	YES	YES	G	YES	Cholera, dysentery, rabies, sleeping sickness, schist
TONGA	—	—	—	—	C	—	Dysentery, dengue
TRINIDAD AND TOBAGO	YES	—	YES	YES	C	—	Worms
TUNISIA	YES	—	YES	YES	—	—	Rabies
TURKEY	YES	Rural areas March–Nov	YES	YES	—	—	Dysentery, rabies
TURKMENISTAN	—	—	—	—	A	—	Dysentery
TUVALU	YES	—	YES	YES	C	—	Filariasis, dengue
UGANDA	YES	ME	YES	YES	H+C	YES	Cholera, dysentery, rabies, schist, TB, plague, filariasis
UKRAINE	—	—	—	—	—	—	—
UNITED ARAB EMIRATES	YES	PC (northern rural only)	YES	YES	—	—	Dysentery, rabies, schist
URUGUAY	YES	—	YES	YES	—	—	Cholera, dysentery, rabies, leish, flukes, worms, chagas
USSR	—	—	—	—	—	—	Tick encephalitis
UZBEKISTAN	—	—	—	—	—	—	Dysentery
VANUATU	YES	Resistance is a problem	YES	YES	—	—	Dengue, filariasis

VENEZUELA	YES	PC OR ME (rural areas)	YES	YES	H+C	—	Cholera, rabies, leish, schist, worms, chagas, filariasis
VIETNAM	YES	ME (rural areas) YES	YES	C	—	Dysentery, dengue, rabies, leish, filariasis, plague
VIRGIN ISLANDS	YES	—	YES	YES	—	—	—
YEMEN	YES	PC	YES	YES	C	—	Dysentery, rabies, typhus, leish, schist
ZAIRE	YES	ME	YES	YES	G	—	Cholera, dysentery, rabies, typhus, sleeping sickness, filariasis, plague
ZAMBIA	YES	ME	YES	YES	—	—	Cholera, dysentery, rabies, schist, filariasis, sleeping sickness
ZIMBABWE	YES	ME	YES	YES	A	—	Cholera, schist, worms

Excepting the above circumstance, I maintain the philosophy that the more bugs a child is exposed to when they are young and strong, the better. I always imagine the immune system as a muscle. The more exercise it gets, the bigger and stronger it becomes. Vaccinations help flex this 'muscle' without putting the child at risk from the disease.

A recent article in a respected Sunday newspaper concluded that children who attend nursery schools at a very young age have a much stronger immune system later in life. Other studies suggest that a better-developed immune system will protect against problems such as asthma, and even cancer. There is some evidence that the incidence of leukaemia in children is much higher in middle-class children who have been kept at home and sheltered from common illnesses. Tumours may be the result of viral invasion. If your immune system is in good fighting order, you are less likely to fall victim. This is readily illustrated in AIDS patients whose immune system is failing. Many will develop characteristic cancers, for example, Kaposi's sarcoma.

Unless you intend to keep your child at home in the UK for the rest of its life, you protect them by immunisation. A healthy child's body is fit for fighting off infections and designed to cope with vaccinations. Very few will react to immunisations unpredictably, although if your child has any allergies you must tell the doctor. Some vaccines are derived from eggs and others contain antibiotics, so an allergy to either constituent must be declared to avert a potentially serious allergic reaction. At the same time, discuss any concerns you have and take into account the particular vaccine and from what age it is recommended to be given.

Note that pregnant women should avoid vaccines which contain live organisms, for example, polio or yellow fever.

Further information
Most vaccines are low doses of the bacteria or virus that would normally cause the illness. The offending bug has usually been altered in some way (attenuated) or killed so that it is incapable of causing the disease. Instead of becoming ill, the body is given time to learn to recognise the particular bacteria or virus and

develop antibodies ready to attack the bug the next time it is introduced into the body.

All manufacturers of vaccines have a medical information department that is usually willing to help and advise patients, either over the telephone or in writing. They will be informed, up-to-date and the best possible source of data on their products. The employees working in the medical information section of any pharmaceutical company are either trained medics or qualified scientists whose knowledge in their field is excellent and unbiased. They are not salesmen and will often be more cautious about the details they give you than your own doctor. They may either reassure you or confirm your fears. Either way, they are likely to help you to make your decision.

Ask the doctor or nurse in your health clinic which vaccine they use and, if possible, the name of the manufacturer. Your local pharmacist will then be able to provide you with the manufacturer's address and telephone number. Don't be inhibited about contacting them by phone. Once through to the main switchboard, ask for the medical information department. When you are put through ask anything you want to know. Some questions might be:
1. How long has the vaccine been available?
2. How many people have received the vaccine over the years?
3. What are the side effects?
4. Can it be given to toddlers?
5. Is a penicillin, egg, or any other allergy, going to interefere with the vaccine?

Even if the voice on the other end of the phone asks you to hold while they check or look up the information, you should be confident that they are giving you good advice.

The importance of age
Children in the UK very rarely catch measles or chicken pox before they are twelve months old. This, to me, is amazing. It is possible that the immunity passes on from the mother and gradually wanes over the first year. Then why do children suffer more with common illnesses the older they get? Teenagers in particular often present with much more severe symptoms than younger children presenting with the same infection. I vividly

remember catching chicken pox from my younger brother. He was about five years old and had thirteen spots in total. I was ten years old and developed over 300. They were everywhere, including inside my mouth, my nose and my eyelids. My son Paris caught chicken pox from nursery school when he was two years old and didn't even notice.

Measles struck me when I was thirteen and I lay like a limp rag for two weeks while my youngest brother ran around me, covered in spots. Measles and most other viruses are invariably far more aggressive in teenagers and young adults who are usually society's fittest and strongest members. Measles and bacterial meningitis may kill a sixteen-year-old but when the same measles virus or meningitis bacteria attack a seven-year-old brother or sister, complications are far less likely to arise.

Also worthy of note is that although the triple vaccine is given from one year old in the UK, it is not licensed for adults.

So, although we may imagine that young children would be more vulnerable to a particular vaccine, provided the dosage administered has been tested by the manufacturers and is correct relative to the age and size of the child, we need not be unduly worried.

Figure 3. Minimum age and booster guide for the use of the principal travel vaccines.

Travel vaccine	Minimum age children can safely be given the vaccine	When are booster doses necessary?
Diphtheria (usual childhood course)	2, 3 and 4 months (3 doses)	3 years old
Tetanus	2, 3 and 4 months (3 doses)	After 10 years
Pertussis (Whooping cough)	2, 3 and 4 months (3 doses)	
Polio	2, 3 and 4 months (3 doses)	School entry (5 years old) Booster should then be given 10 yearly
Yellow fever	9 months (single dose)	10 yearly
Meningococcal meningitis A&C	2 months (single dose) (May be less effective under 18 months)	3 yearly

Hepatitis A + B (Twinrix paed)	1 year (3 doses)	Hepatitis B booster after 5 years Hepatitis A booster after 10 years
Hepatitis A Immunoglobulin	No minimum age (single dose)	Protection lasts just 2–6 months
Hepatitis A Havrix Junior	1 year (single dose)	Booster given 6–12 months after initial injection. Gives protection for up to 10 years
Hepatitis B	No minimum age (3 doses)	Every 3–5 years
Rabies	No minimum age given (3 doses)	Every 2–3 years
Japanese encephalitis	Vaccine is available for children only if requested for specific named cases (3 doses)	After 2–4 years
Tick-borne encephalitis	No minimum age given (3 doses)	After 1 year
Typhoid injection	18 months (single injection)	Every 3 years
Typhoid given orally	6 years (3 oral doses of one capsule)	Protection lasts 1 year
BCG (Tuberculosis)	Usually given at 6 weeks old	Booster may be required after 15 years
MMR (measles, mumps and rubella)	1 year	
Hib Meningitis	2, 3 and 4 months	

PROPHYLACTIC ANTIMALARIAL DRUGS FOR CHILDREN

If malaria is a risk in the country you will be travelling to, you must ensure your child is protected with the correct dosage of the recommended drugs. Malaria has killed more people than any other disease in the history of mankind. Although some parasites attack in purges, malaria is unabating and is always present in many parts of the world. Two million people worldwide die each year from the disease. Those most at risk are children under five years and pregant women.

In the UK, around 2000 cases of malaria are diagnosed each

year. Of those, very few cases are fatal but death has been known to occur within 24 hours of symptoms developing.

Unfortunately anti-malarial drugs do not give complete protection and symptoms may develop up to a year after your holiday. This is confusing and may go undiagnosed by your doctor. It is likely that he will never have seen a case of malaria before and because so much time has lapsed between your holiday and the illness, you may neglect to mention that you visited a region where it was a problem. It has been suggested that malaria is the most misdiagnosed illness in the UK. Many patients are considered to have flu.

Malaria, its drug treatment and signs and symptoms are detailed in chapter 12, page 232.

When you arrive at your destination, you must be aware of the risk and concentrate on reducing the number of mosquito bites received. Getting a child to comply with the dosages below is not easy but it is very important.

If you are travelling to a country where the malaria is drug resistant and you may not be easily able to seek medical help, it is advisable to carry quinine and fasidine for treatment in an emergency. Discuss this with your doctor.

Conclusion

1. Confirm that you do actually need the vaccine by checking with a travel clinic. Note that you may only need a particular vaccine if you are visiting a certain region of the country or travelling outside the cities or tourist resorts.
2. Discuss allergies and any other issues that concern you with either your own doctor or a nurse at a travel clinic.
3. Check that the vaccination you are considering is licensed and recommended for your child's age group.
4. It is essential that your child is well when the vaccinations are given.

If you have come to the decision to take advantage of the protection offered by immunisation you should feel confident and guiltless. It may even be that in future years you will find that you have benefited your child in other ways by keeping his immune system 'on its toes' and protecting against other problems. Also consider that even if your child has a minor

Figure 4. Anti-malarial drug dosage guide.

Age	0–5 weeks	6 weeks–11 months	1–5 years	6–11 years	>12 years
Weight			10–19 kg	20–39 kg	>40 kg
Chloroquine Weekly dose	37.5 mg or 3.75 ml syrup	75 mg or 7.5 ml syrup	150 mg (1 tablet) or 15 ml syrup	225 mg (1½ tablets) or 22.5 ml syrup	300 mg (2 tablets)
Proguanil Daily dose	25 mg (¼ tablet)	50 mg (½ tablet)	100 mg (1 tablet)	150 mg (1½ tablets)	200 mg (2 tablets)
Mefloquine Weekly dose	Not recommended (N/R)		N/R <15 kg 2–5 years ¼ tablet (62.5 mg)	6–8 years ½ tablet (125 mg) 9–11 years ¾ tablet (187.5 mg)	250 mg (1 tablet)

N.B. The most important gauge for dosage is weight. An underweight child must be treated as a younger one, or they might overdose. An overweight child must be treated as an older child, otherwise they might not receive a therapeutic dose.

reaction to the relatively innocuous vaccination, imagine how he would have suffered if he'd come into contact with the real thing. It may have killed him. The immunisations that have received the worst press are the diphtheria, pertussis and tetanus vaccine, together with the measles, mumps and rubella injection. I thought long and hard about immunising Paris but I justified it to myself by thinking that if he reacts badly to the vaccination, how on earth would his little body cope with the full-blown disease?

Note
The diseases for which vaccinations have been developed can all cause serious risk to human life without treatment. Thankfully the diseases which have been historically catastrophic can now be prevented and contained with the benefits of modern medicine. However, even when protected by all the available vaccines, common sense is still your most powerful weapon against similar and related illnesses:
1. You must pay stringent attention to what and where you eat and drink (see chapter 10).
2. Avoid being bitten by mosquitoes and other biting insects and creatures.
3. Beware of stray or wild animals, including bats, which can carry rabies. Avoid being scratched or even licked.
If you pay careful attention to the above guidelines you will avoid many other transmittable diseases for which there are no available vaccines.

DISEASES PREVENTABLE BY VACCINATION

The following facts on preventable diseases and their vaccinations have been compiled to help you to make an informed choice to protect yourselves and your children from contracting major illnesses while travelling abroad.

Cholera
Cholera is caused by a toxin-producing bacteria that lives in the intestines of infected humans. The illness is acquired from contaminated water or food. Although insanitary water plays the main role in the transmission of the disease, shellfish can harbour the responsible bacteria in high concentrations, and

any food – even fresh fruit and vegetables – which has been in direct contact with infected human excreta or contaminated water can pass on the infection.

Symptoms
Sudden onset of painless, profuse, odourless diarrhoea. The volume of diarrhoea is enormous and is predominately water with flecks of mucus, similar in appearance to rice water. After the diarrhoea begins, vomiting usually follows, which is characteristically effortless. This drastic loss of fluids causes severe, life-threatening dehydration with associated muscle cramps and extreme weakness.

Prevention and treatment
Cholera outbreaks often make news headlines and so you will be able to avoid taking your children into areas of danger.

Unfortunately the vaccination is no longer very effective and is estimated only to give protection levels of around 50 per cent. This, combined with the fact that the disease is relatively uncommon among travellers, has led to a decreased level of demand for the vaccine. It is no longer widely recommended and no country now requires the immunisation as a condition of entry, unless the border staff are trying to extort a bribe.

Even if you do opt to have your family vaccinated against cholera, you must be scrupulously careful of what you eat and drink. Vigilance in this area will help to avoid a whole plethora of other contagious illnesses and food poisoning while you are travelling (see chapter 10).

If you are visiting endemic areas, such as Bangladesh, go prepared. Buy commercially available sachets or tablets of sugars and salts to take with you. These include Rehydrat and Dioralyte which are both available to buy over the counter in most pharmacies (see page 226). When added to clean water, these provide effective oral replacement of vital electrolytes (e.g. salt) and fluids, so if there is any delay getting a doctor, you may be able to prevent your child getting so drastically dehydrated that he or she will need intravenous fluid replacement.

With adequate oral – and in more severe cases intravenous – fluid and electrolyte replacement, recovery from the symptoms of cholera is remarkably rapid and there is a very low associated death rate in children and adults.

While fluid replacement is the most important aspect of treatment, the required volume of fluid may be enormous and an effective administered antibiotic will dramatically reduce the duration and volume of diarrhoea by rapid eradication of the causal bacteria.

The recommended antibiotic treatment is tetracycline. The recommended dose is 10–12.5 mg/kg, every 6 hours, for 48 hours. This drug should not be used in pregnant women or generally in children under eight years old because it causes discolouration of the teeth and is laid down within the structure of growing bone. However, because dosing is only for 48 hours, such a short treatment should have no adverse effect. An alternative to pack is co-trimoxazole (Bactrim or Septrin). This antibiotic has a variety of uses and is indicated for children as young as six weeks old.

Diphtheria

Diphtheria is a very serious, highly contagious illness caused by a toxin-producing bacteria. It is very rare in developed countries due to the extensive immunisation programmes in very young babies. However, in many parts of the undeveloped world, diphtheria is still a common and tragic illness. Diphtheria can progress to a life-threatening illness within a day of the appearance of the first symptoms. It is easily transmissible by dust or coughing and sneezing.

Symptoms

Fever, sore throat, difficulty in swallowing and enlarged lymph glands in the neck. The toxin released by the bacteria causes destruction of the upper airway's tissue cells and the formation of a greyish-yellow membrane that can obstruct the upper air passages, causing asphyxiation (choking). The toxin also enters the bloodstream where it can cause serious, permanent damage to the heart, nervous system or the kidneys.

Prevention

The vaccine is an important standard childhood immunisation. It is highly effective, long lasting and a very important defence against a potentially tragic condition.

The usual course is of three injections given to infants

between three and six months old along with the tetanus and pertussis (whooping cough) vaccines. If you have followed advice, it is more than likely that your children will already have been protected as babies but if you have any doubt and your doctor or health visitor has no records, you should ensure that your children are vaccinated before travelling. In many parts of the world, diptheria is still a killer.

Treatment
Treatment of the actual disease would be with administration of antitoxin which needs to be given before the toxin is able to cause all its damage. An antibiotic, for example, penicillin, should also be given. If your child is allergic to penicillin, erythromycin is the next best option.

It is important to note that even with good medical treatment, there is a one-in-ten chance that diphtheria will be fatal. In places with low standards of healthcare, the incidence of death will be much, much higher.

Keep up to date with boosters (see page 128).

Hepatitis
Hepatitis is a serious infection of the liver caused by any one of a number of viruses, most commonly hepatitis A or hepatitis B.

Symptoms
Jaundice, fever, lethargy, chills, headache and digestive problems, fatigue, feelings of weakness, aches, pains, loss of appetite, nausea, vomiting, abdominal pain, dark urine and light-coloured faeces, yellow skin and, in severe cases, the whites of the eyes may turn yellow.

Hepatitis A
Hepatitis A is the most commonly travel-acquired illness and is endemic in many areas of the world. It is caused by a water-borne viral infection that poses a significant risk to travellers of all ages.

Hepatitis A may infect children or adults without producing any symptoms at all. Even in its most severe form, it is unlikely to be deadly. However, it is a serious illness that can incapacitate its victims for several weeks.

Because the incubation period of hepatitis A is between three and five weeks, it is unlikely to ruin a fortnight's holiday. However, a number of viruses are shed in the faeces after infection before symptoms show, which means that there is a good chance that it will be passed on to family or friends unknowingly.

Hepatitis A is spread from the intestines of an infected host by contaminated water and food. Outbreaks can often be traced to uncooked food or food handled after cooking. Raw and inadequately cooked shellfish are associated with a high risk of hepatitis A infections. All age groups are at risk.

In tropical climates, most cases occur during the rainy season, with low incidence during the dry periods.

Prevention

Spread is reduced by hygienic measures and extreme care with food and water intake.

Immunisation against the hepatitis A virus is readily available either by injection with human immunoglobulin or with the more recently developed Havrix or Twinrix, both of which contain inactivated hepatitis A viruses. Twinrix gives added protection against hepatitis B.

(a) *Immunoglobulin* This has been widely used for a number of years and has successfully controlled the outbreak of hepatitis A in, for example, nursery schools.

It is an injection of concentrated antibodies which can help the body fight off an entire range of bacteria, fungi and viruses and so can help defend against many of the bugs a child may encounter on holiday, including measles, German measles, and, theoretically, even minor infections and stomach upsets.

It is safe enough to be given to pregnant women who have come into contact with rubella to prevent them from catching the illness that would damage the developing foetus.

The only concern voiced by some is that the immunoglobulin is derived from pooled human blood products and so there is a tiny risk of contacting some as yet undiscovered disease, as was the case with HIV. This, however, is a 'what if?' and a purely hypothetical situation.

The positives for immunoglobulin are that it gives immediate immunity. It can therefore be given just two to three days before you travel. Therefore, if you book a last-minute trip, you will still be able to get protection. In fact, the injection should be as close to departure as possible, as the immunity is at its most effective during the first few weeks and then gradually becomes less and less effective over three to six months.

The negatives are that it is thick and viscous so must be given through a wide gauge needle. The injection is therefore painful and it stings. You may be well advised to ask for the jab in your child's bottom which is less tender than a skinny little arm.

I recall a particularly painful immunoglobulin injection during which the doctor had to withdraw the needle and change it because the solution proved to be too thick to pass down its gauge. He changed it for a much wider one which really hurt (incidentally that doctor was my dad!).

Immunoglobulin should be given after all the other travel vaccines have had the chance to work. If not, some of the effect of the immunisation program would be lost.

(b) *Havrix* Until recently, immunoglobulin was the only vaccination available for hepatitis A and so it was widely used and heavily indicated. Now specific hepatitis A vaccines – for example Havrix – have been developed which offer immunity for up to ten years. You therefore have two options although your doctor or travel nurse may have a preference.

Havrix Junior monodose can be given to children over one year old. It is administered as one dose that will be effective for three years. If a booster is given six to twelve months later, protection against hepatitis A lasts ten years.

Side effects are that there may be some discomfort or redness around the injection sites and a child may have very mild symptoms of the actual disease such as slight fever, malaise, fatigue, nausea and loss of appetite, but these symptoms could be a fraction of the severity of the full-blown disease.

A feature of Havrix is that it must be given approximately three weeks before departure to allow the immunity to build up.

Although Havrix is far more expensive and because it is new, there is not as much information available or experience of using the product. It is more easily administered and for the regular traveller is probably the best option.

Treatment

If any member of the family were to contract hepatitis A, in general there is not much you can actively do. You must wait for the healing process, which can take many weeks. The liver has amazing powers of rejuvenation, but when it is preoccupied with fighting infection, it can't mop up all the toxins from the blood efficiently and the patient with hepatitis will feel terrible.

Fatty foods, processed food, all alcohol and some medications should be avoided. The best treatment is to rest, eat plenty of fresh food and drink plenty of fresh, boiled water.

Hepatitis B
Hepatitis B usually develops 60–180 days after injection of human blood or plasma or use of inadequately sterilised syringes or needles. It can also be sexually transmitted.

Because of the mode of transmission of hepatitis B, it is unlikely your child will catch it under normal circumstances. The only real threat would be if your child were to need hospital treatment, particularly a blood transfusion. In this instance, you are likely to have a great deal more to worry about, but you should be aware of the risks in many parts of the world where screening all blood and blood products is economically impossible.

Hepatitis B is a serious illness and although the symptoms are similar to those of hepatitis A, hepatitis B is a chronic, recurring illness which can cause serious liver damage and may progress to liver cancer.

Prevention and treatment
If you intend to travel abroad for a long time (more than six months), or live in a country that does not share Western healthcare and screening standards, you should have your child immunised against hepatitis B. In some parts of the world there is a 15–20 per cent incidence of hepatitis B in the local population. If you are living amongst them, your family should be protected.

Twinrix paediatric gives protection against both hepatitis A and hepatitis B.

Hepatitis C, D and E (Non A, Non B Hepatitis)
New strains of virus responsible for causing hepatitis in man are being steadily uncovered. It is possible that others already exist or may develop in the future. Research is ongoing.

Hepatitis C, like hepatitis B, is transferred by blood and

blood products, so prevention measures are the same. A vaccine is currently being developed.

Hepatitis D has been classified relatively recently. Immunisation against hepatitis B does afford some immunity. Hepatitis D is transmitted in blood and blood products so prevention measures are the same as for hepatitis B.

Hepatitis E is transmitted by the same mechanisms as hepatitis A – by infected food and water intake. The greatest danger is to pregnant women. Prevention is by careful attention to hygiene and great care with food and water ingested.

None of the above poses great risks to the traveller of any age at present.

Japanese Encephalitis

This is a rare infection causing inflammation of the brain. It occurs primarily in rural Asia, especially during the rainy season. The disease is caused by a virus mainly transmitted by the bite of rice-field breeding mosquitoes. It can be fatal.

Symptoms
Fever, headache and vomiting. Convulsions in children may be the first sign. Lethargy is common and there may be confusion and delirium that progresses into coma. The duration of the illness is very variable but recovery is long and young children are the most prone to complications, including mental impairment and personality changes.

Prevention
Because Japanese encephalitis is rare, the vaccination available is only recommended for those going off the beaten track for a long time, and there are no guarantees about its effectiveness.

The vaccine is not licensed in the UK for wide general use. It is only available in specialist health clinics in the UK or by special request by your doctor from the manufacturers. The vaccine is indicated for children but for the majority of travellers, the first line of protection is to avoid being bitten by mosquitoes as far as is possible. (See page 236.)

Treatment
There is no specific treatment recommended for the disease.

Measles

Measles is a highly infectious and potentially very serious viral disease. It is caught by inhaling infected droplets and is rare in children under six months due to the passive immunity passed on from the mother. Most children who are not immunised would be most likely to develop measles in their second year of life. Measles can be caught worldwide.

Symptoms

The incubation period is seven to twelve days and the child is infectious from a few days before the rash appears until five days after it goes.

The symptoms are fever, a sore throat, cough, headache, runny nose, red eyes, general misery and an irregular, red, mottled, raised rash which starts behind the ears, spreads, lasts for about a week and then fades. White spots in the mouth (Koplik spots) are a sign doctors look for to confirm measles.

Vomiting and diarrhoea are not uncommon and complications include ear and chest infections which must be treated to avoid long-term damage. There is a slight risk of encephalitis.

Prevention

The vaccine is usually given in the UK at about twelve months along with mumps and rubella. As with all vaccines, it is strongly advocated by the medical profession as a safe alternative to the infection. The side effects of the vaccine are generally mild symptoms of the illness, local and allergic reactions. The vaccine is effective after two to three weeks and gives long-lasting protection.

It is not advisable to go abroad immediately following the vaccination just in case there are any adverse reactions.

It is important to note that the measles, mumps and rubella vaccine may interact with some travel injections and should not be given within one month of any other live vaccine (e.g. polio) or within three months of immunoglobulins.

Severe allergies to eggs are a contraindication for the vaccine.

Treatment

If you decide not to vaccinate your child and your child contracts the illness, it is advisable to seek a doctor, then concentrate on keeping your child comfortable and rested with plenty to drink. Paracetamol will ease discomfort and lower the temperature. Wash crustiness away from the eyes with clean, warm water. If the temperature remains high after the fever has begun to subside, your child might have developed a secondary infection, possibly in their ears or chest, and will need antibiotics to prevent any lasting damage which could occur if left untreated.

Meningococcal Meningitis

Meningitis is an inflammation of the membranes covering the brain and spinal cord. Children are particularly susceptible and the disease – which might be caused by a virus or bacteria and transmitted by contact with an infected carrier – can be fatal.

Viral meningitis is usually the less severe form and although the symptoms are similar to those seen with the more aggressive bacterial infections, most children make a complete recovery.

Bacterial meningitis is more serious and life threatening. The strain most common in the UK is quite different from the meningococcal bacteria that cause epidemics in sub-saharan Africa and Asia.

In Africa and Asia the age group most at risk are five to fifteen year olds. Compare this with the UK where those most at risk are under five years old.

Symptoms

Severe headache, confusion, drowsiness, fever, rising temperature, stiff neck, nausea, vomiting and photophobia (sensitivity to light). Convulsions might occur in young children. Babies have a characteristic high-pitched cry and the fontanelle (soft spot) may bulge outwards and feel tense. A rash of red spots might occur which does not disappear when pressure is applied to it. Test this by pressing a drinking glass on to the spots on the child's skin. If the rash is still visible, it might have been caused by the toxins produced by the meningococcal bacteria interfering with the blood-clotting process.

Prevention

Infants are given three separate 'Hib' vaccinations between two and twelve months old to protect against the strain of meningitis common in the UK. Check your vaccination records or confirm with your doctor or health visitor.

The 'Hib' vaccine, however, is different from the one

required for protection in Africa or Asia from group A and C meningitis. A safe and effective vaccine against group A and C is available but is not normally required unless travelling to an area of a current epidemic. Long-stay visitors and those undergoing rural travel should also consider being protected.

It is worth noting that visitors to Saudi Arabia on Haj (the annual Muslim pilgrimage) are required to receive the vaccination.

The vaccine is safe from two months old but children under eighteen months old have a reduced duration of protection. Boosters should therefore be given sooner. Over eighteen months of age cover lasts for three to five years.

Treatment

If the vaccinations have not been given and either strain of the disease is contracted, a child might become gravely ill within hours and might pass rapidly into a coma. It is crucial to get urgent medical attention without delay.

Children treated in time with antibiotics nearly always recover from bacterial meningitis. Antibiotics may be administered by injection.

In sub-saharan Africa and certain parts of Asia it would be advisable to carry your own needles and then, if anything were to happen, you must insist upon their use. The economy in these areas does not allow for blood screening and good sterilisation techniques. HIV and AIDS are rife.

Your child will need hospital treatment, but if there is going to be delay in getting your child there, you should seek out any doctor, nurse, midwife, pharmacist or even a vet to give your child an injection of benzylpenicillin.

The recommended doses to be given by injection into a muscle are as follows:

Children under

1 year: 300 mg (dissolved in a few ml of pure water)
1–9 years: 600 mg (dissolved in a few ml of pure water)
>10 years: 1200 mg (dissolved in a few ml of pure water)

Injectable amoxycillin is an alternative if benzylpenicillin is unavailable. If your child is allergic to penicillin, injectable co-trimoxazole or erythromycin would be advisable.

If you are outside the realms of medical help and injectable antibiotics are unavailable you must give high doses of more than one oral antibiotic. The best would be a combination of amoxycillin and co-trimoxazole. Your child is more at risk from the infection than from antibiotic overdose, so aggressive treatment is necessary. If my child were very ill with suspected meningitis, I would give at least double the standard dosages for the first 24 hours or until he showed some sign of improvement.

Mumps
Mumps is a viral infection most commonly affecting children. The illness causes fever and a characterisitic swelling of the main pair of salivary glands in the lower cheeks to such an extent that the child has a hamster-like appearance.

The disease is spread by sneezing and coughing. It is rarely serious in children, who might not even feel particularly unwell.

Symptoms
The incubation period is approximately two to three weeks.

The symptoms are fever, headache and tender, swollen glands below the ears and beneath the chin. There will be difficulty swallowing and chewing but the illness is invariably mild. A less common symptom is painful testes in boys.

Very occasionally meningitis, encephalitis and pancreatitis are complications.

Prevention
The vaccine is usually given in the UK at about twelve months of age along with the measles and rubella vaccines. The side effects are generally fever, malaise, local and allergic reactions.

Due to the mildness of the illness, it need not be a major concern on holiday if a child has not been vaccinated beforehand.

Treatment
If your child presents with the symptoms of mumps while you are on holiday, you should concentrate on making them comfortable. Give them plenty to drink, ease pain and fever with paracetamol and, if possible, liquidise or mash their food to make it easier for them to swallow.

Pertussis (Whooping cough)

This is a highly infectious bacterial disease occuring almost exclusively in children under five years old. It is easily spread by coughing and sneezing and can be fatal. The infection clogs the airways with mucus, making it difficult for the child to breathe. If not fatal, the illness can produce lasting lung damage.

Symptoms

The incubation period for the disease is between seven and nine days. After one or two weeks of cold-like symptoms, a severe cough with a distinctive sound develops that lasts for several weeks. A whooping sound is produced when the child desperately sucks breath into their lungs after a coughing fit but this might not occur in babies or very young children. The coughing can be so racking that the child may turn blue due to lack of oxygen and vomiting often happens when the coughing ceases.

Attacks are more common at night. The whole illness is exhausting for the child and those caring for it. There are a number of complications associated with the illness including lung collapse, hernias, pneumonia and convulsions or, more severely, brain damage as a result of lack of oxygen in the blood reaching the brain.

Prevention

Children who have received all the usual childhood vaccinations will have been immunised as babies. This will have been done along with diphtheria and tetanus in the triple vaccine, the child having received three injections, four weeks apart, between the ages of three and six months of age.

The vaccination should be considered if travelling abroad with children under five years old who have not been immunised, particularly babies and infants. Children over five years old are not at great risk. If you have opted not to have the full protection of the vaccine, you should keep your children, as far as is possible, away from infected children, even those who just seem to have a cold.

Treatment

If the illness is contracted, your child will need effective antibiotic therapy and might need treatment for dehydration if the vomiting has been severe. Cough medicines are of no value. The bacteria responsible for the illness are sensitive to a range of antibiotics including erythromycin, but only during the early stages. If the antibiotic is not started before the severe coughing stage, it will not be effective.

Poliomyelitis (Polio)

Poliomyelitis is a viral infection which can cause untreatable meningitis and paralysis. Until the relatively recent advent of the vaccine, the illness was a serious epidemic world health problem and was the most common cause of paralysis in children. It was also a common cause of death.

The virus responsible inhabits the intestine and is passed in the stools in large numbers for up to six weeks after the start of the illness. It is spread by the faecal contamination of food and water, even in swimming pools. It can also be transmitted by coughing.

Symptoms

The patient is anxious, irritable and feverish with a severe headache. They might complain of stiffness and pains in the neck, trunk and limbs. Paralysis usually occurs during the fever, rarely afterwards, and might be the first distinct sign of poliomyelitis in infants or very young children. Death can occur from paralysis of the muscles used for breathing.

Prevention

The oral polio vaccine is a safe, effective and painless means of preventing the tragedy of childhood paralysis and death. If you have followed the advice of your doctor and health visitor, your child will have been immunised as a baby, but if you neglected to take your children to be vaccinated when they were very young, you should seriously consider protecting them before you take them outside Western Europe, the USA, Australia or New Zealand.

The vaccine is usually given by mouth at two, three and four months of age, or in older children similarly as three doses, four weeks apart. A booster should be given at the age of five which lasts for approximately ten years. It is very safe.

It is important to note that the polio vaccine takes eight weeks to be effective and so the course should be given well before you intend to travel.

Polio and typhoid vaccines should be given three weeks apart. If you opt not to take the safe option of protection by immunisation you should adopt very high standards of personal hygiene and pay scrupulous attention to what your children eat and drink. Be very careful where they swim and even who they play or have contact with abroad. Naturally, avoid other sick children.

Treatment
Once the infection progresses, it cannot be effectively treated.

Rabies
Rabies is endemic in most parts of the world. Only a few countries remain rabies free. These include the UK, New Zealand, Australia, Taiwan, Japan, Hawaii, Western Malaysia and Antarctica.

Rabies is a viral infection that is spread by an animal bite or scratch. If the skin is broken, even a lick from the infected animal can result in the infection being passed on. The animal carrier can be wild or domestic and apparently tame. Foxes, wolves, raccoons, mongooses, skunks and bats all transmit the virus, but in 90 per cent of cases in man worldwide, rabies is caught from a domestic cat or dog.

Rabies is an infection of the nervous system and, if not treated before symptoms develop, is usually fatal.

Symptoms
The incubation period following the bite ranges from four days to many years but is more usually 20–90 days. It tends to be a shorter incubation after bites to the face than after those on the limbs. The illness usually starts without specific symptoms over the first few days. Fever, chills, weakness, tiredness, photophobia (sensitivity to light), muscle pain and mood change then occur. The victim might become anxious, irritable and depressed. There is also likely pain in the area of the healed bite. Most patients then develop furious rabies which is distinguishable by the characterisic fear of water. As the illness progresses the patient might display terror even at the mention of water.

Patients with furious rabies produce excess saliva and have painful muscle spasms in the throat; as a result, they do actually foam at the mouth. There are many other severe and distressing mental signs, including delirium, hallucinations, raging and convulsions. The virus is passed on in milk so following a bite from a mammal, a mother should not breastfeed.

Prevention prior to travel
The rabies vaccination is only deemed necessary – and so recommended – for those travelling into remote areas at some distance from medical treatment, or for those who may be exposed to an unusual risk of infection.

Protection is afforded by a series of three injections given over a month, and is effective after 30 days for up to three years. It is often given injected into the stomach muscles where it can cause some local pain. Other side effects include fever and malaise.

Prevention and treatment following a bite, scratch or lick from an animal
IMPORTANT: Even if your children have been immunised, you must still seek urgent medical attention if there is any possibility that they have been bitten by an infected animal. In addition to the risk of rabies, there are many other infections that can be passed on by a mammalian bite, including tetanus.

Once someone is bitten by an infected animal, the virus takes time to multiply in the bite area. After days, or even weeks, the virus gets into the nerves. It then travels up the nerves and into the brain and spinal cord where it multiplies further. Because of the delay before the virus begins to attack the nerve system, you should have time to get to a hospital. A friend was once bitten in Nepal by an animal which she was never actually able to identify. She was taken calmly but urgently back to Kathmandu by one of the guides to get treatment. It was three days' trek for them alone but although her holiday was ruined, she survived.

If you or one of your children is bitten, you should wash the wound immediately. Wound cleaning is an effective way of killing or removing the virus from infected wounds and is therefore very important. Wash the wound meticulously and thoroughly for at least five minutes with soap or detergent and water. Your child might cry but at least they will survive. Remove any foreign material and rinse with plenty of clean, plain water. If possible apply alcohol (at least 40% vol) or tincture of iodine, both of which will kill the virus. Spirits, including whisky, rum, gin and vodka, are usually 40% alcohol. Then get medical attention fast. It will be too late once the symptoms start to develop. A course of rabies vaccinations should be started as soon as possible. If there is any option, request the human diploid vaccine.

If the animal was not wild or a stray, try to identify the owner and note their name, address and telephone number. The animal should be kept under observation to detect any changes in its behaviour. If it does remain healthy for five days you are unlikely to contract rabies, but the animal should still be checked for two weeks.

If the animal does become ill or dies you must complete the course of vaccinations and should be given an additional serum which will further protect you.

If you were bitten by a wild animal, a stray or a domestic animal that is unavailable for observation, the same applies, especially if the bite were on the face, neck, head or finger.

Children must be warned not to play with, or touch, any animals whilst on holiday. Even visiting farms, zoos or conservation programme sites, be respectful of animals. You may not be able to read warning notices and you will have no idea what the animal's health status is. The standards in zoos vary drastically around the world and certain sights may even be upsetting.

All wild animals should be kept at a distance, even those that gather at feeding areas around tourist spots and look perfectly healthy. Baboons in Africa and monkeys in Asia, might appear friendly but can carry rabies and other infections. They may attack if they learn that you have food with you.

Avoid any animal acting strangely and remember that 90 per cent of rabies infections in man worldwide are as a result of a cat- or dog-bite.

Rubella (German measles)
German measles is a viral infection that causes a rash. The illness is usually mild in children.

Symptoms
Incubation period is usually two to three weeks.

Small red spots appear first behind the ears, then spread to the face and all over the body. The child will have a mild fever and the lymph nodes at the back of the neck will be enlarged. There is a slight risk of encephalitis. The child will be infectious one week before, and at least four days after, the rash first appears.

The greatest danger of rubella is to pregnant women as the virus can cause birth defects.

Prevention

The vaccine is usually given in the UK at about twelve months of age along with the mumps and measles vaccines. The side effects of the vaccine are generally mild symptoms of the illness, local and allergic reactions.

Treatment

Usually children with rubella don't even feel ill, so you need not worry about travelling abroad before immunisation, but if you suspect that your child has contracted the disease you must keep him away from anyone who might be pregnant.

Any pregnant woman who has had contact with German measles and who is not up-to-date with her vaccines should seek medical advice. She should be given an injection of immunoglobulin, which will help protect the foetus.

Tetanus

Tetanus is a dangerous disease caused by a bacterial infection of the nervous system. The bacteria produces a toxin which causes violent, painful muscle spasms.

It is caught by the introduction of spores into the body through even a slight wound. The spores are found in soil and faeces – and even in dust or the air – all over the world and so anybody and everybody is at risk.

Deep wounds are a greater concern because the bacteria like to live in an environment without much oxygen, but even a minor trauma should not be dismissed, as even a prick from a thorn, which introduces soil into the skin, could be deadly.

Symptoms

Early signs are spasms in the chewing muscles. It is difficult to open the mouth. There is difficulty swallowing and an infant would be unable to suckle. Fever and severe stiffness progress to increasingly regular, violent muscle contractions that grow in severity over a week.

A baby's cry would be stifled with the face wrinkling up at the same time. An older child's face would have an altered expression caused by contraction of the facial muscles, often described as a sardonic smile. Their body would have a stiff, ramrod appearance.

Death is from exhaustion or asphyxia during convulsions.

Prevention
Children who have received the usual childhood vaccinations will have been immunised as babies along with diphtheria and whooping cough in the triple vaccine. They will have received three injections, four weeks apart, between the ages of three and six months. Protection then lasts for ten years. Children of ten and over will need a booster before travelling if they have not had one since infancy. The only side effects likely would be tenderness around the injection site and/or a slight fever.

Immunisation is a very important protection against the tetanus bacterial organism in every country of the world and it is sensible to ensure that your child is protected from this terrifying, deadly disease. Even if you decided not to vaccinate your child as a baby, it is a good idea to consider it before travelling abroad, especially if good medical treatment is not readily available. Children are constantly cutting and scraping themselves on road surfaces and mucky sticks so they are at real risk. At the very least, and if travelling to a country with good healthcare standards, ensure your child is taken to hospital and given a protective dose of the vaccine if they are cut, bitten or injured.

Treatment
The incubation period is just ten days. If your child falls ill while you are away, they will need injections of antitoxin, large doses of antibiotics and good hospital care.

Tick-borne Encephalitis
Tick-borne encephalitis occurs throughout Central Europe, from Scandinavia, USSR, Czechoslovakia and Germany through to Austria. It is caused by a virus related to dengue and yellow fever. The parasite involved is very different from the

organism that causes the tick typhus and does not respond to antibiotic treatment.

Symptoms
There may be an area of redness or inflammation at the site of the bite. Fever and encephalitis will follow.

Prevention
A vaccine is available which should be considered when camping in Central Europe. It is unlicensed in the UK but available through your doctor who will have to request it direct from the manufacturers, specifically.

It is important to advise children that they should keep to woodland paths and not walk through tall grass or foliage with bare legs or skin, even at the edge of the campsite. They should also be protected with insect repellent sprayed on to clothes and uncovered regions of skin.

See page 247 for advice on important grooming and removing ticks.

Treatment
If a victim becomes ill following a tick bite in Central Europe, it may be advisable to have an injection. This must be given within four days of the bite.

Tuberculosis
Tuberculosis is increasing worldwide, although in the UK, extensive immunisation has brought the disease under control. In Britain during the Industrial Revolution, tuberculosis – known then as 'consumption' – was a killer, weakening its victims, including the Brontë sisters, over months or years.

It is a highly contagious bacterial infection which most commonly affects the lungs, but if left untreated will also affect the kidneys, brain membranes and joints. The mode of transmission is usually by inhalation or ingestion of the infected droplets produced when a sufferer sneezes or coughs.

Symptoms
Early signs include a dry cough, fever, night sweats, reduced appetite and in children, a failure to thrive. If young children who are infected are left untreated (particularly infants or under-fives), the symptoms will become more severe, and

complications will develop, including, pleural effusion, blood in the sputum and meningitis. Although this may not be until months after the early signs began, the disease is then likely to be fatal or cause long-term damage.

Prevention

Most young children born in the UK over recent years are vaccinated at six weeks old with BCG to protect against tuberculosis. Check with your doctor or your own records to confirm whether or not your children have been immunised. You may remember it as a single injection given separately, possibly at the hospital, which developed into a small blister at the site of the needle puncture.

Although tuberculosis is widespread, the infection does not pose a major risk to the traveller unless staying for more than a month in Asia, Africa, Central or South America. However, if you and your children are likely to be staying with, or in close contact with, local people, including close family, it is advisable to be protected.

Even if your children did not have the vaccine as babies, they could have acquired some immunity. A simple test called the Heaf test is carried out to determine whether or not this is the case. It uses a multiple puncture technique but is completely painless. This should be done well before your departure date because if the Heaf test determines that your children do need the vaccination, it should be given eight weeks in advance. Teenagers over fifteen years old who are travelling with you should also be tested as the BCG vaccine given to babies might not always give lifetime immunity.

Treatment

If your child were to become infected with tuberculosis, the illness takes time to develop and does not present as a medical emergency in the early stages. You will have time to get them home where they will usually be admitted to hospital, mainly to prevent the spread of infection. Treatment will be given in the form of a combination of antibiotics which need long-term administration for up to a year.

Typhoid

Typhoid is a widespread and potentially fatal infection caused by the ingestion of the bacteria Salmonella typhi.

The infection is passed on via contaminated food, milk and water and can be spread by human hands, flies and other insects. It can also survive freezing and drying and so might be carried on to food and into drink from the water supply, sewage, dust, ice and shellfish.

Although no age group is exempt, typhoid is generally a disease of older children and young adults. Children under two years old rarely catch the illness. It is even more unlikely in those under one year.

Symptoms

Headache is the most common symptom in children, which is unusual and clinically distinctive as this severe, frontal headache seen in children with typhoid fever is relatively rare in paediatric medicine. There might be a high fever but the heart rate will be slow. This again is unusual. Cough, diarrhoea and abdominal pain are frequent symptoms and vomiting can occur.

A rash often appears on day seven to ten of the illness. It is characterised by a variable number of rose-coloured spots which are usually first noticed on the abdomen and disappear with pressure. Sometimes each spot is capped with a small blister. After two to three days the spots can disappear, leaving brownish stains which are much harder to notice on darker skins.

Untreated typhoid lasts for around four weeks. The most serious consequence of the illness is destruction of the gut tissue, which can lead to haemorrhage and perforation. This does not usually happen in the early stages of the illness but treatment needs to be sought before the stage has the chance to develop.

There is also the potential of renal, cardiac and liver complication and increased risk of abortion in pregnancy.

Prevention

The typhoid vaccine was at one time a monster, after which you were left feeling sore, disorientated and weak for days. An improved injection has since been developed with fewer side effects, limited to local irritation and discomfort at the injection site, or mild symptoms of the illness including headache, fever and malaise. It is claimed that side effects are lessened if the injection is given into the skin (intradermally).

Oral protection against typhoid is probably the better option but is not recommended for children under six years old (the injection can be given at eighteen months) and boosters need to be given yearly (the injection gives protection for three years). The side effect of the oral capsules may be a mild tummy upset.

Immunisation should be given ten to fourteen days before departure. It is important to realise that immunisation still does not protect a child from massive doses of ingested bacteria. The vaccination is only about 60 per cent effective and so careful attention must still be directed towards avoiding ingestion of this aggressive bacteria.

Treatment

If your child is feverish and you suspect he has typhoid, seek medical attention. There are a number of antibiotics useful in treating the illness, but the more effective ones have a number of side effects which should be monitored in children. If you cannot get medical assistance, co-trimoxazole or amoxycillin are both effective. The 'strong' option of ciprofloxin is very effective but its use in children should be reserved.

You must ensure that the child does not become dehydrated or that his temperature does not reach dangerously high levels. Oral replacement therapy should be started immediately (see page 226). This will save your child's life. Paediatric paracetamol will help with the pain and fever.

Paratyphoid

Paratyphoid is similar to but milder than typhoid and caused by a different strain of the same bacterium, Salmonella paratyphi A, B & C. Strain B is most common. Paratyphoid runs a shorter and gentler course than typhoid with relatively little toxicity.

Yellow fever

Yellow fever is a disease caused by a virus transmitted by the bite of a particular species of mosquito. It is active in several African, South and Central American countries. In about five per cent of cases the illness is fatal, usually as a result of liver or kidney failure.

Symptoms

After a three- to six-day incubation period, the symptoms begin as headache, backache and fever, which progress to nausea and vomiting. The victim has a flushed and swollen face and a bright red tongue, then begins to show a bleeding tendency. The gums begin to bleed, the patient produces black blood-filled vomit and the stools are full of blood. The disease can progress to a form of lethal hepatitis affecting the liver, although most victims actually recover. It is during the recovery phase that the patient might become jaundiced and the skin will have the yellow tinge that has given the fever its name.

Prevention

Infection can be prevented by a safe and highly effective vaccine which gives protection for ten years. A number of countries require proof of immunisation if you have passed through endemic countries. You must present your vaccination certificate, which is valid ten days after the injection.

The vaccine can be given to children over nine months old at specialist yellow fever centres. It produces few side effects, although many countries who stipulate that travellers must have their certificate state that children under one year are exempt.

The hitch is the expense. The yellow fever vaccine may cost as much as £30 per person (average cost around £21). It is also important to note that children or adults who have an allergy to eggs or chicken protein should not be given the vaccine.

The vaccine is live and so should not be given to pregnant women.

Treatment

Treatment is largely to control the symptoms by replacing fluid and electrolytes in the patient. Blood transfusion is sometimes required to correct blood loss following haemorrhage.

PART TWO: PREPARATION

6 Essential Papers and Insurance

CHILDREN'S PASSPORTS

If you are applying for a British passport for your child for the first time, they will not be added to your passport as they were allowed to be before October 1998. After October 1998, even a one-week-old baby will need its own passport with a photograph unless the child is already on your passport or your husband's. The child will still be able to travel on your passport after October 1998 but only if it is already named on it, either

 a) until your passport expires or

 b) until you apply for the child's own passport. At this point your child must be taken off your passport.

Applying for a Child's Passport

1. Request a passport form for a child under sixteen years of age at your main post office (smaller post offices do not carry the form).
2. Complete the form which must be countersigned by a professional who has known you for at least two years.
3. The form should then be sent off with the child's birth certificate and two passport-sized photographs.
4. The post office offers a service which guarantees that your passport will be returned to you before your day of travel. It costs £3.20 extra. The cost of a child's British passport is £11.

You will be advised to pay registered postage if you leave your application until within a couple of weeks of travel. The total cost for your application will then be £17.70 per child. The minimum period required for this service is four working days, not including the day you take your form etc. into the post office. If you have less than four working days to apply, you should go in person with the completed form, the birth certificate and two passport-sized photographs to your local passport office. Be prepared for a return journey the following day.

All prices are correct at time of writing.

A child's passport lasts five years but the photograph must be updated at predesignated intervals by the passport office. The charge for changing the photograph is the full £11. Between the ages of one and two, or one and three, you should change the photograph, but it is not considered necessary between the ages of two and three. When you apply for the passport, ask when you need to update the photo.

VISAS

Visas are a frustrating, hopeless bureaucratic anomaly. Requirements change constantly. Sometimes you can get visas at the borders, sometimes you can't. It is better to apply before you go.

Contacting the embassy concerned is the best way of finding out whether or not your family need visas to enter the country. Unfortunately, if you try to do this by phone, it will often cost £0.50 per minute for a recorded message which might not answer all your questions.

When applying for my family's Chinese visas, I spent around £10 listening to all the information at premium rate and still didn't find out what I needed to know. Did I need a separate visa for a child on my passport and, as I had booked the trip so near to departure, did I have to travel to London to get it? I wrote off to the embassy asking both questions and received three visa forms back without any covering letter or even a note. Running out of time and to be safe, we all travelled to London. The Chinese embassy only accepts visa applications between nine and twelve o'clock so we were obliged to stay in London overnight to be certain of arriving in time. At 9.05 a.m., after queueing for a short time, I presented the three completed forms.

A Chinese woman stamped everything about six times then told me to return in three days. I explained that I couldn't and that I had travelled down from Manchester. She barked back at me, 'Unless you travel today you not get visa today.'

I stared at her. 'But I wrote to you and now I have come all this way and I need my visas.'

She looked at me blankly and told me that I could have applied to the embassy in Manchester. I could have screamed. I felt like jumping over the counter and throwing all her papers into the air and inconveniencing her as much as she had inconvenienced me. A simple scribbled line would have avoided a 500-mile round trip and a £120 hotel bill. However, I was helpless in the face of bureaucracy and was forced to leave empty-handed.

We finally got our visas three days before we were scheduled to travel. Paris did in fact require his own, although he was on my passport.

Important points

1. Printed travel brochures giving visa information are usually accurate.
2. Some larger travel agents have dedicated visa information sections that are kept up-to-date and accurate. If they are unsure, they will also provide you with the addresses and telephone numbers of the relevant embassy.
3. Apply in good time if you are applying by post.
4. If you are short on time, consider using a passport and visa agency who will take your application into the embassy and pick it up for you as soon as possible. The cost is approximately £18 per visa. This is usually cheaper and far less hassle than a trip to the embassy yourself.
5. You can apply to most embassies in person in London but be prepared for a return trip a few days later.
6. Some embassies have a branch outside London where you can apply in person. If you have no luck finding out this information, telephone the overseas student department in your local university. If they don't know, they should be able to tell you who does.
7. Some countries do not require a separate visa for children travelling on your passport but many do. This information will only be reliable from the embassy itself. If in doubt, apply for a separate visa anyway. Although the price of a child's visa is the same as an adult's – it may cost £10–£35 – it is a small price to pay relative to a cancelled trip.

TRAVEL INSURANCE

You will often find that you will get free travel insurance for infants – and even older children up to the age of twelve – on your own policy. This indicates to me how low the risk of a child's illness or injury abroad requiring medical attention actually is. Insurers never give something for nothing and by their nature would demand a high premium if there was a high probability of a claim.

Even if you don't normally get insurance for yourself, consider getting it for your children. Medical treatment abroad can be very costly and run into tens, even hundreds, of thousands of pounds.

If you have private health insurance this may cover trips abroad but check it carefully and compare the terms and conditions with those of a specialised travel insurance policy.

You must be covered for an emergency flight home. From European resorts and cities you might have the option of an air ambulance. From farther flung destinations, you could need a combination of a helicopter and an entire section of the aircraft with a full medical team in attendance. Someone has to pay for all this.

If you are well insured, it might be advisable to have your child treated abroad immediately, but in many Third World countries your child could be more at risk from a visit to the hospital than the illness or accident. In addition, in many underdeveloped countries, the cost of screening blood is prohibitive and so if your child needs an operation or blood transfusion, he would be at serious risk from HIV and hepatitis B. In such instances, get them home.

There should be a 24-hour emergency service included on your policy with a freephone or collect call telephone number that you can ring for advice and assessment of your situation. This would be of invaluable help if you were to run into problems. Carry a note of it on you at all times.

The other main advantage of travel insurance is that the family will be covered for cancellation. My son presented with full-blown chicken pox three days before a trip to EuroDisney. The holiday would have been a total waste of time. Children have a habit of doing this and it is advisable to avoid travelling when your child is ill. A simple cough or cold wouldn't be a problem but anything more serious is likely to mean that you would all have a miserable time. A child with a serious ear infection should not fly.

In my experience, travel insurance companies do pay up. I have made a few small claims over the years and they have all been settled satisfactorily through the post.

NB: It is absolutely imperative that you get a theft report from the police or your holiday rep and retain all the receipts for purchases, medication or treatment. You will need to present documentation to the insurance company on your return as proof.

Also check the small print of your policy. Some insurance policies do not cover watersports, diving, skiing, or even car hire.

THE E111

In countries within the European Economic area – which consists of the fifteen member states of the European Community plus Iceland, Norway and Liechtenstein – production of a valid E111 will entitle you to free or reduced-cost medical emergency treatment. Cover is not as comprehensive as that offered by travel insurance policies and might be complicated. For example, in Germany you have to locate specific listed doctors to receive free treatment.

To obtain a form E111, you must go to the post office, where it will be stamped and signed and returned to you. It will only be of any use if it is validated in this way.

RECIPROCAL HEALTHCARE AGREEMENTS

Outside the EEA, some countries have a reciprocal healthcare agreement with the UK. These countries include Anguilla, Australia, Barbados, British Virgin Islands, Bulgaria, Czech Republic, Falkland Islands, Hungary, Malta, New Zealand, Poland, Romania, Russia, Slovak Republic, St Helena, Turks and Caicos Islands. However, cover is often limited to hospital treatment and not that in doctors' surgeries.

Details of which countries accept E111s or have reciprocal agreements with the UK can be found in the leaflet 'Health Advice for Travellers' produced by the Department of Health. To order a copy, telephone the Health Literature Line on 0800 555 777.

7 Planning and Packing

Once you decide where to go, where to stay and how to get there, you need to prepare for your trip. Before children, you may have booked at the very last minute, packed in seconds and taken off at a moment's notice. With children, everything changes. Detailed organisation and planning is crucial.

Travelling with children takes ten times more preparation than travelling without. They will need immunisations, a passport, travel insurance, their own visas (if applicable) and ten times more luggage.

Provided all the groundwork is done, you can relax and look forward to your holiday. You should be able to avoid any major inconveniences and mishaps and have a thoroughly relaxing time. Minor illnesses and traumas are not unlikely but if you are well prepared with knowledge and a well-packed medical kit, they should never ruin your holiday. Holidaying with children is often a challenge, if not an adventure, but the chances are good that the sensible pre-planning will prevent your trip abroad becoming a disaster, even without experience.

Try to pack sensibly, although I know first hand that this is virtually impossible when you take a young child away for the first time. Before having a baby, I had become a master at packing and would travel around the world for three weeks with one tiny rucksack small enough to carry as hand luggage.

At the airport on the first trip abroad with my baby, I found myself with three large suitcases, six pieces of hand luggage, a camcorder, a car seat and a pushchair. We were only going for a week. With a baby under six months you will need a lot of luggage to ensure a comfortable holiday.

The best way to keep your luggage to a minimum is to pack long before you need to. After a few days, repack, then again after another week and remove all the items you will be able to survive without. Resist the urge to add anything extra, unless it is absolutely essential.

If you want to use or wear items in between time, writing a checklist will make sure you don't forget them and that you don't grab everything in sight 'just in case' before you close your suitcase for the last time.

Imperatives

The most essential things to remember are the following. As long as you have them you will survive:

- Passports and visas
- Tickets and hotel reservations
- Insurance
- Credit cards, cash and/or traveller's cheques
- Baby food, bottles, formula milk, sterilising equipment
- Medical kit
- The things money cannot buy – such as comforters or your child's favourite toy.

Plus, if you are taking your family on a driving holiday or picking up a hire car don't forget a driving licence. We once arrived in Southern Ireland on a Sunday and tried to pick up our rental car. Unfortunately Simon and I had both expected each other to pack a licence and we found we were without one between us. No licence meant no car. We had to go to our hotel in Dublin then return to the airport the following morning when the DVLC was open and the rental company could check our details. This, thankfully, they did and handed over the keys as soon as they received facsimile confirmation from Swansea.

BULKY ITEMS

Pushchair or baby buggy

You may not be able to decide whether or not to take a baby's pushchair or buggy with you, but for under-threes, it will be invaluable in most instances.

Even for slightly older children it may be useful in the airport, on train stations, waiting at bus stops or while walking out at night. Your child can sleep (theoretically) while you go shopping after dark or eat in restaurants.

It will be an asset in the airport, especially if you have a night flight. You will be able to transport your sleeping child right up the point of embarkation where the crew will take the buggy from you and put it in the hold. At bus stops and on train stations your child will be secure and unable to lurch out into the road. It may be advisable to take a sling, too. Walks on the beach, up mountains, across rough terrain and on pavements in poor condition are impossible with a buggy.

Many countries have only narrow, rough tracks by the roadside and use of a pushchair will be dangerous. In my experience Latin, Caribbean and other hot-blooded drivers are usually maniacs and you will often find yourself jumping off the path into a surrounding field as a car screeches around a sharp bend. This is impossible with a trolley.

If you think that your best, warm pushchair may be more of a hindrance than a help, buy an old second-hand buggy from a car boot sale. It will probably only cost you a few pounds. Give it a good clean and take it with you. You can use it in the airport, and if you find it cumbersome when you arrive at your destination, abandon it.

Even if you are trekking, it is likely that you will have a base where you will be able to leave the buggy. If it only cost you £4, it doesn't matter if it disappears while you are trekking. There are three-wheeled strollers on the market that are suitable for use on any terrain, but they are expensive at around £300.

Travel cot

Even if you imagine that your baby will not sleep in any cot other than his own, he will. Older babies may take a short time to adjust, but it won't take long. If you are tense, your clever baby will play up to this, just as they would in any other situation, but within a few days your baby should settle just as happily in a strange cot as he would do at home.

Take a few familiar toys, books and blankets and don't forget any comforters your child is attached to. It may even be worth buying and taking a back up comforter. A familiar music box or mobile may be awkward to pack but this would often be a more practical solution. For most babies, taking a heavy and cumbersome travel cot halfway around the world is unnecessary.

It is important to prearrange a cot in your hotel room or apartment before you go. Eighty per cent of the time, when you arrive at your hotel, even though the receptionist assures you that your cot is already in your hotel room, it is not. However, they usually arrive fairly swiftly. This minor inconvenience is repeated the world over and is surely an international ploy of housekeeping to secure more tips.

If you intend to stay in real budget hotels you are unlikely to be able to acquire a cot. If you plan to move around, prearranging cots in a series of different hotels will be impossible. In these instances, you must be prepared either to sleep with your baby or to improvise.

A friend of mine who was brought up in Ireland with eight brothers and sisters once told me that the youngest baby of the family always slept in a large drawer. This has a rather romantic tinge about it and a practical sense too, especially if you are not finding it easy to sleep with your wriggling progeny. In desperation, try it.

Travel car seats

If your baby is younger than nine months old he will probably still fit in a baby carrying car seat. If so, it is definitely worth taking it with you. It will be useful on the plane if you don't get an aircot. It will also be essential for feeding them on the move plus you can jump in a taxi with your baby and go to a restaurant in the evening with them strapped in their seat. The theory is that they will fall asleep in the taxi and not wake up again when you all get out. Instead, they will remain as good as gold, sleeping peacefully in their familiar seat while you enjoy a nice meal and a good bottle of wine.

We found that this does happen a lot of the time and is far superior to juggling with trolleys. Babies are guaranteed to wake up when shifted from taxi to pushchair and it is a matter of luck whether or not they go back to sleep. For toddlers and older children it is only worth taking their bigger car seats if you are hiring a car at the other end.

When prearranging your car hire from the UK, remember to

request one that does have rear seat belts as your car seats will be useless without them. Developed countries do offer the option of children's car seats. Ask if they can guarantee this option at the time of booking.

Feeding arrangements

Many hotel dining rooms will not have high chairs. Even if they do, they might be occupied by the time you make it to dinner, or even be unsafe.

The carrying car seat is great for children under nine months old. For older babies, a portable feeding chair that fixes on to any table edge with screw contraptions might be useful (unless the tables are all glass as happened to us once).

Booster seats and fabric pouches that rely on a certain chair structure are of limited value. You have no way of knowing whether or not they will fix to the hotel dining room's chairs.

With older babies and toddlers the best bet is likely to be feeding them sitting in the buggy.

Baby walkers

Don't bother. They are treacherous contraptions at the best of times. There are thousands of accidents every year when babies fall out of them into fires, down stairs and on to stone floors or sharp objects. You don't want to see your baby sinking into the swimming pool in his.

Baby bath

No way. Take a sponge.

Potty

Holidays may be a good time to begin potty training. You are all more relaxed and accidents on a tiled floor are better than on your carpet. Buy the cheapest one you can find and then you don't need to bring it home.

Bouncy Chair

Anything that keeps your baby quiet will help make your holiday peaceful.

ELECTRICAL ITEMS

When taking electrical items abroad, don't forget your travel adapter, but also be aware that most of the electrical items made for use in Britain are useless in countries where the electricity supply is 110/120V (such as the USA) even with an adapter. The adapter in effect just changes the shape of the plug.

To change between 240V and 110/120V, you would need a transformer, too. Our 240V hairdryers will do nothing more than puff air, and kettles will never boil on a 110V supply. When travelling abroad, check your appliance for suitability in your destination before you pack it.

Practically all specially designated 'travel' appliances will work off both 110V and 240V supplies, usually automatically. However, if you arrive and your travel kettle, hairdryer or other appliance doesn't work, check for a hidden switch that changes the voltage manually.

Travel kettle

A travel kettle is one of your most essential travel companions when travelling with a baby. Even with older children, an emergency pot rice or noodle may be a godsend. You can't rely on hotel staff in the kitchen having the same hygiene standards as you, and in some countries, water needs to be boiled for five minutes (three or four times in your kettle). If you are absolutely certain your room or apartment will have one, then you needn't bother but otherwise, don't forget yours.

If you are relying on the hotel kettle, it may be scummy. It is a good idea to boil it filled with sterilising fluid before you use it for making up your baby's feeds.

When you buy a travel kettle, make certain that it will boil at 110/120V and not just 240V. Test that the kettle works before you leave home. If you then arrive and it doesn't boil, be patient. You may need to flick a switch to make it respond to a lower voltage or it may just be that it takes longer to boil. My travel kettle takes about fifteen minutes to boil in the Caribbean off the 110V supply and around seven minutes at home in the UK.

Baby listener

I was once at a New Year's Eve party in an exclusive hotel. Whilst everyone was dressed in all their finery and sipping champagne, one over-zealous mother danced around a baby listener she had plugged in next to the dancefloor.

I never actually got on with my baby listener and so never

really tested its range in hotels. But judging by that mother's response to the flashing light on hers, it was working perfectly, despite her baby being four floors away.

If your room is close to the pool, a battery-operated listener may be useful when your baby is having his afternoon nap and also in the restaurant at night. However, if your hotel room is at risk from intruders, don't leave your baby sleeping in the room alone.

If you usually use a listener at home, it will be at its most useful abroad in your own apartment or villa and if you don't take it, you might miss it.

Don't rely on the plug-in adapters unless you are travelling to a 220/240V country. Take a battery-operated listener.

Camcorder battery chargers

Remember your plug adapter and it should work, whatever the voltage.

Bottle warmers and sterilising systems

You should be able to cope without your bottle warmer for a fortnight. You might even find your child will prefer cool milk on a hot night. You are unlikely to want to take your bulky plug-in steamer-steriliser on your travels, but if you are used to this method and can't imagine any other, there are compact travel steam sterilisers available which fit two bottles. However, I have only seen them for use with a 220V supply and so they cannot be used in the USA or the Caribbean.

Travel bottle-warming pouches that do not need batteries or a power supply are available. The pouches must be put in boiling water to be re-energised.

If you normally use sterilising solution, take everything with you. Even if you don't, consider it while abroad as an alternative to the steam method. However, do practice it once or twice at home before you leave.

If you are no longer breast-feeding, you will already have all the feeding bottles, teats and bottle brushes. You don't need to buy an entire new sterilising system, just some sterilising tablets or fluid and a reasonable-sized plastic container with a lid. The sterilising fluid or tablets dissolved in a small amount of water have the added benefit that they can be used to wipe down the bathroom, kitchen surfaces and floor areas. This will at least keep the bug level down in your accommodation.

Sterilising tablets are better than fluid for travelling with. They are lighter, less bulky and you need have no fear of them leaking. Fluids such as Milton bleach clothes, so it is not a good idea to pack them in your suitcase. If you do take fluid, carry it in your hand luggage wrapped in a plastic bag. When using a foreign water source, boil all the water you use, even though you are adding sterilising tablets. Each sterilising tablet then needs to be dissolved in a set volume of water as marked on the packet. If you use bottled water check the seal is intact. It still may be a good idea to boil bought water as a precaution. Note that even in the UK, bought bottled water must still be boiled before it is given in any form to babies.

You can use the feeding bottles to measure the volume of water needed to make up the sterilising fluid. Don't forget they have fluid ounces and millilitres measurements graduated on their sides. If you prefer, measure the set volume per tablet (and per two tablets) in a measuring jug at home, then with a waterproof pen, mark the level this reaches on the plastic container you plan to take with you. You then know where to fill the container up to each time. If you are camping, simply boil all your bottle-feeding equipment in a large, covered pan for at least twenty-five minutes.

Presterilised bottle kits are available to buy. They are basically a system of sterile plastic bags but may be useful as a back up.

FOOD AND NUTRITION

Under One Year

Breast-feeding
If you have established breast-feeding and are very comfortable with it, then you can travel anywhere in the world easily. Although I would never be deterred from travelling with a bottle-fed baby, there is little doubt that it is easier to travel farther and wider and to more remote places with a baby who is breast-feeding. Do be sensitive about the other culture's modesty and follow the lead of local mothers. Carry a shawl for privacy and warmth as you feed.

Breast-feeding is well recognised to be better for babies and when travelling it offers significant advantages. Many constituents of breast milk have potent antibacterial activity and anti-rotavirus antibodies are secreted in maternal milk. This will protect your baby from stomach upsets, diarrhoea and other illnesses while travelling. It is also very convenient. Preparing bottles without a reliable electricity supply, although possible, is very hard work.

I struggled with breast-feeding but persevered for five months. When I booked a trip to Tobago, I decided to stop because I didn't want to risk the complications I was suffering while I was abroad on holiday. I regretted having stopped just a couple of times but I did have the comforts and facilities of a hotel room and restaurant. Once was during the plane's descent when Paris was screaming with the discomfort in his ears. I knew that he would have suckled at the breast, despite not being hungry, which would have eased the pressure and his pain. The second time was when we arrived at our hotel late at night and I had to start boiling kettles and mixing feeds for the night. The rest of the time it was fine and no more inconvenience than it was at home.

There are few disadvantages to breast-feeding, the only significant one being if the mother were to fall ill. If she were suffering from diarrhoea and vomiting, it might be transmitted to the baby, as some food-poisoning bacteria can be passed on in maternal milk. If the mother then became dehydrated, her milk supply would be compromised. For this reason, it might always be worth packing a bottle, a teat, some sterilising tablets and a small tin of formula milk, just in case. In desperation, a baby can be fed from a spoon but it will be very frustrating for both the baby and feeder. The bottle would also be invaluable if your baby were to fall ill and needed oral rehydration therapy.

While breast-feeding in hot, humid conditions, you might develop thrush on your nipples that can transfer to the baby's mouth. You must both be treated together with an antifungal agent or reinfection will occur.

Bottle-feeding

Ideally you will need a reliable electricity supply. A refrigerator is a great asset but a kettle is essential. If not, bottle-feeding is still possible but will be far more difficult.

An acquaintance once told me the tale of her daughter planning a two-week driving/camping holiday in France with her husband and six-week-old baby. She packed the car with cartons and cartons of premixed formula. Everything was planned to the last detail. She got in to northern France and lasted two days before coming home. This was very ambitious and would need a great deal of energy which you don't always have as a new mother. Things would probably have been a lot different if the child were that bit older or if she had been breast-feeding.

If you have a kettle and a fridge, bottle-feeding is no more inconvenient than it is at home. You will need to pack all the formula milk your baby is likely to drink while on holiday. You will probably be able to buy a brand of formula milk abroad, but, as they all taste different to your baby, you might find it's a battle to make them adapt to the unfamiliar taste when you should be relaxing and enjoying your time together.

You are the best judge of what quantity your baby will get through in the time period. Calculate what you will need then take extra, especially if travelling to a hot climate. Your baby will be thirstier and need more to drink. Appetites of any age group tend to diminish in high temperatures and at least if your baby is getting plenty of milk over the duration of your travels, he will stay healthy.

If your child will tolerate ready-made cartons of baby milk it may be a good idea to take some with you. They are about the right size for a bottle and are very useful on the plane or beach in an emergency. If you arrive late at night at your destination they will be a much easier alternative to boiling up kettles and mixing powder scoops. Unfortunately, Paris would never drink them but, fortunately, I bought and tried them before we travelled. They are bulky and heavy but are a convenience.

Although we stop sterilising babies' bottles at six months in the UK, it is advisable to continue doing so if you are abroad and cannot guarantee tap water quality.

Solid feeds

If your baby is fussy, it is a good idea to take a full supply of jars, cans and packets with you. Foreign supermarkets may only stock a few ageing, familiar branded cans.

In many European or Caribbean resorts, Australia, America and other countries of Western standards, you will be able to buy baby food easily, but you may not be able to buy your baby's favourite. It is a safer option to go prepared. Jars can smash easily in your luggage and so packets of powdered food or cans are easier to transport. Rusks are a light option to pack, too.

Toddlers

Milk feeds

Although, after twelve months, you will be giving your child fresh cow's milk at home, in many countries of the world this is not to be recommended. If milk is not pasteurised, it can harbour many bacteria and pass on many illnesses.

If your toddler will still drink formula milk for the holiday, your life will be relatively easy. Paris would switch back from fresh cow's milk at home to formula milk on holiday until the age of eighteen months. From then on, we took several one-litre cartons of longlife milk with us on a trip. They were very heavy but gave us the time to hunt out where we could purchase pasteurised milk.

In most places we found that we could get it in branded tetra-packs, even in China, but a few times we were obliged to leave the milk out of the diet. At home, if we ran out of milk it would be an emergency, but when we were abroad a couple of times and unable to get any milk for days, Paris would accept it and drink juice, bottled water and sodas.

With toddlers and children, don't be too concerned about their lack of milk intake for the duration of a short holiday. Even in the worst case scenario, a two-week diet of chips and coke will not do any lasting damage.

Supermarket powdered skimmed milk is not recommended for feeding children under a year old, but above this age you can try it. Most toddlers don't like it, but if yours does, it is a useful, lightweight backup to mix with boiled water for the first few days of your trip.

Solid feeds

Feeding toddlers abroad can be a doddle or a nightmare, but don't get stressed. You may find that they have a drastically reduced appetite in the heat but this is natural. Their bodies aren't burning up calories as fuel to keep themselves warm.

It is a good idea to apportion part of your suitcase for snack and emergency meals for toddlers. Paris was, and still is, a fussy eater. I knew I would be lost without taking all his meals with us on every journey until he was over two years old. I packed dry instant noodles, small pasta shells (if you sit them in boiling water for five minutes they soften to an edible level), raisins, crisps, cereal, bread sticks, cheese biscuits, pretzels and glucose sweets for an instant sugar burst. Supplemented by milk and local fruits, this stock would give him plenty of carbohydrates and fats, plus the sugars and salt that are important in the heat. These were not, perhaps, in their most desirable form, but we would always survive for a week or two and have a pacifying snack at hand wherever we were.

Persuading the hotel staff to prepare a meal before the restaurant opens can be a stressful and costly business. You are much better with a kettle and a few pasta shells. Many toddlers will eat pasta alone. They like bland foods and so don't worry that there is no tomato or meat sauce on it. If your child refuses plain pasta, try a little instant soup on it. This will transform it into, for example, tomato or chicken flavour. Otherwise try the instant flavoured noodles.

Small children

If you are staying in a hotel, just pack supplementary snacks. Small children might demand a bowl of instant noodles before the hotel restaurant opens, but you are less of a slave to their stomachs than you are to a baby's or toddler's.

If you are self catering, then pack a few back-up favourites and snacks for emergencies. Cereal is handy but remember, in many countries, you won't be able to get the milk to put on them. If you can't, you can always pour yoghurt or flavoured, sterilised milk drink over the cereal and hope the children like the novelty of it.

You may decline into a holiday of crisps, chocolate and coke but the worst of that is the battle you have when you get home and the child wants to know why they can't have the same diet at home (see page 208, Feeding Children Local Food).

Older children

Hopefully they will be able to pick from a restaurant menu. If they are being faddy, don't make mealtimes an issue. Help them avoid choosing high-risk foods (see page 208, Feeding Children Local Food).

NAPPY CHANGING

Nappies and wet wipes

In many countries of the world, disposable nappies are not available. In others, they are prohibitively expensive. In Beijing, Western branded nappies are approximately £20 per pack. It is therefore advisable to take your disposable nappies with you. They may be bulky, but they are light and will leave a gap in your luggage by the end of the holiday for any souvenirs. If you do use them abroad, be sensitive when disposing of them. Don't put them down toilets, use nappy sacks. A soiled nappy is a potential breeding ground for disease when abandoned.

Refastenable nappies are preferable. You can take them on or off in between dips in the sea or pool. A pair or two of padded washable training pants are a back up. It is important to save some nappies for the plane journey home. If you begin to run out, use training pants instead for the last few days on the beach.

If you consider baby wipes to be too expensive, take plenty of tissues, cotton wool and baby lotion. A wipeable changing mat is useful, although not essential. A hotel towel will suffice. Pocket size, padded and waterproof changing mats are available.

SWIMMING AIDS

Inflatable baby seats

Inflatable baby seats which float are popular with many mothers and keep even very young babies reasonably stable in the water provided they keep still. You need to stay close by, just in case your baby launches itself sideways out of the seat and under the water.

Paris enjoyed the novelty for about four minutes then refused to go back into the seat. I didn't force the issue because I couldn't quite understand the benefit myself. The seats are not stable enough to give a baby any independence, nor do they help build confidence as they set the child above the water level, which removes the sense of being in the water. They are really just a little boat with the legs cut out. I preferred to hold on to Paris in the water and give him confidence with closeness and smiles. However, other mothers I have asked have told me that their babies enjoyed the seats.

Arm bands
For very young babies, arm bands are of little use. Babies are unable to support their own heads enough to keep them out of the water, even though their bodies will be kept afloat.

Arm bands do help to build confidence and if you do intend to teach your child to swim using them, it is a good idea to get them used to the idea when they are very young. At 18–24 months your child will be able to enjoy independence in the water with the aid of the correct sized arm bands.

Rubber rings
I was ten years old when I learnt to swim and did so with a rubber ring. Inflatable rings are useful for older children or to increase smaller children's buoyancy with the added safety of arm bands.

Special swimwear
There are a whole host of new swim suits that provide buoyancy in the water, with either 'polystyrene' floats that slip into pockets sewn on to the body of a swimsuit, or inflatable back and front pads. These are excellent. They allow a child to move their arms freely, they are not as uncomfortable as arm bands and allow enough stability and support for children as young as eighteen months to be completely independent. There is also the added benefit that as your child becomes more confident in the water you can gradually reduce the buoyancy in line with their swimming ability.

CHECK LIST OF ESSENTIALS

For babies
1. (a) Bottle-feeding equipment
   - A bottle brush (if you forget one use your toothbrush).
   - 3–4 bottles
   - 3–4 teats
   - Sterilising tablets or fluid (tablets are better for travelling)

- A plastic container to sterilise in.
- More formula milk than you think you will need.
- A few cartons of ready-made formula, heavy but useful in an emergency.

(b) Breast-feeding equipment
- Breast pads
- Standby bottle-feeding equipment:
- 2 bottles, 2 teats, sterilising tablets, bottle brush, a small pack of formula milk.

(c) Packing for solid feeds
- Jars, cans and powdered foods, rusks.
- Plastic bowl and spoon.
- Feeding cup (non-spill cups are available and do not spill drink even if held upside down).
- Bibs (especially important if you are travelling to a cold environment to prevent your baby being damp).
- Tissues.

2. Travel kettle (check that it works with 110 and 220V).
3. Wet wipes for every occasion.
4. A sponge and flannel.
5. Baby shampoo and soap.
6. Security objects or comforters (blankets, dummies, toys or mummy's nightie).
7. Disposable nappies, cream and nappy sacks.
8. Fabric nappies, pins, plastic pants etc. NB Even if you use disposables, a few back-up fabric nappies might be useful if you begin to run out.
9. Training pants. Ideal on the beach or when swimming but are washable.
10. Pushchair or baby buggy (sun parasol and/or rain cover).
11. Carrying sling or back pack.
12. Carrying car seat (insect net to fit).
13. Favourite toys, books and blankets.
14. Comforter (it would be advisable to take a spare).
15. Insect repellent.
16. Swimming aids.
17. Clothing:
    - Swim wear
    - Sun hat

- Cool cotton T-shirts
- Shorts
- Long-sleeved tops and long trousers in cool, natural fabrics to help avoid insect bites when out in the evening
- Socks
- Cotton sleep suits or long-sleeved and -legged pyjamas to protect from insect bites in the night
- Soft shoes
- Warm clothing (important for air-conditioned buildings and transport even if you expect the weather to be warm).

18. Bibs (particularly if travelling to a cold climate where you need to avoid a damp, sticky mess down your child's clothing).
19. Liquid clothes wash.
20. Sterilising surface cleaner.
21. Small bottle of washing-up liquid to wash bottle and bowls etc.
22. Highest factor sun block suitable for babies' skin, water resistant rather than waterproof.
23. Shawls and a blanket.

Non-essentials

1. Wipeable foldable changing mat. Alternatively, use a towel.
2. Baby listeners.
3. Travel cots.
4. Music boxes or mobiles.
5. Bouncy chair.

Additional needs for toddlers

1. Milk feeds:
   - Formula milk, UHT cartons of milk or powdered semi-skimmed milk
2. Solid feeds:
   - Favourite snacks
   - Raisins
   - Cereals
   - Dry instant noodles
   - Small pasta shells (if you sit them in boiling water for five minutes they soften to an edible level)
   - Crisps

- Bread sticks
- Cheese and sweet biscuits
- Pretzels
- Glucose sweets for an instant sugar burst.
- Long-life/'stay fresh' bread (will last up to 14 days).
3. Portable feeding chair.
4. Reins, wrist attachment, audible distance alarm.
5. Potty (useful for camping).

For all age groups

1. Documentation: passport, visa, E111 or health insurance details, vaccination certificates.
2. Insect repellent containing DEET (Diethyl toluamide).
3. Plug-in mosquito killer (or coils) and nets.
4. Camera and spare camera film and batteries.
5. Camcorder, blank camcorder tapes and battery recharger.
6. Beach shoes or old pumps.
7. Comfortable shoes that children can walk well in (warm, water resistant shoes for cold conditions).
8. Swim wear.
9. Sun hat, essential for travelling on water.
10. Swimming aids.
11. Bucket and spades.
12. Toothbrush and paste.
13. High factor suncream, sunblock.
14. Towels.
15. Phrase book with section on medical symptoms.
16. Sunglasses.
17. Spare pair of prescription glasses.
18. Plug adaptor.

Older children
Their own little bag for them to pack and carry themselves.

THE MEDICAL KIT

Essentials

1. Sachets of oral replacement salts, e.g. Rehydrat or Dioralyte.
2. Paracetamol syrup, e.g. Calpol or Disprol. Will provide pain relief, alleviate fever and reduce inflammation.
3. Malaria prophylaxis tablets.

4. If travelling into a malarial region outside the reach of medical help, drugs to treat malaria should be carried, such as Quinine combined with Fansidar.
5. Antiseptic powder spray, e.g. Betadine/Savlon (povodine iodine).
6. Antibiotic treatment:
   (a) Antibiotic oral tablets.
   Check doses for your children's age groups when you pick up the prescription. Carry at least one but preferably two (one as a back up).
   - Naladixic acid is useful for gastro-intestinal and urinary infections.
   - Co-trimoxazole is useful for many bacterial infections, including stomach upsets, urinary tract infections and general respiratory tract infections.
   - Amoxycillin and Augmentin are useful for many bacterial infections, including general respiratory tract and skin infections.
   - Metronidazole or tinidazole for amoebic dysentery and giardiasis.
   (b) Antibiotic eyedrops/lotions.
   - Fucithalmic is effective and non toxic. Allergic reactions are quickly limited by discontinuing use.
   (c) Antibiotic powder is better in the humid tropics for skin infections. Cream is very efficient for skin infections (e.g. impetigo) in temperate climates.
   (d) Eardrops are effective for infections in the outer ear.
   (e) If your child is prone to middle ear infections or tonsilitis, consider taking specific antibiotics with you to treat flare ups.
   (f) If your child has an existing medical condition, pack enough routine medication to last the duration of the trip. Keep a written record of the generic (not trade) name of the drug, so that if you need to buy the drug abroad, you will be able to do so.
7. When travelling with a young baby, you may be advised to take an electronic thermometer with you. Dummies with a built-in thermometer are claimed by the manufacturers to be accurate to 0.1°C.

8. Canesten cream for superficial fungal infections.
9. Motion sickness tablets (Dramamine, Phenergan or Stugeron, depending on child's age).
10. Jet lag/sleeping tablets (debatable).
11. Sudocrem antiseptic, good for nappy rash, sunburn and bites.
12. Calamine for sunburn, prickly heat and itchy bites.
13. Phenergan for motion sickness, sedation, bites and allergic reactions to antihistamines.
14. Water sterilisation tablets.
15. Water purification tablets (iodine) for emergencies, if you anticipate travelling to where you will be unable to buy bottled water, or boil your own supply.

THE FIRST AID KIT

1. Packet of absorbent cotton wool
2. Sterile gauze squares in various sizes
3. Plasters
4. Bandages
5. Triangular bandage
6. Adhesive surgical tape
7. Safety pins
8. Tweezers and scissors, or a Swiss army knife with both
9. Two 5ml syringes
10. Five needles (preferably two different sizes)
11. One dental needle
12. One intravenous cannula
13. One skin suture with needle
14. One packet of steri-strips or other skin closure mechanism
15. Alcohol swabs for cleansing the skin

Additional items such as an intravenous blood-giving set and blood substitute solution may be worthwhile additions to the luggage if travelling to remote, rural areas. Discuss with your doctor.

NB: Keep what you will need for your first night at the top of your suitcase, and remember infants (children under two years) often have no weight allowance on the plane.

PART THREE: WHILE YOU ARE AWAY

8 Settling In

ON ARRIVAL

Transfer

If you don't have transport included in your package, your first trial is the journey from the airport to your accommodation. Many opportunists tend to gather around and outside airports to squeeze the tourist's purse when he is tired and jet lagged, and hasn't yet had the chance to get to grips with the currency. Thankfully, in many Third World countries, the locals are kept out of the arrivals hall and so you have time to gather your wits before you are bombarded. If you arrive in daylight hours, you will have various options. Every airport in the world is serviced by some method of local transport, otherwise it would find itself with a shortage of employees.

At quieter times and in the middle of the night your options will usually be either a taxi or sleeping in the airport until morning. I have done the latter on a couple of occasions but would not choose to do it with accompanying children.

Unfortunately, taxi drivers seem to be internationally committed to extortion. The only country of the world in which I would get into a taxi without first haggling the fare is Japan. In every other country, before setting foot inside a taxi, I would either ensure that there was a visible meter or negotiate a fixed rate in a specified currency (local or US dollars), especially outside airport arrivals.

Before leaving arrivals, you should always ask someone inside the airport terminal what the approximate cost of the fare to your destination will be and insist that this sum is all you are prepared to pay. Tourist information should be able to help. If everything is closed, ask a member of staff. Most airports do try to aid their tourists in transit and will recommend the best means of reaching your destination cheaply.

Tips

1. Always negotiate your fare before getting into the taxi or insist that the meter is switched on.
2. Confirm the currency or you may get to the end of your journey and the driver will claim that he meant $20 US not $20 Hong Kong.
3. Try to have the right change on you then if he does try to squeeze any more money out of you, you can claim that this is all you have on you at the moment.
4. Don't follow anyone to a 'taxi' outside a designated taxi pick-up zone. The taxi is bound to be unlicensed and the state of the car questionable.

ARRIVING AT YOUR ACCOMMODATION

Room allocation

In a resort hotel with babies and young children, try to secure a room on the ground floor. Lifts and balconies are both treacherous with toddlers. Stairs are wearying after a long day, especially with buggies and car seats. The best spot in a hotel with an accompanying infant is a ground-floor room that backs out on to the pool. You can leave your child sleeping peacefully in the cool while you laze by the pool a few feet away.

The disadvantages of a ground floor room are that there are more likely to be flying and stray crawling insects around. No matter how clean a hotel is, the occasional stray cockroach may find its way in. It is postulated that after an atomic war cockroaches may be the only creatures to survive. They are hardy, ancient creatures which, although repulsive, are not always a bad sign. In the course of my studies I was once handed a roach in a box and told that it had been in there for six months without food and water and was still alive. They thrive in the humid tropics and even the best hotels constantly fight and spray to keep them at bay. If you see a solitary one, try not to worry unless more begin to appear.

With older children, rooms or apartments on higher floors

mean that you will be able to keep your windows open at night with less fear of mosquitoes or intruders, but with younger children, you need to keep the windows locked anyway.

If your child is unlikely to settle in a strange cot alone and likely to end up nuzzled next to you, request a king-size bed. If there is one available, the hotel will usually oblige. Big bed often also means big room.

If you are having to prepare milk feeds, a room with a fridge or minibar (to use as a fridge) is a distinct advantage. Many hotels do not have this facility but check with reception if this is an option before your room is allocated.

COMFORT AND SAFETY IN YOUR ROOM

Don't be surprised if, when you arrive in your room, there are too few beds or no cot at all. It happens all over the world. Even in the best hotels, housekeeping seem reluctant to supply all the extra sleeping arrangements until you all actually arrive. This minor inconvenience is repeated the world over and is possibly an international ploy of housekeeping to secure more tips. I have been standing at reception numerous times and been reassured that yes, the cot is definitely in the room. It very rarely is. On our last trip there was a bed missing. It is slightly irritating but is usually one of the more immediate things to be corrected. Often when the cot does finally arrive, it will have bars missing but relax, you're on holiday.

On arrival it is a good idea to do a safety checklist. Most mothers will do it instinctively but if you are tired and jet lagged, you might crave the days when you were child free and so could just fall into bed then unpack in the morning. It is incredible how young children are when they work out how to escape from a hotel room. Paris was eighteen months old when he managed to open our door in China. When he was three years old he determined how a series of locks on the door of our apartment in Spain were opened in sequence to escape. It was so complicated that on the first day it had taken us fifteen minutes to leave and lock the room, yet a few fiddles and Paris was out. Luckily both times I heard the door go, but he was already halfway down the corridors when I caught up with him. Thankfully I wasn't in the bath!

As soon as a child can reach the locks and the door handle,

you need to double lock the door with a key or in any other way out of your child's grasp, even if you don't imagine they will be able to get out. Most hotel rooms have security chains on the door and some have child locks. Get into the habit of using them. If the windows don't lock properly, you must insist on a room change or repair immediately.

Check list for safety in the room or apartment

1. Check that your children can't open the doors or windows. Ensure they are securely locked out of reach.
2. Tuck away trailing wires and check flexes for fraying.
3. Shield or hide any electric points behind furniture. In many parts of the world they are positioned at fiddling height and look different and more interesting than the ones at home. Don't worry about adjusting the furniture to make the room safer. Electrics in foreign apartments and countries with lower standards of health and safety than ours can be suspect. Sockets might be hanging off. They must be either repaired or shielded by a piece of furniture.
4. Remove all unstable furniture with sharp edges, projecting nails or thin glass tops. Ask housekeeping to remove anything you feel would endanger your child and if they don't arrive, stick it in the wardrobe, the bathroom, out on the balcony or even in the corridor.
5. Remove all breakable objects.
6. Look out for complimentary matches and glass ashtrays and put them out of reach.
7. Move the toilet brush. You really don't want to find your toddler sucking it in the morning.
8. Take up mats that slide on tiled floors or trip up your child. Don't let your child run around on tiled floors with just socks on.
9. If there are any heavy doors inside your room, wedge them so that they cannot crush a child's fingers.
10. If there are any glass doors that your child may run into, they should be marked with warning stickers to make them more visible. If not, mark them in some way yourself, either with draped fabric, washable paints, children's stickers, even squiggles of toothpaste on the far side.

11. Move any unfamiliar flowers or plants from inside the room.
12. Check the safety and stability of the balcony.
13. Look in cupboards and under the bed for poisonous substances including rat or insect traps.
14. Store medicine, razors and scissors out of reach.

Aiding sleep

On the first few nights away, it may be difficult to settle your child. It could be the excitement or the unfamiliarity but it is often a test. Does a different bed mean different rules? In our travels, the answer is 'yes' but if you want to maintain a routine bedtime, settle them with books, blankets and clothing that will smell familiar. For the first few nights respond to them if they cry in the night. If you can tolerate it, allow them to sleep in your room where they can see you, or leave on a light and surround them with familiar things as you tuck them up.

We are always very relaxed about bedtime when we are travelling and have found that, generally, Paris will fall asleep much earlier and more deeply on a settee in a villa or in a noisy restaurant than in a fresh bed. It's not unease or insecurity but re-testing the rules. At home, bedtime is non-negotiable but when travelling, it never quite seems worth the three-hour battle to make him go to bed early. He thinks he's missing something and will rage until midnight, whereas if we simply take him with us, he will fall asleep in his buggy and we can have a night of quiet conversation and peace. When he was younger he slept in his car seat, then his pushchair or buggy. Now if we are out late we will either arrange chairs in a row for him to lie down on, or spread a blanket or coat on the floor and he will snuggle at our feet. He can fall asleep anywhere. We can then just pop him into bed and he never stirs.

Jet lag

If you have had a long journey crossing several time zones, children are likely to suffer from jet lag. The body is used to a regular daily pattern. After long periods in the air in a pressurised cabin, sleep patterns, digestion and circulation will all be affected.

There is a lot of advice about how to avoid jet lag but I never actually manage to do it. Jet lag is something I do suffer from quite badly. Unfortunately, Paris is the same. I don't have the ability to sleep sitting upright and, no matter how sleep deprived, can never sleep in daylight. From being seven months old, Paris couldn't sleep in the daytime either. His father, Simon, can sleep whilst driving or eating, in the blazing sun on the beach, or for the full duration of a fourteen-hour flight. He very rarely gets jet lag while I always suffer for days, up at 4 a.m. watching him sleep. Now I have Paris to keep me company!

The guidelines are to avoid fatty foods, alcohol, coffee and tea the day before you leave and during the flight. Drink plenty of water to help combat tiredness, dehydration and headaches. Apply a moisturiser and wear loose-fitting clothes of natural fibres. Stretch all your muscles by walking around the plane.

But if you or your children have a strong body clock and don't need much sleep they will need time to adjust. Our two worst cases were in China, where Paris would have a nap from 8–11 p.m. (as if it were the afternoon) then be up between 11 and 5 a.m. On that occasion I resorted to the whisky from the minibar to keep me sane. We read book after book after book whilst his father snored peacefully. I was a walking zombie for three days. In Venezuela, Paris fell asleep at 6.30 p.m. but was then up between 4.30 and 5 a.m. for the first five days.

It is generally accepted that jet lag is worse going east. Eastbound, your watch must be put forward (+ hours). Travelling westbound it must be put back (− hours). It is much easier to stay up past your bedtime and sleep well than to go to bed six hours earlier than normal and try to get sleep. Going west is much more bearable but, when going east, the best thing I have found to combat jet lag is a low dose of a mild sleeping tablet for the first few nights.

The group of drugs known as the benzodiazapines are the most effective because they actually relax and reset the body clock. One dose on the first night is often enough to eradicate jet lag. The drug in this class known to most people is Valium. Valium is excellent for jet lag and can be given to children, although I would not necessarily recommend that you do this unless you have a very important date soon after arrival and discuss the option with your doctor.

Valium is usually given to children if they are suffering from night terrors or sleep walking, not just jet lag. There is absolutely no chance of your child developing any dependence after one or two nights. The much-publicised problems with Valium occur after prolonged use with high doses.

I have not yet resorted to giving Paris sleeping tablets. However, I would confidently do so when he gets older.

For children, the better alternative would probably be an antihistamine such as Phenergan syrup. This medication is also used for motion sickness and has significant sedative properties to help your children sleep through their first few nights. Sedatives are especially useful if travelling east.

If medication for such a minor problem seems unnecessary to you, natural tips for minimising jet lag include:

1. If travelling west (to the US or Caribbean) and the children aren't at school, start keeping them up later and letting them lie in as long as possible a few days before you leave. This will help with a few hours of adjustment and there will not be such a vast difference on arrival.

2. On arrival westwards, keep the children up and awake as long as you can. Don't let them go to bed at 4 p.m., they will be up and ready for the day at 3 a.m.

3. Going east, allow them an afternoon nap but wake them up after an hour or so, no matter how grumpy they will be. Then try to keep them up until 10 p.m.

4. They may suffer from loss of appetite on arrival. Give them regular, healthy snacks and titbits.

FOREIGN ROADS

There are more tourists killed on foreign roads than by any of the tropical diseases, parasites or dangerous animals (see page 100, Travelling By Car).

It is hard to drive on foreign roads on the 'wrong' side but it is just as big a change to be a pedestrian abroad. Instead of looking right then left, on the continent we should be looking left then right, but years of conditioning are not going to change on the first day. Encourage your children to follow the 'green cross code'. They must look both ways. Abroad teach them to look right, look left, then right again, then a 'special holiday' left again before they step out on to any roads, or tracks that might be a road. Everything will seem different. Roads may not even look like roads. There might not be a separate pavement which can serve as a mental barrier in the UK. You will need to take extra care, especially on the first few days.

A friend told me recently how she turned her head for one second and her three-year-old girl had jumped out of her buggy and on to a Spanish road. It hadn't seemed like a road to her. I have quite often looked the wrong way myself and nearly stepped out in front of a car. The closest was a tram in Amsterdam. They move so silently and so close to the kerb. Simon caught my arm and the tram driver rang the warning bell, otherwise I would have been in hospital.

If you are hiring a car check all the car seats and check also that there are seat belts in the back of the car before you sign for it.

HOW TO AVOID LOSING YOUR CHILD

1. Protect your child from getting lost by dressing them in bright clothes and keeping toddlers on reins, wrist straps or secured in their buggies in busy areas.
2. Teach children their hotel name and room number as soon as possible. You will be surprised how young they will be able to learn this. Paris was able to remember at three years old.
3. On busy beaches and in theme parks it is advisable to put a wrist strap on your child with your name and accommodation address written in the local language.
4. If your child is old enough to understand, suggest that if they do get separated from you, they walk into a shop and address a female assistant, explaining that they are lost. This will at least get them off the streets.
5. If you do lose your child, be aware that in most countries of the world you need have no fear that any harm will have come to them.

Friends of ours lost their son in Spain for an entire afternoon. They were frantic but the locals reassured them that 'we do not harm children in Spain as they do in England and America'. He was found enjoying a meal with a local family.

Throughout the Mediterranean, the Caribbean, the Far East and South America, children are precious. At the other extreme, a friend's mother once told me how he had been snatched in a market in Jordan when he was a toddler. She tore through the streets and saw him just before he disappeared off the street into a local house.

Terrifying rumours warn that professional gangs haunt children's theme parks and whisk away children. They snatch a child, then take it straight in to the restrooms where they change its clothes and put on a baseball cap to hide the familiar hair-colouring. They may cut or even dye the child's hair, making its appearance so different that its own mother wouldn't recognise it. Incredibly, older children have been rumoured to be drugged to quieten them. Beware, but remember that the chance of this happening is a billion to one.

It is easy to get separated from your child in crowds. On one of my first trips to America I found a young girl wandering lost and alone in Disneyworld. I took her hand and asked her where her mummy was. She was either too young or too frightened to speak and just stared up at me. We stood with her on the spot, expecting her anxious mum to run towards us at any time. After fifteen minutes I gave up and took her to the lost child station. She followed me with mute obliging and sat in the cabin, tearless and bewildered. I am glad I had found her first.

The tales may be sensationalist but if you ever suffer the unbearable experience of a missing child, don't just look for familiar clothes and hair colour. Scrutinise every child of a similar shape and size.

9 Acclimatising to the Elements and Change of Environment

ARRIVING IN THE HEAT

The effects of heat on the body

In a hot enviroment, if the heat lost by the body by sweating and flushing of blood to the skin's surface is insufficient, there will be a rise in body temperature that will lead to hyperventilation, irritability and confusion. If the temperature continues to rise, the body gives up and even stops sweating. The temperature will then continue to rise dangerously. If it rises above 41°C in effect the body begins to cook. The brain is affected first, followed by the liver and kidneys, then muscle cells. As the body's internal temperature rises further, the damage caused is likely to be irreversible. If the internal body temperature reaches 50°C for just a couple of minutes, cells in every organ of the body will be destroyed. Death will follow.

HEATSTROKE

Heatstroke refers to overheating of the body's inner core, not just the skin, which can suffer prolonged exposure to intense heat with the only major damage being blisters and superficial burns.

Babies are unable to sweat efficiently and can suffer dangerous increases in internal body temperature very quickly, so are particularly susceptible to heatstroke.

Children sweat more in hot climates but are generally more active and less able to judge when they are getting dangerously hot. Heatstroke is therefore relatively common when unacclimatised children go on holiday into the intense heat and strong sun of a Mediterranean or Caribbean summer.

Humidity is an important factor. High humidity interferes with the body's ability to cool down. Even adults who aren't exercising can suffer heatstroke if the air temperature and humidity are both high.

Most children will get too hot at times on holiday either by overdoing the running about, spending too long in a hot car or walking in the midday sun. The danger is when they become so hot that the body effectively gives up trying to cool itself.

Symptoms

The skin will look and feel hot but will be dry due to the lack of sweat. In the early stages, your child will become extremely irritable, confused and might complain of a headache. Babies will cry inconsolably until you make attempts to cool them. If this stage goes unrecognised, babies and children will become drowsy, lethargic and might have a rapid pulse rate. Their temperature could rise to 40°C. In severe cases, your child might become confused, have epileptic-like seizures, begin to lose consciousness and even stop breathing.

Heatstroke in the shade

When we visited Tobago with Paris for the first time, he was five months old. We sat down to lunch in the shade and left Paris asleep and plastered in waterproof sunscreen. We enjoyed a relaxed 45 minutes until he woke up and began complaining. We left the restaurant then put Paris in his pushchair under a parasol as we enjoyed the sunshine. At around 3 p.m. we judged that the sun was weaker and allowed Paris to roll on a towel in the sun, plastered with more waterproof suncream. At 4 p.m. he began to complain gently, so I moved him back into the shade. Soon after, he began to cry louder then louder then louder. We tried to soothe him but there was nothing we could do. We eventually left the poolside, very embarrassed at the fuss we had all created.

Paris continued to cry inconsolably for over one hour. Eventually I collapsed next to him on the bed and began to blow over his back and the nape of his neck. He went quiet. I stopped blowing and he began howling. I blew cool air all over him. He became quiet again and after ten minutes of sobbing fell into a deep sleep. Simon and I fell asleep, exhausted, by his side. None of us roused until morning. I realised that what we had been faced with was very mild heatstroke. Clearly a baby is at risk, even if left in the shade.

When I returned to the UK, I telephoned various suncream manufacturers and they confirmed that waterproof creams can worsen heatstroke due to the fact that they act as a barrier to sweating and heat loss from the skin.

How to prevent heatstroke from occurring

- When you arrive at your destination, allow time for acclimatisation. Children will actually acclimatise more quickly than adults but are more susceptible in the interim. They are therefore most at risk in the first day or two.
- Keep children out of the sun during the hottest part of the day. This is not necessarily at midday as humidity rises in the afternoon. Keep babies and young children in the shade for as much of the day as you can.
- Do not apply waterproof sunscreen too thickly. It hinders sweating and heat loss.
- Ensure that your child rests and cools down at intervals. Discourage them from running around too much in the sun. Play energetic games in the morning or evening.
- Encourage them to take regular swims and cold drinks.
- Don't travel in a car at the hottest times of the day without air conditioning.
- Ensure that babies and children wear hats, preferably ones that also cover the back of their necks. Direct sun on the nape of the neck will interfere with the temperature regulatory centres in the brain.

What to do if it your child shows symptoms of heatstroke

Act immediately to cool your child. Get out of the sun and into an air-conditioned room and remove all your child's clothes. Sponge him down from top to toe with cool water. If you don't have a fan, blow all over the skin, particularly on the back of the neck. If you can get an ice pack or anything cold (even a chilled canned drink or an ice lolly in its wrapper) place it on your child's forehead, and run it occasionally over the back of the neck. Make up an ice pack by tying ice into a T-shirt. Monitor pulse rate and if you have packed a thermometer, measure temperature. Give cool drinks and check the temperature continuously until it lowers to 37.5–38°C. You should then stop cooling as you may risk your child becoming too cold.

If the temperature has reached more than 40°C and you feel that your child needs medical attention, call a doctor.

If your child begins to lose consciousness, place them in the recovery position and check breathing. If breathing stops, begin artificial respiration (see page 280) and get help urgently.

In milder cases, Calpol may help to lower temperature and relieve headache.

HEAT EXHAUSTION

Unacclimatised children will lose a lot of salt in their sweat and can become salt-depleted during the first few days of their holiday, leading to 'salt depleted' heat exhaustion. Even following acclimatisation, 'water depleted' heat exhaustion may occur if your child does not have plenty to drink.

Symptoms
Fatigue, weakness, headache, nausea and sometimes vomiting. Muscle cramps are a distinctive sign that the body is salt depleted. Excessive thirst and dehydration clearly indicate that your child needs fluids.

Prevention
- Do not prevent children from adding salt to their foods. Allow them to eat crisps, pretzels and other salted snacks.
- They must also be given adequate water to drink to balance the salt intake. Ensure your child has plenty to drink throughout the day.
- Never embark on long walks or journeys without fresh water.
- Be aware that children will lose more fluid in less humid enviroments and at high altitude. They may not feel too hot but still need plenty of fluids.

What to do
If your child shows symptoms of salt depletion – headache, fatigue, muscle weakness – treat them with oral rehydration salts (see page 226). Mask the flavour with juice.

Give plenty of bottled or boiled water.

PRICKLY HEAT (HEAT RASH)

On my first trip abroad I suffered agony with prickly heat. It was in northern France in moderate temperature, but was the first time my pale skin had seen much sun and I burned slightly. This pain settled quickly but was replaced by tiny, raised lumps and an agonising, prickly itchiness all over my chest and shins that forced me to literally tear off the top layers of skin with my nails. It kept me awake for two whole nights and, as I was with a friend and her family, I felt bound not to complain.

The next time I felt the signs stirring was in Crete. This time, instead of scratching, I splashed my chest with cold water and it never developed to the stage of misery. It was four years later that I realised that I had been suffering from a condition called prickly heat that is caused by excess perspiration trapped under the skin.

- If your child presents with a 'heat rash' of tiny, raised pimples, do everything you can to prevent them scratching. It will make it worse.
- Splash the area with cold water.
- Pat dry (do not rub the area).
- Dab with Calamine to stop the itching.
- If symptoms are severe, a product containing camphor and antihistamines will provide relief.

SUNBURN

Sunburn is something about which there is high public awareness. Severe skin damage as a result of overexposure to the sun early in life may predispose your child to skin cancer later. You must pay overzealous attention to protecting your children from burning.

- Burning is more severe when the sun is at its most intense. This is when it is directly overhead (around midday).
- The sun is more intense closer to the equator in the tropics and can burn the skin in minutes.
- Reflected sunlight from water, sand and snow can burn, even if a child remains in the shade.
- When skiing, reflected sunrays can burn the inside of the nose.
- Sun penetrates clouds.
- Sensitive skin can burn through light clothing.

Avoiding sunburn

- Cover babies and children with sunscreen whenever they are exposed to the sun. Do not expose infants to direct sunlight for any length of time. Use parasols or shade, even for very short walks, when the sun is high.
- Use the highest factor sunscreen available and reapply regularly. Do not apply too thickly.

  NB: For babies and small children who are not in and out of the water swimming, it is unnecessary to use waterproof creams. They have a high fat content and, when applied too thickly, interfere with sweating, heat loss and act as an insulator. This increases the risk of heatstroke in infants (see page 193).
- Protect a baby's scalp with a hat (preferably one that also protects the back of the neck) or suncream. A child with thin hair will burn on their parting or through their hair.
- Protect the soles of the feet with shoes. They will burn.
- Apply sunscreen to the tops of the ears. They burn easily and are a very common position for skin cancer.
- Keep T-shirts on children, even when swimming.

Treatment

Resting, drinking plenty of water and paracetamol for the pain will relieve mild sunburn. Soothing antiseptics containing zinc oxide (e.g. Sudocrem) will help.

Products containing camphor have a cooling effect, and Calamine lotion is soothing. Antihistamines may help and, if the pain and irritation is preventing sleep, a dose of Phergan (promethazine) will be of great benefit.

In more severe cases

Leave blisters alone. They may become infected if burst.

If burns are very severe, a doctor may suggest the use of steroid cream with antibacterial action.

SWIMMING ABROAD

In many parts of Africa, an accidental topple into a lake can infect you with a parasitic illness, so if this does happen, dry your children off vigorously straight away. Always tell older children to keep their mouths tightly closed if they do fall in any fresh water. Many civilisations in the developing world use the river for all their ablutions while others are heavily polluted.

Many doctors advise mothers not to even take their babies swimming in the UK before three months of age. It would seem logical, therefore, that if you have the strength and the inclination to travel with such a tiny baby, you should keep them out of foreign swimming pools.

Many diseases are transmittable in pools which are insufficiently chlorinated or cleaned and so, even when travelling abroad to visit family or friends where you can guarantee levels of hygiene, avoid taking a very young baby into the pool. As you may have already read, President Roosevelt contracted polio in his own swimming pool and was crippled for life. Closer to home, an air stewardess told me that she's certain that the hepatitis A she suffered from for months was due to a brief swim in the pool on a stopover in Mexico.

Be stringent. If you take your tiny baby for a dip in the pool, ensure that he doesn't swallow any water by keeping the head out and cleansing the hands immediately afterwards.

It is debatable whether or not you are often better swimming in the open sea than in hotel swimming pools from the hygiene aspect. My mum swears that whenever we swam in the sea off Abersoch, North Wales as children, we were all sick. Many beaches around the world are heavily polluted, particularly in Europe. You would imagine that the Pacific would be too vast to harbour bugs in a high enough concentration to cause infection but in Lima, the capital of Peru, some years ago, a cholera outbreak was thought to have come from the ocean.

The waters off heavily populated cities or holiday resorts – such as those in Spain when the entire coastline is a mass of tourist resorts bordering tourist resorts for hundreds of miles – are potentially polluted and contaminated with infective illnesses. In the Caribbean or South Seas, where coastal towns are few and relatively small, the sea is unlikely to become a risk.

The other concern, of course, is precautions against drowning. Listen to the locals and ask where they take their children to swim. Look for beaches with families on them and not just windsurfers. Find out about currents and tides if you are straying off the usual tourist beaches. A child can drown in two inches of water. Most drownings occur less than two metres from safety.

Teach your child to swim as early as possible but even when they are competent swimmers, do not let them swim unsupervised. Discourage them from diving into water. A number of casualties break their necks diving into swimming pools in the UK every year. In rivers and lakes, unseen rocks can do untold damage. Ask anybody who speaks English if there are any dangerous sea creatures or coral reefs in shallow water. Coral cuts can be nasty.

Bilharzia is a very real risk in tropical areas and is spread by contact with fresh water in lakes and rivers. However, once diagnosed it can be effectively treated with a single drug dose. Swimming, wading, bathing and even showering in contaminated water can cause infection. If you or your children fall into deep water, towel off thoroughly and quickly. Keep showers short or use a sponge and bucket of boiled water instead (see page 252).

With or without a nappy?
Without. Being in the water seems to suppress the baby's toilet reflexes to a degree and, even if this were not the case, you can buy a range of swimsuits that double up as nappies.

ARRIVING AT HIGH ALTITUDE

At high altitudes the air becomes 'thin', cold and dry. The low concentration of oxygen in the 'thin' atmosphere does affect most people to a lesser degree.

It is likely that the more severe signs people develop are caused by failed and exaggerated responses to a lack of oxygen. Approximately 50 per cent of people who ascend to altitudes of 3,500 m and above, suffer from acute mountain sickness (AMS) and a few are at serious risk from the complications of pulmonary oedema and cerebral oedema, both of which can be fatal. As age increases, the risk of AMS decreases, which unfortunately means that your children are at greater risk than yourself. Whereas you may just feel a little lethargic, they might be suffering from a whole range of symptoms. The other problem is that it is largely unpredictable who will suffer from AMS and it often bears little relation to physical fitness. Strapping healthy soldiers, accustomed to carrying 60lb backpacks, can keel over and be unable to get up because of the severity of their symptoms, yet frail, elderly ladies can be fussing over them and skipping around.

When I have been at altitude, I have noticed a few patterns and, although I have been unable to find proof in any medical text books or clinical papers, it appears that there might be a genetic predisposition to the condition. On a number of occasions, I have observed mothers and daughters or siblings suffering exactly the same symptoms together. Therefore, if you or your partner suffers from AMS, it is possible that your child will suffer too, and to a greater extent. There is some evidence that young children are particularly susceptible to pulmonary oedema, therefore, if your child is unwell, you should descend to a lower altitude and give them more chance to acclimatise. Children do acclimatise more quickly than adults.

Surprisingly, asthmatic children are not considered to be more prone to AMS than any other child. This may be a function of the lack of pollutants and causative elements in the fresh, mountain air but the low temperatures could precipitate an attack. Every parent of an asthmatic child must ensure they carry enough medication for a trip, whether travelling at altitude or not.

AVOIDING AMS

- Speed of ascent is an important factor. The faster you climb, the more likely you are to suffer from AMS. When aiming for altitudes above 3,000 m the ascent should be limited to 300 m per day, with a rest every third day, to minimise the risk of AMS developing. Driving or flying directly into altitudes over 3,500 m should be avoided if possible.
- Strenuous exercise should be avoided. Exertion predisposes to AMS. Your child should be allowed to rest regularly, before they need to.
- Take light meals. Adults should avoid alcohol.

Very high altitudes can be attained with children but to be safe, take your time, go gradually and, if your child is unwell, descend to a lower altitude without delay.

Symptoms
Symptoms rarely begin immediately on arrival at high altitude but generally develop after a day or two. In the majority of

people, AMS may be a miserable condition but it is trivial and passes quickly.

On arrival, the sufferer might feel light-headed, weak and notice a change in breathing patterns after otherwise feeling perfectly fit. Lethargy begins after a few hours and there will be difficulty sleeping. Sleep is disturbed and there is irregular breathing during sleep. On waking, there is a headache which is not helped by pain killers. Keeping on the feet causes dizziness and perhaps loss of balance. Nausea and perhaps vomiting might ensue.

After rest, the symptoms should disappear. If not, you should descend at least 500 m. Dangerous symptoms include a significant increase in breathing and breathlessness at rest with frothy sputum. These are signs of pulmonary oedema. Cerebral oedema is illustrated by incoherence, confusion, drowsiness, unsteady walking, personality changes and irrational behaviour which can progress to coma.

The condition is very hard to diagnose in young children. Even local doctors will be unable to positively confirm the condition, unless it becomes obvious by the fact that as soon as your child descends again, all their symptoms disappear. Look out for irritability, apathy, increased breathing and loss of appetite without a high temperatures. However, any significant signs of illness should be taken as warning signs and you should descend.

What to do?

If you all have minor symptoms, then just take it easy and allow your body to adjust naturally to your environment. Gradually your blood will build up its oxygen-carrying capacity by increasing the proportion of red blood cells and you will all acclimatise until you feel as fit and healthy as the natives.

When I visited Cuzco in Peru, our hotel welcomed us all with a cup of coca tea. This local remedy is deemed to be very effective. Coca tea contains tiny amounts of cocaine which acts as a central stimulant and so helps combat the fatigue many people feel when they first arrive at altitude. Coca leaves also suppress appetite and help abate the nausea. The minuscule amount of cocaine in tourist tea is barely efficacious but still cannot be recommended for children. The best remedy is rest. You could try paracetamol elixir but don't be surprised if the headache doesn't disappear. In mild cases, paracetamol and rest are enough. If not, the sufferer must descend.

Other concerns when trekking or skiing at high altitude

Radiation
With altitude, radiation levels increase. You must pay strict attention to applying sunscreen and be aware that snow, like water, reflects the sun's rays and so the intensity is greater. Burning can be severe, even in very cold conditions.

Dryness
Ensure that you all drink plenty of fluids. At altitude, the dry conditions mean that you lose moisture as you breathe, despite the cold. You should therefore ensure that dehydration does not occur. This naturally would be more likely to occur if complicated with vomiting due to AMS.

ARRIVING IN THE COLD

Newborn babies cannot shiver and so are very vulnerable to low temperatures. Infants are prone to hypothermia in cool surroundings that would pose no threat to an adult. Children, too, are much more susceptible to the cold. They lose heat more rapidly because of their shape and the fact that they have relatively low levels of insulating fat stored under their skin. In fact, cold is more of a danger to children than heat and possibly harder for an adult to judge. We might not feel particularly chilly and so assume our children are comfortable when they might feel as if they are freezing. Toddlers and small children will often rely on you to provide the right environment and do not have the understanding or the vocabulary to express how cold they are. Even six-year-olds may not turn round to you and say, 'I'm cold.' It is left for you to guess. Older children are more insistent in their demands but are still very vulnerable.

When Paris was three years old, we spent Christmas in Munich. It was very sunny but very cold when the sun went in. We took him to the zoo on Christmas Day and, although the air felt crisp and fresh to us, Paris was very quiet and showed little interest. After an hour of walking around, he asked, 'Shall we go back home to the hotel?'. At the windy bus stop he said, 'Can we get a taxi?' yet he never once shivered or told us he was cold.

From Munich, we went by train on to Salzburg where the mountain air was very dry and colder. Paris had developed a cough and when I tried to buy him coke in the buffet car, the German man behind the bar told me off and insisted I buy orange juice.

We checked into a hotel in Salzburg then went out for the rest of the day. Although Paris was really well wrapped-up, he was immobile in his trolley. He kept pleading with us to carry him or let him walk but we judged he was being awkward and forced him into his buggy. We stayed out all day, then in the evening walked around looking at the Christmas lights and eating hot dogs. Paris was very quiet. He just sat in his buggy, silent and still. His face looked warm and although we kept asking him again and again if he was cold, he would just complain about his hands, which we would then warm up.

When we arrived back in the hotel room, Paris just flopped on the bed. As I undressed him, he began to warm up. He turned from blue-white to bright pink and began to rage with a fever. The skin all over his bottom was mottled and chapped. On hindsight, I realise that he must have been freezing. He had been so quiet and miserable which is so unlike him. He was expressing himself so well at three years old that I was sure he would have told me when he felt cold. He was in a roundabout way, but he didn't have the understanding to say, 'Mummy, I'm freezing cold', and because I was walking and warm, I didn't appreciate how cold he had been until afterwards.

He was very ill that night and I hardly slept. He had an infection too, but the intense cold must have lowered his defences and his temperature raged. I still get pangs of guilt when I remember him lying limp on the hotel bed. His little chapped bottom where his blood must have been stagnant against the cold trolley broke my heart.

HYPOTHERMIA

If your child becomes very cold they may become hypothermic which is very dangerous. Hypothermia is very serious because it slows down the functioning of all the body's organs. If the body temperature drops low enough, the organs will stop working and this will be fatal. It is clinically defined as a deep body temperature below 35°C.

Wet and windy conditions are when you are most at risk but as I learnt from experience, even when you feel warm, your child may be losing heat fast. Hypothermia can develop in children after even what we consider to be mild exposure to the cold.

Hill walkers, climbers and skiers are at all risk from hypothermia and frostbite if their clothing is insufficient. Inactivity in the cold makes a child more susceptible.

Symptoms

The symptoms that an older child has hypothermia are usually obvious. They are likely to be shivering, pale and blue. They will be listless, lethargic, confused and quiet.

Babies, who cannot shiver, and small children are harder to judge because their faces may be bright red and they will look warm (as was the case with Paris). They will not complain of the cold but will be quiet, listless and lethargic. The only real way of confirming hypothermia is by taking a child's temperature. Breathing may be slow and, in severe cases, your child may start to lose consciousness.

Prevention

- Irrespective of the level of latitude, the temperature falls by approximately 1°C for every 150 m rise above sea level. If you are planning a trek or a journey or even just a day's excursion into mountainous regions, you must take warm clothing. No matter how hot it is at sea level, it will be several degrees colder at altitude.

- A child who is immobile is especially at risk. If they are being carried or are inactive in a trolley, buggy or backpack, they will get very cold. If a child pleads with you to let them walk, don't make the same mistake as I did. Do allow them to rejuvenate their extremities. An active child is much better able to keep warm.

- Take a warm jumper for each child with you everywhere, especially at night or out on a boat.

- Take a waterproof raincoat or change of clothing if rain is even a remote possibility.
- Good shoes are another essential.
- Never forget that even if you feel warm your child is at risk from hypothermia in cold conditions.

This was part of our problem when Paris suffered mild hypothermia in Salzburg. He had been desperate to walk because he knew he would feel better but things were complicated by the fact that his shoes were totally unsuitable. There was snow on the ground and Paris had on light summer shoes. This may sound neglectful but between the ages of 18 and 40 months, Paris was fanatical about what went on his feet. He refused to wear anything except one familiar pair of shoes that we had to keep buying in a bigger size. Apparently, this is not uncommon in boys and, up until our trip to Austria in winter, had not really caused much of a problem. Unfortunately that day it did. If he had been wearing wellies, I would have let him walk and he would never have become so cold. As soon as he felt better, we took him in to a shoe shop in Austria where he lay on the floor kicking, struggling and screaming hysterically. It took three of us to pin him down and force a pair of warm shoes on to his feet.

Treatment

Get your child out of the cold, even if means knocking on a stranger's door. An obviously sick child will break the barriers of language and race wherever you are in the world.

Warm your child by wrapping him in dry clothing or blankets. Older children can be given warm drinks and a warm bath. Skin temperature is a good indicator that your child is recovering but if possible continue to take his or her temperature.

Allow your child to rest in a warm bed but don't allow your child to sleep until you are certain the body temperature has risen and he is more alert and breathing properly.

10 Nutrition and Hygiene

Children will often suffer a loss of appetite on arrival into a strange environment. Jet lag, excitement, heat and unfamiliar foods all contribute. You should never worry; they won't let themselves starve.

FEEDING BABIES ABROAD

I have always found feeding babies abroad no more or less difficult than feeding them at home. You still need to sterilise bottles, boil water to mix with milk or powdered foods and follow all the rules you have been adhering to since birth. Where's the difference?

If you are having to prepare milk feeds, a room with a refrigerator is a distinct advantage. A minibar is a useful alternative. Budge up the beers and move in the bottles.

If you have forgotten your travel kettle and there isn't one in your room, then try to persuade reception to lend you one. If not, go out and buy one with a local plug on. It will be well worth the money.

It is too risky to travel far from the hotel with ready-mixed bottles of milk in warm weather. This is when ready-made formula milk in cartons is a godsend. The alternative is to take a sterilised bottle of plain, boiled water and carry the dry milk powder separately, but pre-measured, in a small plastic container or bag. Do not mix them before you travel but as you need them.

If the bottle is made fresh on the move with water you have boiled yourself that morning, it will be safe and your baby will never be at risk. The worst scenario is that your baby will have to drink a bottle of cold milk. Your baby might kick up a bit of a fuss if not used to it, but will soon take it if hungry enough.

If you have no boiled water left, then any shop or restaurant serving coffee or tea should be able to give or sell you some. This will also be useful to heat jars or bottles for a feed. As a precaution, sterilise the bowls, spoons and training cups as well as the bottles in areas where you would not drink the water.

Buy local fruit with protective skins for extra vitamins. A banana is easily mashed and prepared. Mango, pawpaw, guava and other tropical fruits are easy to squash to baby food consistency with a fork but buy them and prepare them yourself.

Even on the breakfast table, fruit could have been handled or washed in local water. You need to peel the fruit yourself and take care not to contaminate the flesh of the fruit when you are peeling it. I always clean the fruit's skin with a baby wipe first.

On the move, take a jar of sweet baby food and a spoon with you wherever you go. It is more likely to be eaten than savoury if there is nowhere to heat it.

From around eight months old, you will be able to find food in restaurants to feed your baby even if it is only the bread roll. Most good and obliging restaurants can usually supply one or more of the following, even if it isn't on the menu:
- Eggs prepared fresh and well done either as omelette, scrambled or boiled.
- Chips.
- Fresh rice. In Asia you will often be offered honey sauce to pour over your baby's rice but Western guidelines advise that honey should not be given to children under one year because of a slight risk of botulism poisoning.
- Noodles or Pasta.
- Some form of local bread, pitta, naan, chapatti, ciabatta, etc.
- Fresh whole fruit for you to peel yourselves.

FEEDING CHILDREN LOCAL FOOD

Children who are introduced to different foods early on develop a much broader range of tastes than those who eat one brand of white, sliced bread all their lives out of habit.

Japanese children aren't born liking sushi and seaweed, nor are all Indian children born liking curry and rice. What they grow up liking to eat depends on parental influences, available foods and perhaps, as has recently been suggested, what their mothers ate while they were in the womb or while they were breast-feeding.

A toddler or small child is just as likely to eat something you give to him abroad for the first time as anything new at home.

You will need to be careful what you feed your children but try to persuade them to try different things. Be wary of the high-risk foods highlighted below, but enjoy the fun of discovering different cuisines together. If you are in a local restaurant and thrown by the menu, ask one of the locals or waitresses what they would order for their children. You don't need to speak the language; a few shrugs and a finger pointed at the menu, then your child will usually get the message over.

Wherever you are you will be able to find something that your child will eat and probably enjoy. Paris is so fussy and so stubborn with what he is prepared to eat that I had to have a repeat appointment with the health visitor because he only weighed 22 lbs at his three-year check. At nursery, they stopped trying to feed him and asked me how I coped. Now at pre-school, in spite of my objection, he is regularly made to sit on his own on a 'naughty chair' in a corner of the school dining room for refusing to eat or even try his lunch. He won't eat sandwiches, hamburgers, potatoes, cheese, beans, ketchup, biscuits or even chocolate.

I try never to make a fuss and when he gets hungry enough, he will totally surprise me by eating satay with peanut sauce, garlic, chilli, noodles or black tiger prawn tempura off my plate. Even the fussiest children will find something to eat when they need to. I rarely order anything separate for him but order something for myself that he might like. This saves waste, money and frustration.

A phrase book or dictionary is pretty essential when travelling with children, just in case you have to explain to a doctor the symptoms of an illness. It will help in restaurants too, although you probably won't need it. Even in the depth of Central and South America there is usually someone who knows a few words of English and you will be amazed at how many restaurants in the tiniest corners of the world have menus in English. Even without any help, pasta, pizza, paella, roti, taco and teriyaki are similar in any language.

When ordering from a menu, deep-fried foods cooked through and eaten piping hot are generally safe including chips, spring rolls, fish, meats or vegetables in batter or breadcrumbs. Hot oil can reach temperatures of more than 180°C, well above that needed to kill any living organisms. Small pieces of meat basted with the local flavours of peanut, coconut, soy sauce or sweet sake on a skewer such as satay, kebabs or yakitori are easy to cook through well and generally fine unless they were precooked (they will then be dry and much tougher).

Local bread, pancakes or dry patties made from wheat or corn flour will be filling and nutritious. Children will usually eat noodles made from wheat or rice flour fresh from boiling hot soup stocks. In many countries of the world, the staple foods are rice and fresh fish which, if freshly and well cooked, will invariably be safe. Some large fish can accumulate toxins in their livers and occasionally their flesh, especially if harvested from the ocean during a red tide, which occurs when the sea becomes so full of plankton that it actually looks red. Fish and shellfish feed on this plankton and the toxin gets into their flesh. If it is then eaten, it can cause potentially fatal poisoning. However, you are just as likely to suffer if you buy sea bass, parrot fish or snapper in the UK where it will have been imported by air from all around the world.

In Japan the delicacy of Fugu (puffer fish) kills three to four Japanese diners every year but it is so expensive you would be unlikely to feed it to your children anyway, even if there wasn't the chance of it killing them. I tried one little piece once when I was being entertained in Japan and it really isn't delicious enough to risk your life for.

Yoghurt is usually OK because it is full of harmless bacteria that inhibit the growth of food-poisoning bacteria.

Local fruits which you peel yourself will give your children plenty of vitamins and natural sugars. Pawpaw, pineapple, mango and banana always taste so much better in the sun.

THE ROLE OF FOOD AND DRINK IN SPREADING ILLNESS

Certain foods are judged as high risk because of the likelihood that they will harbour bacteria and viruses that can cause illness. Even if your children have been vaccinated against hepatitis, typhoid and cholera, it is still important for you to avoid these foods and pay rigorous attention to what they drink.

Most of the foods will be no surprise to you but it can be difficult to convince a screaming, hot child that a cool ice cream could make him severely ill. However, try to explain and if necessary tell them 'the secret' that there are lots of little germs jumping around inside the ice cream and even the man selling it doesn't know.

Remember that most foods have the potential to cause illness if they have been contaminated by handling or flies and dust while sitting around uncovered in warm temperatures. Bacteria need food, water, warmth and time to proliferate. Once they are transferred on to moist food, bacterium multiply every fifteen to twenty minutes so that each individual bacterium has the potential to become 1,048,576 in five hours. In contrast, food which has been thoroughly cooked at a high enough temperature and for long enough, then served fresh and eaten piping hot, is virtually guaranteed to be safe, even those deemed as being high risk. While travelling, you will not be able to control the cooking methods and standards of hygiene, so you must choose your restaurant prudently and then select carefully from the menu. If you are uncomfortable about the standard of the food or the temperature at which it is served, send it back. This can be difficult, especially for the polite British, but otherwise, don't eat it.

The number of stars a hotel has for luxury and facilities is no measure of kitchen cleanliness. Remember our cricket team in India? They ate prawns in one of the best hotels in India and were all poisoned so severely that the game had to be cancelled. Even five-star hotels still need to depend on local suppliers and staff who may have low standards of hygiene. It only takes one trainee chef not to wash his hands properly to cause catastrophe. The same problem can occur on cruise ships. Cruise ship kitchens are invariably obsessively clean. However, they depend on produce supplied at the ports and a multitude of staff. If any of the staff are not vigilant with their personal hygiene and are themselves unknowingly disease carriers, they could give rise to an outbreak of giardiasis, hepatitis or E. coli poisoning. So even when cruising with children, it is important to choose the ship and the ports of call carefully.

The sneaky thing about all the bugs pathogenic in man is that they never give themselves away until they are inside your stomach. There is no smell or change in the appearance or the taste of the food. This is, of course, how they have remained so successful in spreading themselves. Food-poisoning bacteria, for example, Salmonella spp. and E. coli, are very different from the food spoilage bacteria that alter the smell, colour and texture of foods and make them taste rotten. Food will still smell and taste delicious while teeming with virulent sickness and diarrhoea-inducing organisms.

Spices and chilli can hide the flavour of rotting meat but they will not defend you against illness. Chilli itself can be an irritant and cause diarrhoea which is distinguishable from early infection by its burning sensation.

Don't become paranoid. Eating local food is one of the pleasures of every holiday but be informed and be careful.

HIGH RISK FOODS

Unpasteurised (unboiled) milk
Unpasteurised milk and cheese made from it can transmit diarrhoeal illnesses, tuberculosis, listeriosis and brucellosis. It should therefore be avoided. This includes milk and cheese from cows, sheep, goats or even more exotic animals such as yaks.

Ice cream
Ice cream is often made from unpasteurised milk or contains some local water. Freezing does not effectively kill the bugs that can cause illness and, in some parts of the world, including many exotic islands, there are frequent power cuts during which freezer contents defrost and bacteria are free to multiply. The ice cream will refreeze when the power is returned but will be even more potentially toxic than before.

Cream

Like milk and ice cream, cream may harbour any number of proliferating bacteria if it is not pasteurised then kept sufficiently cool. Fresh cream cakes are often responsible for food poisoning, even in the UK, which is why local summer school fêtes no longer accept cream cakes on their stalls.

Salads, vegetables and fruit

All are potential sources of infection as there is a good chance they will have been washed in local water before they get to the table. Even before preparation, there is every likelihood that they will have been contaminated during transit, storage or even while growing. In some parts of the world, human faeces is used as fertiliser for growing crops, including the innocent strawberry. Unless the produce is carefully washed with purified water, illness is a certain consequence for the unlucky consumer.

Seafood

Shellfish are renowned for their disease-harbouring qualities. The method in which they feed by filtering vast amounts of sea water ensures that if there are any nasty bugs floating around in the water, they are likely to collect in the shellfish and even proliferate, drawing their own nutrition from the filth filtered by their host. Shellfish often thrive near open sewers and in water contaminated with human excrement. Lobsters collect on the seabed around the effluence and feed on the debris. Severe illnesses including cholera and hepatitis plus many other diarrhoeal illnesses are spread in this way. Steaming seafood is not sufficient. The only defence is thorough cooking. In addition to causing infection, eating seafood harvested on the red tide can result in poisoning (see page 210).

Eggs

Raw or lightly cooked eggs and products made from them, for example, custard, mousse and mayonnaise, can be responsible for food poisoning anywhere in the world, not just in the UK. The American love of coleslaw means that in many parts of the world a dollop is often added to your order, whatever it is. Coleslaw and potato salad containing fresh mayonnaise are more likely to cause diarrhoeal illness than a regular salad.

Sauces

Many fancy sauces contain cream, lightly cooked eggs, reheated meat or chicken stock. The low temperatures required to cook a sauce for a short time will not kill bacteria.

Chicken

Salmonella is not just a problem on the surface of cooked chicken. The bacteria can penetrate the muscle of chicken while it is living and so can be present deep in breast meat if it is not cooked thoroughly. The problem is more common in intensively farmed chicken and the old farmyard hen in Peru is less likely to contain salmonella than the one on your supermarket shelf at home. Still, it is important to only eat chicken that is freshly cooked and piping hot.

Meats

The bacteria that thrive and multiply in meat do so mainly on the surface. However pork and beef must be cooked thoroughly to avoid tapeworm infection. Mince, beefburgers and sausages may be contaminated at their core and must be well charred, in and out.

Rice

Rice is a potential hazard. Fresh cooked rice is rarely a problem. However, cooked rice that has been sitting at room temperature for a number of hours might be contaminated with *Bacillus cereus*, which can cause severe vomiting or diarrhoea.

Bacillus cereus is of serious concern to environmental health departments in the UK. Despite this, few people realise that food poisoning after a meal in the local Oriental restaurant is just as likely to be caused by the rice as by the chicken or shellfish.

HIGH RISK DRINKS

Local water

Most travellers now accept that it is foolish to drink the local water and, as a result, diarrhoea and sickness are mainly contracted from food.

Don't be tempted to drink local water, however thirsty you may be, until you have boiled or treated it. Do not use local water for brushing your teeth. I once travelled with a group in Peru who all had mild to moderate stomach upsets, except for just two of us. We had all eaten in the same restaurants but I found out that while the two of us who were symptom-free had both used bottled water to brush our teeth, no one else had. I am certain that this made the difference.

If you are unable to get purified bottled water, local water should be boiled to 100°C for a few minutes. When using a kettle to purify drinking water for myself, I boil it once. If giving it to Paris, I boil it twice. When he was a baby I boiled it three times and although this may appear paranoid, it worked.

Chemical sterilisation is not as effective as boiling and often makes the treated water undrinkable for fussy children. Iodine tablets or drops added to water are fast acting and effective but taste strongly and most young children will refuse to drink it. It is also important to note that there is a risk of damage to unborn foetuses with this form of chemical sterilisation.

NB: It is important to remember that other drinks may be mixed with the local water.

Bottled mineral water
I will never forget the vision of a small boy in India filling used mineral water bottles he had collected with water from a tap in the street. He then carried off the local water to be sold to the unsuspecting as purified mineral water. This is not uncommon in poor countries, when people desperate to make money will sell you anything. Always check that the serrated seal is intact. If you have a choice in a shop or supermarket, buy the most popular brand. They have a reputation to protect.

Ice
Ice is often made from local water and is as hazardous as drinking a cup of water from a tap on the street. You must avoid ice religiously. Many countries do recognise the problem and make ice from purified water. For example, all the good restaurants on the Cayes off Belize are supplied by the same ice manufacturer who uses only purified water. Around the world many good hotels will do the same, but you need to check.

Fruit juices and cocktails
Both may be diluted with local water or contain crushed ice. Even if the juice is made fresh from 100 per cent fruits, there is no guarantee that it was prepared in clean, dry vessels.

Alcohol

Although directly irrelevant to children, they do need you to look after them. Excesses of alcohol can cause diarrhoea all alone, but in some countries the alcohol is diluted by the local water to make more profit or hide the bartender's quick slurps. This is interestingly prevented in Kenya by serving gin from sachets as if it were ketchup!

CHOOSING WHERE AND WHAT TO EAT

Hotel buffets and displayed cooked foods

If food is cooked well, and served and eaten immediately, the chances of infection are minimised.

A hotel buffet supplies food, water, warmth and time, all the optimum conditions for bacterial multiplication. Even if the food has been cooked well initially, it might have been handled and so become contaminated when it was displayed. A perfectly healthy but careless guest could have sneezed on it, spreading *staphylococcus* everywhere, which, given time, will cause havoc.

Flies carry a multitude of bacteria on their hairy legs and, as a fly flits between your hotel buffet and human excrement, it spreads many diseases. Dust and dirt can float bacteria which can comfortably settle on uncovered food.

Most foods, once contaminated, will allow bacteria to live and multiply on them. It is important that you select the hottest, freshest, covered and least-handled dishes on offer. You will be easily able to judge the turnover of food on the buffet. If it is too slow, ask for a well-done omelette or some chips for your children, claiming they are very fussy. Most hotels will oblige.

Choosing a restaurant

Generally, a busy restaurant has a high turnover of food. Theoretically, this means the food will be fresher, although this will depend on the care and skills of the chef at rotating stock and avoiding contamination during preparation and storage.

Restaurants busy with locals are not necessarily a good choice as the indigenous stomach sensitivity will differ greatly from your own.

For some of my time spent in India I was looked after by my friend's brother-in-law. He went to great efforts to ensure I never drank the local water, although he did so himself without any ill effects. He told me that even children who grow up in India must drink bottled water and be careful where they eat when they visit on holiday, 'because their stomachs become soft'.

If you really are floundering, choose a restaurant recommended by your hotel concierge, your tour guide or another tourist. The best option is a restaurant where food is served fresh and not reheated. Reheating foods is commonly the source of diarrhoea and vomiting worldwide, unless they have been pumped with all manner of preservatives and additives, as have our Western, packaged ready meals.

If food is not rewarmed for long enough and the core temperature does not reach high enough levels, bacteria will not only survive but multiply. Many meats such as chicken or shellfish would need to be reheated for so long to cleanse them of bacteria that they would turn to rubber and lose all their nutritional value. It is therefore advisable to avoid reheated foodstuffs altogether if you can.

If you want to find out if a dish is precooked, you should ask if a single ingredient can be missed out, for example, garlic or onion. If the answer is no, it is more likely that the food is precooked. If the dish is being freshly stir-fried or baked, it will be easy to miss out one ingredient.

If the dish you ordered comes to the table lukewarm, don't eat it. Another indication of how fresh food is is how long it takes to arrive. Generally, the longer it takes, the fresher it is.

If you are feeling a little lost, international chains are usually predictable. When I was a university student, I worked in Macdonalds during the summer and know that their hygiene standards are virtually idiot-proof. If I am really unsure where to eat, it really is a good fallback, especially with children. Other chains with worldwide reputations to protect are equally careful. In any city throughout the world there will always be one famous name to opt for as you get your bearings and build your confidence.

Buying food on the move
Most little grocer's shops will have something to offer, even if it is local bread and bananas to make a sandwich.

You will often be amazed to find familiar brands of miniature cheeses, peanut butter, tinned tuna fish, Delmonte fruit juice and crisps in even the remotest corner of a rural community next to the Coca Cola fridge and the Kodak film.

Just follow the rules and, as long as the packaging is intact or, if the produce is fresh, or you are able to peel it, it will be fine. Wet wipes are useful for washing smooth fruits, as well as hands. This will help ensure that you do not contaminate the contents of the fruit as you peel them.

Street stalls may smell delicious if you are hungry, but feeding children from them can never be recommended. No matter how hungry you are, or how good it smells, never eat off train stations. The odds aren't on your side and it isn't worth the risk.

Buying drink on the move

As well as witnessing the young boy in India filling used mineral-water bottles from a tap in the street then trying to sell it, I have also been sold local water in China in a mineral-water bottle. It is very important to check the seal is intact when you buy bottled water. Avoid buying drinks with flip-off bottle tops and corks which can be replaced if removed carefully the first time. Sealed cans are safe, as are bottles of branded drinks.

Check that glasses used are clean and dry. I once bought a bottle of Coke from a street vendor in Thailand and as I stood by drinking it (thankfully from the bottle) he stepped out from behind his stall and did his washing up in a puddle!

Barbecues

Everybody loves barbecues and they are put on for tourists all over the world.

If you attend one, choose the food from the barbecue yourself. Don't let the chef give your children one of the burgers pushed to the edge of the grill that was cooked some time ago. Insist on the freshest and hottest. Check that it has been cooked through and is piping hot in the middle, not just charred on the outside.

Preparation to help avoid the bugs

Since diarrhoea is the most likely problem you will encounter on holiday, you must pay careful attention to avoiding it as far as possible. There can be few things worse than looking after sick children in a hot, strange environment, especially if you are ill yourself after having eaten the same contaminated meal. However, such situations are largely avoidable.

Simple, preconsidered preparation, such as always carrying a snack and drink for your children, will ensure that you don't take unnecessary risks. If you are stuck on a remote train or bus station at mealtime, raisins, bread sticks, crisps, chocolate, glucose tablets or just sweets will take the emergency out of a child's appetite and stop them crying so that you can think clearly enough not to be tempted to risk the hovering street trader's delicious smelling, but infested, offerings.

It is estimated that half of all international travellers suffer from an incidence of diarrhoea every year but rest assured that most cases are mild to moderate, causing discomfort and inconvenience rather than being life threatening. Your children are well nourished and are far better able to fight off bugs than children who are underfed and really at risk. In fact, well-nourished children often shake off diarrhoeal illnesses far better than adults who have been introduced to a bug for the first time.

Children are most at risk of being ill with diarrhoea in between weaning on to solids and three years of age. This is true for all children, whether at home, at nursery, on holiday in their own country or abroad. A child's stomach builds up resistance.

Be careful, not paranoid
On a trip around South America, I met a mother and daughter who spent the entire holiday munching their way through a suitcase full of cream crackers and processed cheese they had taken with them from home. There were approximately 40 of us on the trip and most people suffered minor upsets. Only one of our number was severely ill and he had eaten a meat sandwich bought from a grubby-looking hawker on a Peruvian train station. No one was surprised or sympathetic.

I was more cautious than most. After finding a long, black hair in my meal on a train across the Andes, I refused to eat it. This didn't seem to bother anyone else and no one seemed to suffer any ill effects. I was extra careful for the first few days but slowly gained confidence. I ate well in the hotels recommended by the tour guide and remained perfectly healthy.

The irony was that, after eating just bread, cheese and crackers for three weeks, the mother and daughter were taken out to eat in Buenos Aires by a work contact of the daughter's and she got food poisoning! Perhaps you can be too careful.

11 Avoiding Illness: Diarrhoea and Sickness

PREVENTION IS BETTER THAN CURE

Remember that in most cases, diarrhoea and sickness are avoidable. There is no reason for you to consider that a bout of diarrhoea is an acceptable part of your holiday or refrain from travelling abroad for fear of it.

Understanding how the illnesses are spread is vital, and knowledge of how to cope with your child if he becomes dehydrated may save his life (see page 226).

Diarrhoea is often caused by infection but not always. It can be the result a change of diet, over-excitement, over-indulgence, excess fatty foods or a high mineral content in the local water, all of which can easily upset the unacclimatised stomach and may induce a runny tummy for a few days after you arrive. In these cases, the symptoms will usually pass quickly and there will be no temperature rise.

When the symptoms are caused by an infection, the responsible organism will most commonly be a virus or bacteria (e.g. salmonella). Occasionally, in the tropics, more persistent diarrhoea is caused by little single-celled animals called protozoa (e.g. giardiasis and amoebic dysentery).

Most of the organisms responsible for causing diarrhoea and sickness are predictable in that they have to be swallowed to work their worst and many of the bugs need to swallowed in significant numbers. If you pay careful attention to personal hygiene, what your child eats and drinks and where he swims and bathes throughout your time abroad you should have no problems.

I have travelled all over South and Central America, India, China, South-East Asia and parts of Africa without anything more than minor discomfort. I have fallen seriously ill on holiday three times in my life, once as a child, in Wales and twice as an unsuspecting adult in America!

Letting your guard down

On one of my very first trips abroad to Florida, at the end of a day spent in Disneyworld, I began to feel terrible. It could have been something I ate or caught from contact with one of the multitude in the park.

My now-husband Simon and I arrived late in Daytona and booked into the first motel with rooms free. A notice in reception instructed us that refunds would not be given under any circumstances. I have since grown to appreciate that that notice is usually in keeping with an abundant in-house cockroach population. Even the few snatched minutes of sleep I managed in between violent bouts of illness were disturbed by dreams of cockroaches scuttling across my lips. We moved motels at 7 a.m. the following day.

After three days of vomiting every twenty minutes, day and night, I found a doctor. I felt so ill and miserable when he began to examine me, I burst into tears and began to sob with exhaustion. I had such agonising pains in my stomach that it felt as if the lining had been stripped. He diagnosed gastro-enteritis and prescribed a magic formulae of antibiotics, anti-ulcer drugs and the drug meclopramide to ease the sickness. He brought such relief that I can still remember his face.

The second time I fell ill on holiday was in California, the morning after a day spent in Universal Studios. I lay in the back of a convertible hire car and considered that nothing on earth was more important than health. I couldn't walk or talk without wanting to collapse. Simon set out to find us a room. I remember pointing out a reasonable place to stay, not caring about the cost. He disappeared, checked us in and then helped me to the room. I was violently ill then fell into bed pleading that the curtains be shut tight. I slept for 36 hours.

Both times that I was ill, I had let my guard down. I felt over-confident that the American hygiene standards were high enough for me to eat tepid hot dogs and drink iced sodas. I was wrong! I have had a few other odd days' discomfort in China, Turkey and Japan but they were insignificant compared to my earlier trips.

AVOIDING DIARRHOEA AND SICKNESS

1. Always carry a snack and drink for emergencies to avoid being tempted to take risks when your child is screaming for food or local water. Never feed children with food bought from hawkers on train stations.

2. Always pack wet wipes and use them to cleanse your children's hands thoroughly before eating.

3. Avoid all high risk foods (see page 212), unless you can be absolutely sure that they were hygienically prepared and are thoroughly cooked. Reheated meats and steamed sea food are likely sources of infection.

4. Do not give your child local milk unless you are 100 per cent certain or you boil it yourself.

5. Don't give in to the battle; don't allow your child to eat local ice cream or have ice in their drinks.

6. High prices and plush surroundings are not a measure of cleanliness. You can still be made very ill in the finest hotel restaurant. If your diarrhoea has cost you a small fortune, it will be even more infuriating.

7. At the dining table, ensure all your eating utensils are clean and dry.

8. Don't let children drink the bath water. If you are concerned about the water, drop a few sterilising tablets into a shallow bath.

9. Drink only bottled or boiled water. You must use bottled water for brushing teeth.

10. Public conveniences are horrible places at the best of times. Having been buffeted off a toilet seat in South America by a swarm of flies, then sitting eye-to-eye with a resident tarantula in an Amazon outhouse, I avoid them whenever I can. I think you are often safer wandering off into the jungle. If you do use toilets, don't let children touch anything. Even in hotel or restaurant restrooms, avoid touching the soap, the flushing handle, the taps and even

the door handle. All can spread illnesses. Instead use wet wipes and cleanse their hands thoroughly.

11. Become a veggie for the week.

    Although eating raw vegetables may cause illness, well-cooked vegetables are far less likely to transmit disease than similar dishes containing meat. In diarrhoea hot-spots such as Nepal, Egypt, Peru and India, a diet of local bread, fresh rice and well-cooked vegetables, supplemented by packaged nuts, tofu, chick peas and lentils with a chocolate bribe would be the safest option.

12. Be careful where your child swims. Can you smell chlorine in the pool? It sometimes runs out. Does the pool look clean and well filtered? Filter systems do break down.

13. The sea or ocean off heavily populated cities or crowded holiday resorts is likely to be contaminated with human effluence. The last cholera outbreak in Lima, Peru was thought to have come from the Pacific.

14. Keep children's hands clean and out of their mouths as much as possible. Illness can be caught by sticking dirty fingers in mouths after playing in soil or wet sand, sucking thumbs after crawling across a dirty floor and simply holding hands when playing with local children.

TREATMENT

Don't despair. Most cases of diarrhoea will pass within 48–72 hours without any treatment at all. Thankfully, vomiting usually passes even more swiftly. It is part of your body's natural defences to eliminate a bug, toxin or poison and, although very unpleasant, being sick protects the body by trying to get rid of the problem via its point of entry. Diarrhoea will then take over and flush them out at the other end. In children the combination of vomiting and diarrhoea for longer than 48 hours can lead to severe dehydration which is very dangerous. Small babies can deteriorate much more quickly and become very ill in a matter of hours. Positive steps should be taken to prevent dehydration as soon as the symptoms begin to show. As soon as vomiting and diarrhoea begin:

• Your baby or child must be encouraged to drink plenty of clear fluids. Persuade them to drink slowly and continuously.

- Until vomiting subsides, encourage babies and small children to take the breast or half-strength formula from the bottle, or alternatively, boiled water from a spoon every few minutes. Older children can be offered their favourite drink which should be left by their side for them to drink continuously.
- They may need medication at a later date but although drugs can wait, fluid intake can't.
- If you suspect your child is in danger of becoming dehydrated, begin oral rehydration therapy immediately (see page 226). Rehydration is absolutely crucial and might save your child's life. Even illnesses as aggressive as cholera and typhoid can be thwarted by oral rehydration therapy.

Every local population will have their own local panacea which is often in line with the strain of bug you are most likely to be coping with. I have heard remedies as diverse as salted, fresh mango juice and Coca-Cola mixed with fresh, grated ginger. There is logic in most of them.

There is some controversy as to whether sweet, fizzy drinks are a good idea when a child is suffering from diarrhoea and vomiting but Beechams seem to think Lucozade does the trick. As fizzy drinks are acidic, they may not be very gentle on an upset stomach but they are not very gentle on the bugs either who are already being attacked by the stomach's natural acid.

If a child is in danger of dehydrating, anything they will drink plenty of, whether it be water, juice, fizzy drinks, green tea, clear soup or fresh coconut 'milk' will be a life saver. It is the quantity that is important. If a child can tolerate and keep down sweet drinks, they will help. Water is absorbed from the gut into the bloodstream much more easily and efficiently in the presence of sugar. The only drink to avoid is milk but this will probably be swiftly returned if you attempt to give it anyway.

If your child feels like eating, let them. There is no benefit to withholding food if your child is hungry. If your child is taking in fluid steadily, don't force them to drink more.

As the appetite begins to return, avoid fatty foods but try giving dry biscuits or toast, possibly some dry cereal, and slowly reintroduce their favourite foods. They will soon be scampering around again.

LOOKING FOR SIGNS OF DEHYDRATION

In children under eighteen months old, you will be able to gauge whether or not they are becoming dehydrated by their fontanelle (soft spot) on the crown of their head. If it is sunken, your baby is dehydrated and you must start oral replacement therapy immediately then seek medical help.

For babies and children, check the inside of your child or baby's mouth and tongue. If it is dry, your child might be becoming dehydrated. Headaches and dark, infrequent passages of urine are potentially dangerous signs.

If your child takes on a sunken appearance around the eyes and if you are able to detect a looseness of the pinched skin, your child needs hospital treatment and will probably require urgent intravenous fluid replacement.

Oral Rehydration therapy

This is not a drug or medicine but is a calculated balance of salt and sugar which, when mixed with water, as per instructions on the packet, will help combat severe dehydration.

Oral replacement salt sachets or effervescent tablets are available commercially as Rehydrat or Dioralyte. These can be found on the shelves of virtually every chemist in the UK in a whole range of flavours. Less expensive alternatives are obtainable but in fewer pharmacies. They may taste awful when you are healthy but when your body is depleted of sugar or salts they can taste like nectar.

If you haven't packed any, or it has disappeared in between hotels, you may be able to buy some locally. If not, you can make up a substitute yourself that will be just as efficient and much less expensive. In scientific terms, the ratio of salt to sugar is 1:8 level teaspoons per litre of safe, boiled water. That is, measure a litre of boiled water and add one level teaspoon of salt plus eight level teaspoons of sugar. Water is absorbed from the gut into the bloodstream much more easily and efficiently in the presence of sugar. Fluid replacement alone is often insufficient. Salts and sugars must be replaced too.

Persuade your child to drink slowly and continuously.

Remember, even life-threatening fluid loss and dehydration caused by cholera which would otherwise need intravenous fluid replacement can be avoided if oral rehydration treatment is started early enough.

GETTING MEDICAL HELP

If the illness doesn't abate, seek medical help where possible.

Describe to the doctor how the illness started, anything your child may have eaten that could have been the source of infection, and the stools' characteristics. If they contain blood, don't forget to mention it. All details will help the doctor judge what treatment to prescribe. If the doctor prescribes an antibiotic, you must complete the full, prescribed course unless the symptoms worsen or your child suffers side effects.

In some parts of the world, a doctor may also prescribe an antidiarrhoeal medicine such as Lomotil or Imodium. These should not be given to children under four years old or if there is blood and mucus in the stools.

OUTSIDE THE REACHES OF MEDICAL HELP:
TREATING YOUR CHILDREN WITH MEDICATION

It is estimated that 30 per cent of cases of travellers' diarrhoea are caused by a virus called rotavirus. This bug is also known as the 'infantile gastro-enteritis virus'. It exists all over the world and is endemic in most countries. Your child is as likely to catch it at home or at nursery school as when holidaying in an exotic country. Rotavirus is thought to be responsible for 20–30 per cent of cases of diarrhoea and vomiting in the UK in winter in children between three months and three years. It also affects many adults.

This particular diarrhoeal illness can start with mild upper respiratory tract symptoms and it is possible that it is passed on by coughing or sneezing at this stage. This makes it much harder to avoid as it can be passed on in the street or in a crowded theme park.

Viruses are associated with watery diarrhoea of abrupt onset, often preceded or accompanied by vomiting that is normally self-limiting with a peak incidence in children at 12–18 months. There may be a rise in temperature, but not necessarily. The incubation period is two to three days and generally the disease lasts two to three days.

If you suspect the cause of the illness is viral, you should not give an antibiotic to your child. Intensive rehydration is the essential treatment. The good news is that your child will usually recover more quickly from a viral than a bacterial episode. It is very likely that signs of improvement will start to show after 24 hours. Paracetamol will help ease headache, aching limbs and stomach and bring temperature down.

Antibiotic treatment: the double-edged sword

If you are unable to get any medical help, you might need to consider administering an antibiotic yourself but be aware that if used incorrectly, they can do more harm than good.

You should not give your child antibiotics until you have seen a doctor unless you are unable to get medical help and:

1. The illness has been prolonged (more than three days in children; five days in adults).
2. There are no signs of the illness abating.
3. If there is a high fever with blood and mucus in the stools.
4. If the symptoms are so severe you suspect your child may be suffering from cholera or typhoid.

The reasons that you should avoid giving antibiotics initially are as follows:

1. If the illness is being caused by a virus, antibiotics will be useless.
2. If you give your child antibiotics blindly, without being sure which bacteria are causing the illness, you could give the wrong one. If the problem bacteria are not sensitive to the antibiotic you choose to give, you will worsen the situation. The problem bacteria will continue to flourish, building up resistance while normal, harmless bacterial competition in the gut may be wiped out by the drug.
3. Many antibiotics cause diarrhoea in their own right and so may worsen the situation.
4. In many cases, patients given antibiotic treatment do not recover any more quickly than those given placebo.
5. Using antibiotics incorrectly or for minor illnesses may contribute to an increase in worldwide bacterial resistance. Bacteria are able to communicate resistance between species.

If you go to a doctor and they are able to isolate specific species of bacteria and effectively treat with the antibiotics, the chances of resistance are lowered and the efficacy is increased.

Which antibiotic, if any?

When you visit a doctor and describe the symptoms of the diarrhoea, they will prescribe an antibiotic on a best-guess policy. Only by taking a faecal sample and culturing it will they be able to be sure that the antibiotic they opt for will work.

You might have to do the same.

One of the few antibiotics specifically indicated for gastro-intestinal infection and recommended for use in children is Nalidixic acid. This is available as Negram suspension or tablets in the UK. The drug should not be given to infants less than three months old.

Co-trimoxazole is effective against a wide range of pathogens including many that infect the gut.

DIARRHOEAL ILLNESSES REQUIRING SPECIFIC DRUG TREATMENT

Blood and mucus in the stools (dysentery) should be treated to avoid complications.

Bacterial dysentery

Bacterial dysentery caused by *shigella spp.* is characterised by an explosive onset with high temperature and abdominal pain. Amoxycillin and co-trimoxazole are both effective treatments.

Anti-diarrhoeal drugs must not be used.

Amoebic dysentery (Amoebiasis)

Amoebic dysentery is caused by *entamoeba histolytica*, which has a worldwide distribution. Infection occurs when cysts are passed on in the faeces of a carrier and ingested by a new victim. Once ingested, the cysts 'hatch', live and multiply in the gut, feeding on the natural bacteria there. A large infestation in the gut will result in acute diarrhoea.

Some of the parasites mature in the cells of the gut causing ulceration and necrosis, leading to blood loss and mucus in the faeces. Carriers may never have any symptoms but will pass on the disease. They need to be treated because they are a serious potential source of infection to others.

Metronidazole is the drug of choice when amoebiasis is confirmed.

Giardiasis

If the diarrhoea is persistent, low grade, with foul-smelling and bulky stools, it is likely to be giardiasis. Anorexia, nausea and flatulence are common symptoms.

This illness is caused by infection with a protozoa and is more common in children than in adults, although the symptoms are more severe in those who are infected for the first time in middle or old age. Transmission from one person to another is by ingestion of food and water contaminated with faecal matter containing the cysts. In areas with poor sanitation, the population is often heavily infected.

The symptoms of giardiasis are effectively limited and controlled by treatment with the drug metronidazole. Treatment might need to be prolonged or at least require a second course.

If the illness is prolonged and antibiotics have no effect, you should consider that diarrhoea and vomiting could be a symptom of an illness that needs proper diagnosis and treatment. There is a possibility that your child has acquired an intestinal parasite or is suffering from malaria, Chagas' disease, or schistosomiasis.

ANTI-DIARRHOEAL AGENTS

Do not give children under four years anti-diarrhoeal drugs, including Lomotil or Imodium. These are very effective drugs but paralyse the gut and may cause abdominal distension and even perforation. They also allow the pathogens to linger longer as they will not be flushed out by diarrhoea which is the body's natural defence. The decreased gut motility increases the number of bacteria and may encourage incubation of large numbers of toxin-producing bacteria in the intestines.

The manufacturers of the drugs do recommend them for children over four years old and Imodium is available as a syrup but you need to decide on balance whether or not they are really necessary. Some doctors are firmly opposed to the idea.

Perhaps if you have a long journey ahead, you could administer 5ml of the Loperamide (Imodium) syrup which should be effective for 6–8 hours for children of 4–8 years. The manufacturer's guidelines recommend a maximum of 5 ml, 3–4 times per day for a maximum of three days; children aged 9–12 years might require 10 ml, four times daily for up to five days.

12 Nature's Adversaries and the Diseases They Can Cause

When travelling, you must always put things into perspective and it is important to recognise that your major adversary is the mosquito.

These tiny creatures are the curse of mankind. They transmit many tropical diseases and mosquito bites cause millions of deaths each year. It is estimated that over two million people die each year from malaria. Dengue, yellow fever, encephalitis, and various other parasites are also transmitted by the female as she descends on her human victim to drink the blood she needs to be able to make her eggs.

All other creatures including snakes, spiders and sharks cause an insignificant number of tragedies each year by comparison.

BITING INSECTS
MOSQUITOES

In addition to spreading malaria, yellow fever (see page 154), Japanese encephalitis (see page 139) and the eggs of the horrid Bot fly that hatch into a maggot under the skin, mosquitoes are responsible for Dengue fever and elephantiasis.

Malaria
Malaria is the most common tropical disease. It kills two million people worldwide every year. Those most at risk are children under five years old and pregnant women.

It is caused by the plasmodium parasite that is transmitted to man by the female Anopheles mosquito who must feed on blood to produce her eggs. The parasite invades the red blood cells, eventually causing them to burst. As the parasites multiply in the blood stream, more than half of the red blood cells can be infected and destroyed. The host will become anaemic and characteristically suffer from a pattern of symptoms that every parent should learn to recognise.

Falciparium malaria is more severe because infected blood cells adhere to internal organs. If this occurs in the brain, it may result in coma and death if untreated. It is most common in higher temperatures.

Symptoms
The first signs will be non specific and include headache, vomiting, general malaise, intermittent fever, joint pain, backache and diarrhoea. Often this may be confused with other infections including flu or even food poisoning. A child may seem quiet, uninterested in anything, dejected and miserable.

If the early warning signs go unheeded, after approximately one week, the cycle of typical malaria attacks will occur every 48 hours. They comprise:
(a) A cold stage with rigors and violent shivering. The patient will feel as if they are being plunged into deep icy water.
(b) A hot stage with high temperature and severe headaches.
(c) Profuse sweats as temperature falls.

The abdomen becomes distended over the liver and spleen as the body tries to cope with getting rid of all the burst red blood cells. Complications may include cerebral malaria with fits and coma.

Prevention
Avoiding malaria infection is by drug prophylaxis combined with protection against mosquito bites.

As no anti-malarial drug treatment is 100 per cent effective, minimising the number of mosquito bites your child suffers is just as important as administering the drugs.

Be prepared for a battle when you try to persuade your child to take the tablets. They taste terrible. A crushed tablet in a spoonful of jam may help (for dosage regimes see page 131). The appropriate anti-malarial drug treatment will be dictated by your choice of destination. (see page 113, Figure 2). Chloroquine, Chloroquine plus Proguanil, Mefloquine and/or Maloprim will be indicated in line with up-to-date information.

Chloroquine and Proguanil are both available either on prescription or over the counter. 'Travel foil packs' are double the price for exactly the same number and type of drug. Ask your pharmacist for loose tablets in a bottle if you are confident you will not forget the doses.

Chloroquine: Chloroquine has been available for over 40 years without toxic effects in infants or pregnant women and is considered very safe with few associated adverse effects.

A syrup is available but is bitter and difficult to get down. You will have to try different techniques to see which works best for you. For a child between one and five years, the dose is 15 ml. This will be a battle. You may discover a brief tussle with a spoonful of crushed tablet in jam is better than trying to get three teaspoons full of sticky syrup down.

If I force Paris to take a spoonful of anything, including Calpol or antibiotics, he promptly makes himself sick. As a baby, the only way I could get medicines down him was by disguising them in small portions in a strongly flavoured fizzy drink such as coke or blackcurrant juice. On a trip to Africa when he was three, we had a week of fighting over his daily dose. I then discovered that a spoonful of sugar really does help the medicine go down, and crushed the tablet into white sugar. However, by the third week, and after seeing other, older children popping their tablets into their mouths and swallowing them whole, Paris did the same, happily taking his dosage whole with a drink.

Chloroquine and Proguanil: The combination offers added protection in areas where falciparum malaria shows some resistance to chloroquine alone.

This regime is difficult to give to children because Proguanil must be given every day, there is no syrup available and the tablets taste disgusting. However, there is no record of toxicity in pregnancy or in infants so you can be comforted that you will not be harming your child by forcing them down.

Adverse effects do occur and include nausea and diarrhoea which are less likely if medication is given after a meal. Itching and mouth ulcers may be uncomfortable.

Mefloquine (Larium): In regions of highly chloroquine-resistant falciparum malaria, mefloquine is the recommended drug. The benefit is its once weekly dosage. The negatives are that it is a new drug with more side effects than older treatments and can cause severe toxicity.

Convulsions, coma and psychotic disturbances have been reported. Minor side effects include dizziness, sleep disturbances and thought disorders.

At present, the safety of the drug in pregnancy has not been established because in animal studies very high (near-toxic) doses were shown to have an adverse effect on the developing foetus. It is recommended that you avoid becoming pregnant for three months after the last dose. This is something I have studied in great detail because I fell pregnant while taking Larium.

I had been in South America travelling extensively, with irregular meals and sleep. I had been at different altitudes, levels of latitude, temperatures and levels of sunlight that had turned every cycle of my body into turmoil. The day I returned to my husband, I fell pregnant at a time when I would never had done so under usual circumstances. I always maintain that Paris was determined to be born and he decided when he was coming, outsmarting me in the process.

My body gave me no clear sign that I was carrying a stowaway. Female cycles continued virtually as normal. As the weeks went by, I felt more and more ill and was admitted to hospital twice. No one once suggested I might be pregnant. Eventually I had a scan and discovered I was carrying an eleven-week-old baby. I remember turning to the nurse and saying, 'Well, it can't possibly be alive.' 'Yes,' she said, 'and it is very lively.'

During those eleven weeks, I had drunk alcohol, taken antibiotics, been to the gym, been arrested in Russia and taken Larium. I began to panic. I looked up every drug I had taken and discovered that Larium was strongly contraindicated in pregnancy. The drug was still very new and there was not much information available. After contacting the manufacturers, I became aware of the startling facts that there were approximately 900 recorded pregnancies and of those, 600 had been terminated! This meant I had to make my decision on very scant data. I was reassured by the fact that out of the small number of pregnancies that had gone to term, there had been no strong link of any adverse effect on the foetus.

At the hospital I was offered a termination. I read every clinical trial available and the manufacturers of Larium were very concerned and very helpful. My obstetrician was also very reassuring. I opted to continue my pregnancy with extra monitoring and under close observation. I was worried throughout and never allowed myself to get attached to my baby until he was actually in my arms. Paris was born perfectly healthy and extraordinarily busy.

There is still no conclusive evidence that Larium is safe in pregnancy but there is no longer a contraindication on the data sheet but instead a special precaution. Paris is now a statistic.

Maloprim: Maloprim should only be used when other drug treatments are unsuitable.

Check malaria tablets are not secretly spat out instead of being swallowed.

Protection against mosquito bites

Avoiding mosquito bites may seem like an impossibility but if you do take steps to prevent them you will dramatically reduce the chance of contracting malaria.

The Anopheles mosquito only bites between dusk and dawn and is most active after nightfall. Take precautions to protect yourselves:

1. As evening falls, change your children into long trousers and long sleeves. Ensure that they wear shoes and socks. Mosquito bites are often concentrated around the ankles and feet.
2. Spray repellent containing diethyltoluamide on to the exposed areas of skin and the outside of the clothes, especially around the socks and wrists. I have often been bitten through tight, light clothing and above the sock line under loose trousers.
3. Wearing wrist and ankle bands soaked in diethyltoluamide will mean that less has to be applied to the skin. This is an advantage in children because there have been reports of toxicity following excessive use of repellents.
4. If walking out at night with a baby, you must cover the pram with a fitted net. Fitted insect nets are now also

available to buy for car carrying seats. These are excellent for young babies who may be still sleeping targets.

5. Mosquitoes are attracted by soaps, perfume and shaving lotions. Don't use them at night.

6. The contrast of light clothes is possibly an attraction.

7. Take spray repellent out with you at night. Most preparations wear off after a few hours and need to be topped up. Any persistent mosquitoes are more easy to spray away than swat.

8. Sleep in rooms which are screened. If the rooms cannot be made completely safe from insects, use an impregnated mosquito net (a net doused in insect repellant) tucked in tightly all around under the mattress so that nothing can get under it.

   Kits for impregnating nets are available. One treatment lasts several months. However, impregnated nets are readily available everywhere from travel clinics to shops stocking travel accessories, as well as many high street chemists. The repellent on the nets is much more effective at deterring greedy bugs than the net alone. A determined hungry insect will go to any lengths to get under a net that is not sprayed or already dipped in chemical repellent.

9. Use a knock-down insecticide (even aerosol fly spray will help) sprayed all around the room one hour before bedtime. Do not put a light on early in the room you all intend to sleep in.

10. Use a plug-in vaporiser. Change the tablet each morning and each night to protect from any mosquitoes entering your rooms during the day. Carry mosquito coils in case there is a problem with the electricity or there are no sockets near to the beds (high-frequency buzz offs are not proven to work as efficiently as vaporisers).

11. If likely to kick off their covers, encourage children to sleep in long cotton night-clothes and socks. Keep babies in a cotton sleeper suit.

12. Air conditioning also reduces the risk slightly.

13. Don't assume, because your child is not showing any allergic reaction (red lumps) to bites, that they are not being bitten. Some people react more than others.

Treatment

If you are travelling out of reach of medical help for longer than one to two weeks, you should consider carrying Quinine and Fansidar. Treatment should be begun within eight hours of symptoms developing. A full course should be completed while continuing with preventative measures.

Figure 5. Doses of Fansidar for curative treatment of malaria in children.

Age		Weight	Dosage
Children under 4 years		5–10 kg	½ tablet
	4–6 years	11–20 kg	1 tablet
	7–9 years	21–30 kg	1 ½ tablets
	10–14 years	31–45 kg	2 tablets
Adults			2–3 tablets

Drugs should be given as a single dose and not repeated for at least seven days. The most important gauge for dosage is weight. An underweight child must be treated as a younger one, or they might overdose. An overweight child must be treated as an older child, otherwise they might not receive a therapeutic dose.

In severe cases, Quinine may be added, preferably as an injection if medical treatment is available. Quinine injections are available in most hospitals and clinics throughout the tropics and subtropics.

Returning home

Malaria might develop even several months after leaving a malaria-endemic area.

DO NOT FORGET: A fever that presents itself in your child when you return home could be malaria. You must not neglect to tell your doctor who could easily mistake the symptoms for flu. This is especially important if you have visited tropical Africa. Months later, children can rapidly deteriorate and die without prompt diagnosis and treatment.

Dengue fever

Dengue fever occurs throughout the tropics and subtropics. It is endemic in regions you might not associate with tropical disease such as the Caribbean and North-Eastern Australia. Dengue is also common in South-East Asia, the Pacific Islands, West Africa, Central and South America.

Sporadic outbreaks occur in many other countries of the world, occasionally in South-Eastern USA and even in southern Europe. The disease is transmitted by infected mosquitoes but classic dengue fever, although unpleasant, does not pose a grave risk to the travelling family.

Symptoms

In adults and older children, the illness begins with the sudden onset of fever, headache, pain behind the eyes, chilliness and generalised pains in the muscle joints. Between days three and five of the illness a rash usually appears on the trunk and later spreads to the face and extremities.

In young children dengue fever may never be suspected as the main symptoms are similar to a respiratory infection.

After ten days the patient will usually be completely recovered, although a few may feel weak for some time afterwards.

Prevention

There are no prophylactic vaccines against the disease, and the only real defence against dengue fever is to prevent mosquito bites (see page 236)

Treatment

There is no specific treatment other than paracetamol to relieve the pain and control the temperature. Therefore Disprol or Calpol will make your child feel much better while their bodies fight off the infection.

Dengue haemorrhagic fever

Dengue haemorrhagic fever is a much more serious illness and is often fatal. However, the syndrome is almost entirely confined to local children.

SANDFLIES

Sandflies inflict nasty bites and can spread Leishmaniasis throughout the tropics and subtropics of every continent except Australia.

Leishmaniasis

Kala-azar is the most serious form of the disease but the most common presentation is a local lesion of the skin often called tropical ulcer or yaws, which take a long time to heal.

Specific and effective drug treatment is available.

THE TSETSE FLY

Sleeping sickness

Sleeping sickness (African trypanosomiasis) is caused by single-celled parasites and spread by the painful bite of the tsetse fly.

In the early to mid-part of this century epidemics of the disease caused hundreds of thousands of deaths. The incidence of sleeping sickness has progressively decreased so that now only a few thousand cases are reported each year, among which might be just a handful of tourists.

Symptoms

Approximately five days after being bitten by an infected tsetse fly, a boil-like swelling will appear at the site of the original bite. Weeks or months after being bitten, the patient develops a fever and general malaise.

The parasite then enters the central nervous system and the patient will undergo a personality change. They usually then begin to sleep excessively during the day. If the patient remains untreated, they will continue to deteriorate and will eventually stop eating and die.

Prevention

The principal defence against sleeping sickness is to first recognise and so avoid the bite of the offending tsetse fly.

It is approximately one to two times the size of the house fly, has a brightly coloured abdomen and folds its wings in a characteristic overlapping, scissor-like manner across its back. Any safari tour guide will be able to confirm their identification.

Tsetse in Eastern Africa are often found in game parks and are active during the day so the travellers on safari are potentially at risk. The flies are more attracted to the buses, and other larger moving objects they may judge to be prey, than they are to humans on foot. If they get inside the tour bus they need to be sprayed or squashed.

Insect repellents are highly advisable. As with mosquitoes, avoid deodorants or perfumed soap that will attract the flies. Tsetse are also drawn to dark colours, particularly dark blue, therefore light clothes are a further defence.

Treatment

The illness is serious but responds well to rehabilitation and drug treatment.

The diagnosis in the early stages may be difficult, especially with the likelihood that your family doctor will probably never have seen a case of sleeping sickness. It is unlikely to cross his mind unless you point out that you have been bitten by tsetse in tropical Africa.

Because the drug treatment is potentially toxic to use, diagnosis should be confirmed before it is given. Reassuringly, it is very effective and although relapses of the disease may occur, most patients will be completely cured under doctor's supervision.

CONE-NOSED BUGS (ASSASSIN BUGS)

Chagas' disease

Chagas' disease is also known as American trypanosomiasis. It is a disease of Central and South America and is caused by a single-celled parasite called Trypanosoma cruzi (similar to the African parasite responsible for sleeping sickness), which lives in the host's blood and immune system.

It is spread by the bite of cone-nosed bugs in infested houses. The bugs live in the cracks in the walls close to beds and come out at night to feed. They will bite, then sit and feast on their blood meal until they swell and fill. The parasite is carried in the beetle's faeces. Revoltingly, humans are infected when the beetle defecates next to the fresh bite. The bugs are often known locally as assassin bugs and you may be warned by guides or in hotels if the insects are common in the region.

In poor areas of South America, from Brazil to Chile, the disease occurs most often in children under ten years old but unless you intend to stay in low standard, rural mud-housing with the local population, your own children are at extremely low risk.

Symptoms

The bite is unlikely to go unnoticed. A hard, inflamed swelling develops at the site after about a week.

There can then be swelling of the lymph glands and a high fever. Death occurs in a small proportion of patients a few months after infection due to heart failure or meningoencephalitis. Many others develop no symptoms at all and live normal lives infected by the parasite but without symptoms.

Long-term complications can occur and involve various organs, in particular the heart, which can fail ten years after the initial infection. The intestines are also commonly affected.

Prevention
The surest way of contracting the disease is to sleep next to a mud wall, under a thatched roof and with well-used, unwashed blankets. The cone-nosed bug feeds at night in infested houses. To avoid being bitten by the bugs, avoid sleeping in mud houses. If you don't have a mosquito net with you, the chances are that you are better sleeping outside. Chagas' disease is almost unknown in the Amazon basin where the primitive dwellings have no walls.

If you do sleep in a mud hut, you should cover yourself, your children and your mosquito net with insect repellent and make sure that it is tucked in underneath the mattress all around you. If possible, pull the bed into the middle of the room and away from the walls, which is where the bugs hide during the day.

Treatment
Treatment is easiest in the early stages of the disease. Once it has had time to develop, it is much more difficult to cure.

If you suspect you or your children have contracted the disease you should be tested and treated by a doctor as soon as possible. The side effects of the drugs used to treat the disease can be serious so should only be given under medical supervision.

FLEAS

Murine (endemic) typhus and bubonic plague are both carried by rat fleas, the bite of which transmits disease to humans. In Africa and tropical America the female jigger is a subcutaneous parasite.

Typhus
The traveller is more at risk from the forms of typhus transmitted by ticks (see page 246).

Bubonic Plague
Who can imagine anything more fear-provoking than fighting an invisible, deathly assailant you have no protection against as

you have no understanding of how, when or where it will creep up on you? The Plague has wiped out entire communities throughout the world since ancient times. It hit Western Europe with recurring epidemics between 1347 and 1722 with huge death tolls. Bodies were piled up in the streets with no one left to bury them. Some countries lost two-thirds of their population to the disease. Millions and millions died. The Plague came as close to wiping out the human race as any disease ever has. Every race and religion was struck.

We now know that it is caused by the bacillus *Yersina Pestis*, which is transmitted by fleas from infected rats or from patients who have developed a secondary plague pneumonia. These patients will pass on the bacteria by coughing. This airborne form of the disease is nearly always fatal.

It is still present in some countries of the world but is very rare and thankfully it is now curable.

Symptoms
The earliest symptom is a swelling in the groin or armpit, usually between the size of an egg or a clenched fist. The incubation period of the disease is short and it can be just four days after an infected flea bite that a large swelling develops. High fever, excruciating headache and delirium follow within ten days and without treatment 60 per cent of the victims will have died.

Pneumonic plague caught from the breath of a patient has a much more aggressive onset and, once caught, can be fatal in three days. The victims show signs of respiratory distress with a high temperature, dusky face and shallow breathing.

Prevention
A vaccine is available but the chance of a traveller being infected is so very rare that, even if visiting areas of epidemics, it is not recommended.

The best means of prevention are avoiding flea bites by using insect repellent and ensuring that children do not go near rats or any other rodents including sweet little chipmunks, squirrels and rabbits.

Treatment
Treatment with antibiotics is very effective. Medical help should be sought but if this is not available, streptomycin is the best option.

Although Ciproxin is not indicated for children, it is effective and the benefits of giving it to your child would outweigh the risk if you suspected bubonic plague.

Early treatment is essential before complications such as the pneumonic form of the disease have a chance to develop.

JIGGERS (BURROWING FLEA)

Also know as the sand flea. The insect is a problem in Africa and tropical America. The pregnant female burrows into the skin of the feet causing inflammation, redness and irritation. She needs to be removed as prolonged infestation can lead to amputation of the toes.

LICE

In common with fleas, mites and ticks, the human body and head louse can be the vector of typhus (see page 246).

STINGING INSECTS

Bees', wasps' and hornets' stings are usually more painful than they are dangerous. The problems arise if a child is allergic to the sting and develops anaphylactic shock. Your child will rapidly become distressed and will gasp for air. You need specialist help and should seek urgent medical attention.

If you know that your child is allergic to, for example, bee stings, discuss with your doctor the possibility of carrying a prefilled syringe of adrenaline with you for emergency treatment and know how to use it.

Stings in the mouth can be dangerous as they can cause swelling which can obstruct the airways even in people who are not sensitive.

Prevention
Insect repellents are more effective at deterring biting insects than stinging insects. Generally it is advisable to tell the child to keep still but this does not always work. Wasps are vicious and often sting without any threat.

Treatment
Stings should always be scraped off with a knife or fingernail and never removed with tweezers as this is likely to squeeze more venom into the skin.

Soothe with local anaesthetics but not topical antihistamines as they can promote sensitivity and, in my experience, don't seem to make any difference to pain or itching. Oral antihistamines are more effective and may be useful in alleviating multiple stings, although paracetamol will act more quickly to relieve the pain. For a sting in the mouth, give the casualty ice to suck to minimise the swelling.

Insects that can cause skin reaction or allergic responses
Beetles, caterpillars, ants and others can cause intense itching and redness. Antiseptic soothing creams will provide relief.

BITING ARACHNIDS
MITES

Mites are tiny (often microscopic) arachnids, some of which are parasitic to man. Some burrow under the skin, causing scabies. Chiggers, which are the larvae of harvest mites, stick to the skin and cause severe itching.

Scrub typhus is transmitted by mites from infected rodents in Asia, India, Northern Australia and the Western Pacific Islands (see page 246).

TICKS

The principal reason to avoid ticks is that they are wholly unpleasant little characters. They sit in wait for a passing dog, human or other mammal who is walking by unsuspecting and enjoying the landscape. They will then attach themselves as sneakily as they can in hair, in a crevice or just inside any available orifice where they sit and drink blood until they swell from a tiny speck to a huge, red, engorged creature the size of a grape. The size increase can be quite alarming.

They are easily removed and the careful grooming of a child at the end of each day will limit the time the tick has to feed. This, in turn, will limit the chance of developing one of the plethora of diseases passed on by ticks.

Small children are unlikely to notice the tick by themselves and will need your scrutiny. Most of the time, a tick bite will be nothing more than repulsive. In the remaining one or two per cent of cases, the bite may lead to an infection which, without treatment, could have the potential to be fatal.

If you do find a tick on yourself or a child carefully remove it (instructions below). The longer the tick has to feed, the longer it has to pass on diseases. Some, such as Lyme disease, take eighteen hour feeding sessions to be transmitted.

Don't worry, but be practical and, if there are any signs of fever, headache, rash or redness and swelling following a bite, you should seek medical advice.

A tick bite can transmit typhus, encephalitis, Lyme disease, Q fever and tick paralysis.

Typhus
Typhus has several forms and can be transmitted by tick, mite, louse or flea (see Figure 6).

Epidemic typhus is transmitted worldwide by the human body louse. The disease strikes in times of cold, famine, war and human misery. In history it has been one of the most feared human diseases.

The modern-day traveller is at little risk from epidemic typhus but other forms transmitted by ticks or mites can be caught when walking throughout the world.

Often referred to locally around the world as tick fever, or tick flu, typhus is an illness caused by a parasite called a

Figure 6.   Forms of typhus, their habitat, and modes of transmission.

Associated disease	Habitat	Mode of transmission
Epidemic typhus	Man Rats and mice	Body louse Rat fleas
Rocky mountain spotted fever	Man, dog and rabbit	Ticks
Scrub typhus	Rodents	Mites
Rickettsial fever in Queensland	Man and animals	Tick
Trench fever	Man	Body and head lice
Q fever	Mammals	Tick and by contact

Rickettsia, which is neither a bacterium nor a virus but is somewhere between the two.

Symptoms
All types of typhus cause fever, chills, muscle pain, severe

headache and a rash. There is usually a painful sore and spreading redness at the site of the bite.

The illness is likely to last a number of weeks if left untreated.

Prevention

Vaccinations are available against epidemic typhus and Rocky mountain spotted fever but rarely recommended to the traveller.

Prevention centres around avoiding louse, flea, mite and tick bites. This may be done by applying repellents such as diethyltoluamide and dimethylphthalate to the skin and clothing. Repellent-impregnated, snug-fitting hats can provide a weak defence against the ticks hiding in hair, although you should still inspect the hair line.

Wear light clothes out on walks that will help show up the ticks by contrast but also, ticks tend to aim for darker objects.

With children, it is advisable to avoid straying into areas heavily infested with the offending ticks. The locals will always be able to advise you where these areas are or anything else you should know, for example, how to remove them or any symptoms to look out for following bites.

Rambling through scrub, veldt or tropical bush crawling with waiting hungry ticks is where you will pick up trespassers. When out walking in these areas, be meticulous with the application of repellent and dress accordingly in long trousers well tucked into long socks. Long sleeves with snug wristbands and hats are added protection.

If you need to wade through waist-high grass, pop the kids on your shoulders then at least the ticks will get you instead.

Your second line of defence against disease is to remove the tick as soon as possible and give it less time to pass on an infection. When you get home, or even before, you must scour your children for ticks from top to toe. Comb, groom and search through their hair, then look in deep nooks such as their groins and their orifices.

Tick removal

Care should be taken when removing ticks. It can done by smothering the offender in Vaseline and waiting until it drops off voluntarily. Otherwise, touch the tick with alcohol or oil to encourage it to let go 'cleanly', although there is some debate as to whether this 'shocks' the tick and makes it vomit into the bite, passing on any infection it may be harbouring.

Removing ticks with your fingers or tweezers is tricky and needs patience. You must not squeeze the tick or leave the mouth parts embedded. If you do squash the tick you will effectively squeeze into the bite any parasites not yet transmitted. If you leave in the mouth parts, the bite will take much longer to heal and can become infected.

When I visited South Africa ten years ago, I was told that under no circumstances should I attempt to forcibly remove the tick as, if I did, it would certainly pass on the fever in retaliation. Vaseline was the recommended line of defence. Vaseline supposedly tricks the tick into letting go of his own accord and he will leave without revenge. However, it now seems to be generally recommended that you carefully remove the tick yourself. This, of course, has the benefit of being quick.

The guidelines are to grip the tick firmly between finger and thumb, or with tweezers, at the head end and as close to the skin as possible. Then pull steadily away in a perpendicular direction (at right angles, not downwards or upwards against the skin). The mouth parts will be well embedded and you may need to rock the tick gently from side to side to free its grip.

Personally I would go for the Vaseline every time. A squirming child and an inexperienced tick-remover are a hazardous combination but, if you (unlike me) have a steady hand and the patience, many would recommend that you try to extricate it yourself.

As always, local knowledge is the best. The alternative is to ask a native what they would do. It is likely that your tour guide or the elderly lady in the local store are far better equipped for the job. Even if no one around speaks your language, simply show them your problem and doubtless it will resolved and your child will be tick- and disease-free within seconds.

Once the tick is removed, flood the bite with the strongest alcohol available, be it tequila or rum. This will help disinfect the puncture.

Treatment
Typhus responds well to antibiotics.

Lyme disease
Lyme disease is yet another pathological condition resulting from the bite of an infected tick. The infection is caused by a bacterium that is passed on when the tick feeds between deer and man. The species of tick responsible for carrying the infection is found in park- and woodland in temperate climates, such as that of the USA and Europe, including the UK.

If the disease is left untreated, complications will arise, including heart disease, nerve problems and arthritis.

Symptoms
The tick responsible is small and its bites can often go unnoticed but the useful warning sign in Lyme disease is an expanding, red, skin rash accompanied by a headache, muscle and joint ache, and a slight fever.

Prevention
As with other diseases transmitted by ticks, the best way of preventing the illness is by avoiding the tick bite (see page 247).

Treatment
Antibiotics are effective against Lyme disease. The drugs of choice would be erythromycin or amoxycillin. In children, amoxycillin would be the better choice.

Tick paralysis
Ticks picked up either in the countryside or from domestic animals can produce saliva containing a neurotoxin that is passed on by their bites. The poisoning neurotoxicity that results is rarely fatal to adults but can cause fatalities in children. The most common site of tick paralysis is in Northern USA.

A tick needs to be attached for a number of days to begin to be a real danger and so checking for ticks is an important care regime. Your child might have been irritable, 'out of sorts' and have even collapsed after getting out of bed in the morning. The scalp is the commonest place of attachment, although orifices are regular sites.

Treatment

(See above for tick removal). The tick must be detached without being squeezed. Smothered with Vaseline, the tick drops off. Following detachment, a child will usually recover. An anti-venom is available.

SPIDERS

Spider bites, even in Mediterranean countries, can be dangerous.

The red backed spider in Australia can cause death but with a low incidence and anti-venom is available. A friend once told me that when he visited his mum, who was living in Australia, she had been bitten by a red backed spider. This she judged as an incredible inconvenience rather than an emergency and insisted on finishing what she was doing before she went to the hospital for the anti-venom.

Wherever you are in the world, including the USA, you should teach your child to respect spiders. Empty shoes before you put them on and watch out in outside toilets and outhouses where flies are attracted. Spiders often make these their homes and a number of species have been known to hide under toilet seats.

Treatment

You should get your child to hospital as soon as possible for anti-venom treatment. Try to minimise the spread of the venom in the system by keeping the child calm, immobilising the limb and keeping the site of the bite below the level of the heart. (See snake bites, page 256.)

SCORPIONS

Dangerous species exist in Africa, Asia, Trinidad and throughout the Americas including the North. Mexico is home to a number of dangerous species. Mortality is approximately 15–25 per cent higher in small children than in adults.

Avoiding stings

Scorpions are nocturnal and feed at night, especially after rain storms. In the day they find somewhere snug and dark, such as training shoes. Empty your shoes before putting them on.

Insecticides deter scorpions, so good hotels which spray for cockroaches etc. should not be plagued.

Teach your child to be very wary when lifting logs or boulders and not to push fingers and sticks in holes or burrows.

Treatment

If you suspect the scorpion could have been poisonous, you should get your child to hospital as soon as possible for intravenous anti-venom. Try to minimise the spreading of the venom in the system by keeping the child calm, immobilising the limb and keeping the site of the sting below the level of the heart. Most scorpion stings are more painful than dangerous. Give paracetamol for the pain. Cold compresses and oral antihistamine tablets can limit the reaction.

MILLIPEDES AND CENTIPEDES

Children are particularly at risk when they try to handle or even eat these large arthropods.

Millipedes can squirt venom into the eye. Flush the eye with plenty of water to limit the irritation and ensure that infection does not develop in the affected eye.

Centipedes can bite and no anti-venom is available.

LEECHES

Land leeches infest floor and lower vegetation of rainforests. They should be removed by alcohol, salt, vaseline, a lighted match or cigarette burn. Water leeches are common in rivers all over the world, including the UK.

Leeches do not pass on disease but wounds can become infected and need to be cleaned and sterilised with an antiseptic.

Wearing long socks, long trousers and sturdy shoes liberally treated with repellents such as diethyltoluamide helps to deter them from attaching to the skin.

WORMS

An entire plethora of worms can infect man and a whole host of symptoms can result, the most common being enteritis, abdominal distension, change in appetite and weight loss.

Roundworm, tapeworm, threadworm and whipworm have a worldwide distribution and so are not just a blight of the traveller. However, they are more common in tropical areas with poor sanitation.

None will cause a medical emergency while you are away but care needs to be taken to avoid picking them up.

If you suspect that your child may have become infected you should seek medical treatment. All worms can be eradicated by specific drug treatment once they have been diagnosed.

Avoiding infection
Most species of worm are transmitted by eating undercooked food contaminated with cysts. Many flukes are transmitted by eating raw fish or snails. Undercooked meat conveys tapeworm infection. Even watercress and water chestnut can harbour parasitic worms.

Threadworms are highly infectious and commonly infect school children in the UK. They can be passed on by food, water, air or contact. They cause intense itching around the anus, especially at night. A child will scratch and get eggs under the finger nails. These can easily be passed on to other members of the family.

The dragon worm or guinea worm is transmitted by swallowing or drinking water containing the intermediate host. It causes swelling of the skin that can develop into an ulcer. The worm is removed by winding it around a stick although care must be taken to avoid allergic reactions which occur if the worm is broken.

Infected mosquitoes pass on elephantiasis. Blackfly bites transmit river blindness.

Other worms of the tropics and subtropics can actually penetrate the intact skin. Bilharziasis is caught (*see below*) while swimming, wading, bathing or even showering in contaminated water. Certain species of roundworm and hookworm contaminate soil and penetrate the skin, usually through the soles of the feet.

To avoid infection, children and adults should take the usual precautions against consuming undercooked food or drinking unpurified water. Mosquito and blackfly bites should be prevented with insecticides etc (see page 236).

Children should always wear light footwear to prevent penetration by worm larvae.

Bilharziasis (Schistosomiasis)
Bilharziasis is a chronic infection caused by minute worms whose life cycle revolves around fresh water. The disease occurs

throughout the tropics and subtropics in approximately a third of the countries of the world. It chronically infects more than 200 million people at present. It is particularly common throughout Africa, from the Nile delta to Lake Victoria, in Brazil, parts of the Middle East and China. Island paradises from Mauritius to Antigua are also hosts to the disease.

The parasite spends its early life developing in freshwater snails until it swims free. Once it comes across a person bathing or wading, it will burrow through the skin and migrate into the veins of the intestines or bladder in the new found host. Left untreated, it will remain there for up to fifteen years, continually producing eggs. Many of these eggs are not excreted but remain in the host where they cause an inflammatory reaction. Some of the eggs that are excreted in the urine or faeces will contaminate rivers, streams and lakes.

Symptoms
The first symptom may be tingling and/or a light rash around the area where it penetrated the blood stream. Some weeks later a high fever might develop and so may be confused with malaria or typhoid. The patient will feel unwell with abdominal pain and possibly have blood present in their urine.

If untreated, the long-term effects of the parasite include kidney and liver damage.

Prevention
Visitors to areas where bilharziasis is present should avoid bathing, wading or even showering in streams, rivers, lakes and freshwater stores.

Deep water far from the shore of a huge lake is unlikely to be safe either, so it is not advisable to swim from boats.

If, for any reason, you or your children enter or fall into fresh water of any depth, you must ensure that you quickly remove any clothing and vigorously towel-dry the skin. Do not put the clothes back on until they are dry too. The larvae die quickly once they leave the water and so need to penetrate quickly. It is a race against time to brush them off.

Salt water and chlorinated water are safe. However, if you can't smell the chlorine in the pool there may some fault in the pool's system or the chlorine may have simply run out, leaving it unsafe to swim in.

Keep showers in remote, rural areas short, and again, towel off vigorously.

On a number of occasions while in Western India, I was offered 'a shower' and was led into a room containing a sponge and a bucket of fresh, boiled water. This may not be perfect for a family situation but isn't as bad as it sounds. If you are staying in good standard accommodation, the water will be treated and although unsafe to drink it is very unlikely to be contaminated by bilharzia and will be safe to wash in.

If you have any suspicions about any member of the family having either been exposed to or contracting the disease, you should contact your doctor when you return home and arrange for a test. The presence of eggs can be detected in the urine or the faeces but not until 40 days after infection, so any tests before this may give a false, negative result.

Treatment
The drug treatment should not be started without first confirming that the infection is present and eggs have been found in the faeces or urine.

At present, praziquantel is the drug of choice. It is highly effective and usually only needs to be given as a single dose.

MAMMALS

Bites and scratches are dangerous because they can cause infection such as tetanus and rabies; even a lick from an infected animal can transfer rabies. Prophylactic injections should be given (see pages 146 and 149).

If wounds are severe, or if the bite is on the face, your child should also be treated with oral antibiotics to protect against infection (penicillin, aminoglycosides and metronidazole combination).

A child should be taught to respect all animals and be wary of their unpredictability. All animals are potentially dangerous, even if they do not appear aggressive.

The cute little coatimundis all around the ruins and major tourist spots of Central and South America are vicious little creatures. In Tikal, Guatemala, we were warned that one had just attacked a mother for the milk she was trying to give her baby and had severed her finger.

Just because animals gather around tourist spots does not mean that they are tame. Baboons from Capetown to Gibraltar will come to be fed, but will often attack if they want to claim what you are eating. The monkeys which collect around temples in Asia can carry rabies and you would be advised not to show them that you have food with you.

Most bears are dangerous and the polar bear is one of the few mammals that will actively seek out humans as food. Bears in North America and Canada are unlikely to judge you as a meal but they will come looking for your scraps and you should lock all your food, waste or even toothpaste in the boot of your car or suspended up high on a small branch of a tree. Don't keep anything edible inside a tent.

Beasts of burden can trample a child or easily knock them down a mountain side. Always pass animals on the higher side of the mountain track.

Rabbits and chipmunks carry the bubonic plague. Bats, raccoons, foxes and domestic animals carry rabies. Most other mammals can carry fleas, ticks or parasites. Even wild boar are highly dangerous and attacks can be fatal.

Treatment

1. Clean the wound thoroughly as soon as possible with soap/detergent and water (preferably running).
2. Pour alcohol over the wound that is a minimum of 40 per cent by volume. Gin, whisky, vodka etc. are all 40 per cent alcohol. Local rum or spirits are often stronger and so better.
3. Apply an antiseptic such as iodine.
4. Seek medical attention as soon as possible. Your child could need antibiotics and immunisation against tetanus and rabies. Even if your child has already been vaccinated against rabies, they will need additional post-exposure protection if bitten by an animal that could possibly be rabid.

SNAKES

After a snake bite, panic is the greatest enemy. Keeping calm and still will stop the venom spreading.

If the snake remains attached, apply a flame to the underside of the jaw to make it release its grip.

The pain is immediate and severe at the site of the bite but reassure your child, sit him down and try to keep him still. Flush the wound with water. Keep the bitten limb below the level of the heart and immobilise it with a splint or sling. This will help contain the venom locally.

Take a note of the snake's appearance and move your child to medical treatment and hospital as soon as possible. Anti-venom is a life saver.

DO NOT cut and suck the wound. Local incision and suction by an unskilled person is likely to introduce infection and cause further trauma that can lead to extensive bleeding.

Tourniquets may seem a logical approach but are often not advised and are not necessary if the journey to hospital is less than 30 minutes. If you are a long distance from medical help, a local might be more skilled at applying a tourniquet than yourself. It should not be so tight that the extremities become cold and blue and should be released every 30 minutes for at least 15 seconds to allow oxygen to flow into the limbs. If not, the limb may later become gangrenous. A firmly (not tightly) tied bandage or your own tight grip around your child's limb above the wound would be less likely to cause lasting damage.

During transfer to the hospital, lay your child on his side to stop the inhalation of vomit. If you feel it may help, give paracetamol for the pain.

Avoiding snake bites
Boots, socks and long trousers should be worn for walking through undergrowth and deep sand in places where snakes are common. Tell children that even if a snake appears dead, they should not to touch it. The venom is still often effective. Snakes will make every effort to avoid you and so warn them that you are coming. Carry a light at night, tread heavily and beat the undergrowth in front of you with a stick.

Tell children not to poke sticks into crevices, lift logs or boulders, swim in murky water matted with vegetation or climb trees and rocks with dense foliage.

Some snakes can eject venom in a fine stream in an attempt to distract their victims. If the venom gets into the eye it can cause intense conjunctivitis with a risk of further infection. Damage is minimised by flushing the eye with plenty of water and seeking medical attention.

LIZARDS

The Gila lizard, indigenous to southern USA and to Mexico, is the only lizard with a venomous bite although the Komodo dragon from Indonesia is said to bite its victims and leave them to die from the putrefying wounds that result.

SEA CREATURES

In many places of the world you will be invited to swim with stingrays, barracuda, grouper, moray eels and sharks. All are potential killers and you should respect them. However, where there are scores of tourist boats coming to attract and feed them, you need have little fear. Just ensure that your children do not chase, tease or provoke anything underwater.

The most painful wounds are often caused by venomous creatures who are stepped on.

The stingray is designed so that if you step on them, their tails will flick up and inject a painful sting as a defence. However, they are naturally gentle creatures and around most dive sites in the Caribbean, the worst you can fear is a 'love bite' from a young ray who confuses you with food.

Ensure that your children wear something on their feet such as old pumps, jellies or rubber-soled diving shoes that are now available even in baby sizes. Also advise them to shuffle clumsily into the water. This will warn any fish to move. Weeverfish bury themselves in sand in shallow waters all around Britain, the European Atlantic and the Mediterranean and can inflict a very painful wound. Stonefish are found in tropical regions and if you were to step on one, it could be fatal.

Many other species of fish in tropical waters can sting, including lionfish, catfish and dogfish. Starfish and sea urchins also possess venomous spines that can break off in the foot and cause prolonged discomfort and risks of infection.

TREATMENT OF MARINE PUNCTURE WOUNDS

Place the afflicted limb in water as hot as the victim can stand. Keep the limb immersed and the water as hot as you can for 30 minutes. Keep topping up with hot water but ensure that you do not scald your child.

If spines are stuck in the foot, they need to be removed. You can do this yourself by softening the skin with an antiseptic/anaesthetic cream (for example, salicylic acid or magnesium sulphate) then removing with tweezers. Be wary of the spines breaking up and so urge your child to keep still and be patient.

I once went out swimming with my dad off the coast of Jamaica. We were quite a way off shore and sharing a mask and snorkel between us. He swam around while I waited my turn. He then urged me to follow him as there was a huge rock rising from the seabed that I could stand on even though we were a long way out to sea. I allowed him to guide my feet on to the rock. Somehow he neglected to notice a resident sea urchin and guided my toes straight on to its spines. I was more amazed at my dad's imbecility than the pain and, back on shore, was relieved to find that the spines came out quite easily.

I've never let him forget it!

JELLYFISH, PORTUGUESE MAN-OF-WAR, SEA ANEMONES AND CORALS

All these creatures possess stinging cells that can cause extreme pain. The sting of the box jellyfish, which is common at certain times of the year off Northern Australia, is said to cause death due to excruciating pain. Fortunately it does not inhabit the Great Barrier Reef but beaches on the mainland may be closed in the seasons where the box jellyfish is swept inshore.

The Portuguese man-of-war looks like a pretty, blue bubble but gives a nasty sting. Even jellyfish swept on to the beach can still sting if your child picks them up.

Coral stings are irritating rather than acutely painful but coral cuts are very slow to heal as a result of the venom injected when you step on to the coral. Even non-stinging coral is very sharp and can inflict painful gashes that can become infected. Children should not be allowed to walk on or collect coral, as much for the sake of the dwindling reefs as for their own safety.

Treatment of stings

The best antidote is vinegar poured over the stinging cells. This stops more cells firing and limits the damage. If you can then get hold of some talcum powder, dusting it over the area will make the remaining stinging cells clump together, enabling them to be brushed off safely. A rather crude alternative to vinegar is urine. Alcohol poured over the wound will not help.

MOLLUSCS – INCLUDING SEA SNAILS, CONES AND OCTOPUSES

These creatures can be venomous. Blue-ringed octopus bite with their beaks and have toxic saliva that has been known to cause fatalities.

Be aware that the bite from sea cones can cause respiratory paralysis. There is no specific treatment, only management of the developing symptoms:

1. Monitor the casualty's consciousness, breathing and heart rate and resuscitate if necessary
2. Lie in the recovery position
3. Seek medical help.

Sea snakes can also be venomous (see page 255).

In summary

Don't allow your children to pick up anything off the seabed or reefs including corals, anemones, sea urchins or starfish.

Ensure that they adopt a shuffling gait when entering water, that they don't step on to coral reefs and do not chase or tease any sea creatures.

If a dive leader offers them a sea cucumber to hold or urges them to touch a giant clam and watch it gently close, then OK, but children should always be taught the importance of the 'taking only memories and leaving only footprints'.

13 Coping with Illness

COMMON COMPLAINTS

Ear Infections

Ear infections are particularly common on holiday when children are swimming in the sea or pools where they can pick up infections from the water.

Middle ear infections may be the result of a throat or other upper respiratory tract infection that has spread the short distance up into the ears behind the drum. Your children are particularly susceptible while jumping in deep and diving under water, especially if they get cold.

Symptoms
Hearing loss, severe earache and fever. There is also inflammation and redness inside the ear that will be obvious to any doctor on examination. Young children might tug at their ears with the discomfort.

Treatment
Pain with discharge from the ear is usually a sign of infection in the outer ear that can be alleviated with antibiotic ear drops. Paracetamol eases the pain.

Pain in the middle ear is more serious and needs oral antibiotic treatment. Ear drops will not be effective and your child will be more ill generally, probably having suffered from a previous upper respiratory infection.

Prevention
If your child has chronic tonsillitis, or suffers from ear infections on a regular basis, you should talk to your doctor before you leave, and ask about the possibility of him

prescribing an antibiotic for you to take on holiday to use if your child presents with symptoms.

It is likely to flare up on holiday and repeated ear infections can damage the ear drum. There is the added complication that children with severe ear infections should not fly. With effective antibiotic treatment, the infection will be under control or eliminated for the journey home.

Insects in the ear
Lay the child on its side. Pour tepid water or olive oil into the ear. The insect should float out.

Nose, throat and sinus infections
If your child is unwell, paracetamol syrup will alleviate pain, discomfort and fever.

Infections on holiday that are causing a lot of discomfort and are prolonged should be treated with an antibiotic. The cause may be viral but the antibiotic will prevent any secondary bacterial chest or ear infections developing that are likely to occur if your child is in and out of the water swimming.

Chest infections
Chest infections can develop from an infection in the throat, ear or nose and, in young children, are serious because they hamper breathing. Your child is likely to have a cough, producing phlegm tinged green with pus. This is commonly a sign of bacterial infection that needs to be treated with an antibiotic. Your child will feel unwell, with laboured breathing. Paracetamol will keep the temperature down and make him feel better. Do not use cough medicines as the phlegm needs to be cleared from the chest.

Eye infections
If eyes are bloodshot, swollen and weeping there is likely to be infection present.

Infective conjunctivitis is highly contagious and will spread from one eye to the other just by rubbing. It can be caused by a virus or bacteria and can be picked up while swimming.

Your child will need eyedrops, preferably containing an antibiotic. If none are available, rinse the eye with salt water morning and night. If you have packed a syringe, use this (without the needle) to flush the eye clear from pus and crusting.

If there is no relief and the child continually rubs at the eye, there could be a foreign body in it and you will need medical attention.

Cuts, grazes and skin infections
Cuts heal very slowly in the tropics. Wounds do not dry out and scab over in high humidity. Wet wounds can readily become infected. Even small cuts can become problematic. Great care needs to be taken to keep any wounds clean and dry.

Treatment

1. Run cuts and grazes under cold water and wash the wounded area with soap.
2. Dry by patting with clean tissue. Apply antiseptic spray or powder. Betadine or Savlon (povidine iodine) dry powder sprays are very effective.
3. Cover with a sterile dressing.
4. If the cut is deep, hold together wound edges with skin closure tape or crude stitches. If deep and dirty, leave the cut open and flush with sterilising solution, Savlon solution, iodine or alcohol. Consider whether tetanus boosters are up to date.
5. Change dressings daily and watch for signs of infection, including:
   - redness with swelling around the wound
   - increasing pain and tenderness
   - the area around the wound feeling hot
   - more obvious symptoms such as the wound weeping with pus and failing to show any signs of healing.
6. If a skin infection occurs, antibiotic powder or spray would be the better option in the tropics. If the infection is on the middle third of the face or if it is extensive, you should administer oral antibiotics too, as a precaution.

If you are in a less humid environment, antibiotic creams should clear up the infection perfectly.

Bites, allergic or infected
Insect bites will only usually become infected if they are picked or incessantly scratched. If your child is suffering from a large number of bites, an oral antihistamine will ease the swelling and the suffering. On the surface, calamine lotion will relieve

the itching and is a better option than topical antihistamine creams in the tropics.

Paracetamol syrup will help with the pain and discomfort.

If a bite becomes infected, treat as you would a cut with a drying antiseptic or antibiotic powder and cover it with a dressing to keep interfering little fingers away.

Mammalian bites need more intensive treatment. You must seek medical help (see page 254).

Fungal infections: thrush, athlete's foot, ringworm
These are more uncomfortable than serious and will not endanger your child on a short holiday.

Thrush, ringworm and athlete's foot are the most common blights, the former causing the most discomfort. Fungi flourish in warm, moist conditions. If you are breast feeding in the tropics you might find you are infected on your nipples, which can then be transmitted to your baby's mouth and vice versa. You both need to be treated.

Thrush in the nappy region should be kept dry by leaving the nappy off and the bottom exposed for as much of the time as possible.

Anti-fungal medication will be needed. Most anti-fungal creams, powders and treatments usually prescribed for women's thrush are safe to use on children.

If you are unable to obtain any medication try plain yoghurt on the affected area.

Allergies
Existing allergies should be prepared for and if these are serious, and there is a danger of anaphylactic shock, you should discuss with your doctor the possibility of carrying an adrenaline prefilled syringe with you. Allergies to bites, plants, different food or even sunlight which are discovered on holiday should be treated by avoiding the sensitiser and, if the reaction is severe, by administering oral antihistamines such as Phenergan.

Teething pain and mouth ulcers
In my pre-teens I always seemed to get mouth ulcers on holiday. Soothing gels and tablets never worked for me at all. I would even pour neat salt on to my ulcer so that the pain afterwards seemed dull by comparison. Ambesol was brought out some

years ago and it brought me great relief. It is a local anaesthetic which, when applied directly on to an ulcer, brings about total pain relief. It is effective for teething, too.

Urinary tract infection

Severe back pain, fever, blood in urine or pain on urination suggest an infection of the urinary tract. Your child may have suffered from a sore throat a few weeks before.

Your child will need oral antibiotics. Nalidixic acid is useful against many urinary tract infections.

Stomach or abdominal pain

In the tropics, this could be caused by a whole host of organisms that often cause associated diarrhoea and vomiting.

If your child complains of severe, sharp pain in the lower right-hand side of their abdomen, you should suspect appendicitis. They will also have a slight temperature, will refuse food and might vomit. Their tongue will appear coated.

Nappy rash

Good disposable nappies have limited the amount our babies suffer from nappy rash but you may find that your baby will develop a rash in hot, damp, tropical conditions. It may be heat rash, which will improve if you leave the nappy off as often as possible and don't use plastic pants.

Nappies may need to be changed more regularly than normal and if the rash lingers, it could be thrush, which will need treatment with an anti-fungal cream or oral preparation such as Nystan suspension.

Fever without obvious cause

- Very high fever with headache could be malaria even if prophylaxis has been taken.
- Fever with jaundice could be hepatitis or malaria.
- High fever with severe headache, vomiting, neck stiffness and aversion to light could be meningitis.

GETTING MEDICAL TREATMENT ABROAD

In some Third World countries, if you go into hospital, you are more likely to die from insanitary conditions than if you treat yourself. If this is the case, you must concentrate on getting home, accepting only essential treatment.

If, after getting medical help, your child deteriorates, travel home, sooner rather than later.

If you have to visit a hospital, take your passport, details of your health insurance or valid E111 form and any vaccination certificates.

If you feel that the healthcare standards are low and you have packed an emergency medical kit, don't forget to take it to the hospital.

If you do not have health insurance you will still be entitled to free or reduced-cost emergency medical treatment in countries with a reciprocal healthcare agreement with the UK. However, cover is often limited to hospital treatment, not that in doctors' surgeries. In these countries, you would do better to present yourselves at A&E in the local hospital than to visit the local doctor where you will have to pay.

If you need less urgent treatment in most instances you would do better to visit a local doctor's surgery or, better still, get him to come to you. Good hotels will know of a decent doctor or at least find one for you. Often, if you specifically request an English-speaking doctor, your hotel will be able to get one.

If you are staying in budget accommodation and have been unable to get any helpful advice, don't feel embarrassed about stalking into the best hotel in town and asking them to recommend a doctor for you. The chances are that they will think you are a guest or will have no way of knowing that you are not about to check in anyway.

If your hotel has no air-conditioning and is uncomfortable for your sick child, when you telephone your insurance company, ask if they will be prepared to pay the bill for the room if you move hotels.

You must keep all proof of payment for treatment and medicines. Your insurance company will expect to see them unless they agree to settle directly.

If the doctor suggests an injection, ask if there are any alternative oral medicines available. If not, check that the syringe and needle are sterile. If you have any doubts and have packed your own, insist that he uses it. If you do not have your own, offer to pay whatever it takes to get a fresh needle.

Ask the doctor to explain what each medicine is for and, if

you have any doubts about whether or not it is necessary or even safe, telephone home. Ask a friend or relative to ring a British doctor or pharmacist, giving the generic (not trade) name of the drug, the dose, the symptoms it was prescribed for and your child's approximate weight and age. They will then be able to allay your concerns when you call back.

BUYING AND GIVING MEDICINES ABROAD

If you cannot find a doctor or are confident of which medicines you need, you will often find that you are able to buy many drugs, including antibiotics, over the counter.

Be wary; medicines in the tropics may be substandard.

1. Check drugs have not expired.
2. Check that the medicine was refrigerated.
3. If the medicine is a suspension (liquid), confirm that it has not been mixed with contaminated water.
4. Complete the course. Bacteria may develop resistance to an antibiotic and return with a vengeance.

BLOOD TRANSFUSIONS

In many countries of the world, the screening of blood is prohibitively expensive and if your child needed to be given blood or blood products he would be at a serious risk from contracting HIV, hepatitis or other infections. Blood transfusions outside Western Europe, North America, Japan and Australasia should only be given in cases of medical emergency when there is a real risk of death from blood loss.

Most major cities will have one source of screened blood. Contact the embassy to find where this would be or ask your insurance company to try to find out from the World Health Organisation. Do whatever you can to get screened blood.

The best thing you could do for your child would be to give them yours or your partner's blood, but it is essential that the blood types match. If you know your blood type and that of your children, you will be able to help the doctor judge who would be the best donor. It may be a sibling.

14 Coping with Accidents

How you act on the spot will make the difference between whether or not your child survives or has a long-term disability. Your action at the scene should take priority over calling an ambulance.

Reading the theory is a poor substitute for a first aid course. It is a good idea to consider this before travel, especially if you will be outside the realms of medical assistance with your children for any length of time.

CHOKING BABIES

If a baby begins to choke on an inhaled toy or piece of food, you must act quickly.

1. Lay your baby face down and upside down against your bended knee (see Figure 7).
2. Give your baby five sharp slaps on the back.
3. Check inside their mouth with one finger and remove any object that has become dislodged.

If your baby is still in distress:

4. Turn them over on to their back and place two fingertips on the lower side of the baby's breastbone in the centre, just underneath the nipples.

   Give five sharp thrusts into the chest. When you make the thrusts, be firm, but also aware that you could easily damage the baby's internal organs or crack the ribs.

5. Again, check inside the baby's mouth.

Repeat the steps up to three times and, if the baby remains in distress, call for medical help and continue to try to dislodge the object until you are successful or help arrives.

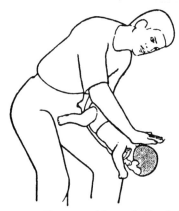

Figure 7. How to position a choking baby.

CHOKING CHILDREN

If a child is choking on a piece of food or a small toy, ask the child to cough and give five sharp back slaps between the shoulder blades with one hand. This will hopefully dislodge the object and free the airways. Check inside the mouth and hook out any obvious obstruction.

If the object remains lodged you must:

1. Grab your child from behind
2. Make a fist and hold it against the underside of the breastbone
3. Grasp the fist with your other hand and thrust into the child's chest up to five times
4. Check inside his mouth

If the object is still lodged:

5. Again, make the fist and place it *below* the breastbone but above the tummy button and, after grasping your fist with the other hand, make a further five thrusts inwards and upwards.
6. Check inside the mouth.

Repeat the above steps three times and then call for help. You must continue the steps until help arrives or the object is freed and retrieved from the mouth.

Fishbone stuck in the throat

Many Asian people will advise you to eat rice if a fishbone lodges itself in the throat and this remedy often works.

On most occasions, although the fishbone feels as if it is embedded, it will have merely scratched the membrane of the throat's lining and moved on.

If a fishbone were lodged, the child would feel progressively worse over time and medical advice must be sought to remove the bone and to ensure that local inflammation of the throat does not interfere with swallowing or even breathing.

Swallowing an object

Most small objects, once swallowed, pass directly inside the stomach and will do no harm. It is the risk of choking when something 'goes down the wrong way' and is inhaled into the airways that is the concern. If there is no episode of choking, you can afford to take things much more calmly.

I recall looking on in dismay as my seven-month-old son suddenly scurried across the bedroom floor and descended on a fallen earring. I made a dash to grab it out of his hand but, within a second, it went from fist, to mouth, to stomach. The earring was sharply hooked and I was frantic.

I telephoned the local hospital and every relative available. However, I calmed down as I was reassured by tales of my sister swallowing a penny when she was a baby and my husband swallowing a strapless watch at around ten months old. Accident and emergency assured me over the telephone that, unless the object swallowed was exceptionally sharp, for example, a needle, all I could do was wait.

The earring reappeared that same evening in a nappy.

If the same thing happens to you and the item isn't extremely sharp, your child will not be in terrible danger.

If there are any severe stomach pains or abdominal distension following the incident, your child will need very urgent medical attention. Otherwise, check for the item in the faeces and, if it has not reappeared by the time you leave, then take your child for an x-ray when you get home. It is more than likely that the x-ray will be clear and you will simply have not checked thoroughly enough.

CONVULSIONS (FITS)

A convulsion is likely to be an intense episode which terrifies you, but it is very unlikely to do any lasting damage.

Typically, all the voluntary muscles of the body will contract violently and there will then be a period of relaxation followed by smaller uncontrollable jerky contractions. More disconcerting attacks can occur when a child lies completely still and rigid, displaying rapid repeated blinking, and is unrousable.

Such attacks are due to irregularities in the brain's 'waves' (electrical impulses) and can be the result of one of a number of obvious causes including a head injury (past or present) or poisoning. Alternatively, there may be no apparent reason at all and a convulsion can occur as an isolated incident. The diagnosis will rarely be epilepsy.

Convulsions in children are not unusual and the most common cause is a high temperature, associated with an illness such as an ear or throat infection. The feverish attack would then be termed a 'febrile convulsion'.

Any parent is likely to be extremely concerned, as their child might well act in a strange, unfamiliar manner, but provided the situation is coped with calmly and correctly, there is very little chance that any complications or problems will be lasting once the fit passes.

What to do
1. Undress the child and cool him.
2. Ensure the child is protected from injury and cannot fall off a bed or settee and bang his head. A carpet, quilting or padding on the floor with space around is safest. Remain by your child's side but do not attempt to intervene or put anything in the mouth.
3. Sponge down from top to toe with tepid water to help cooling. Fan with an electric fan or even by hand with a book.
4. Lay your child on the side and blow cool air on to the upper back and the nape of the neck.
5. Put your child into the recovery position (see page 284) and call for medical help, particularly if this is the first time it has happened, or if the child is running a high fever.

   A high fever indicates illness and could possibly be a symptom of cerebral malaria, meningitis or other serious conditions which will need urgent treatment but don't panic, this is the least likely cause.

6. Try to judge the severity and length of convulsions and in which part of the body (if any) the contractions are more concentrated, as this will help the doctor to diagnose the course of action.
7. Your child will want to rest after a convulsion but while they sleep, monitor their breathing and gently nudge them occasionally to check that they stir.

HEAD INJURIES

Head injuries can be notoriously dangerous and, following a bad bump to the head, you must watch your child carefully for 24 hours. Your child might feel nauseous, drowsy, have visual disturbances and complain of a headache. The real danger signs following a head injury are neck stiffness, photophobia (aversion to light) and vomiting. Any changes in personality are also cause for concern.

Relatively harmless bumps to the head can be dramatic. A scalp wound often bleeds profusely, far overdramatising the real extent of the injury, and a small knock can rise into a pulsating 'Brazil nut' in seconds. Rarely will these have serious consequences.

The bleeding usually stops when compressed with a dressing, and the bumps go down as quickly as they came up. The body is swift to defend the brain and any impact rapidly provokes a defensive cushion of bruising, which quickly subsides.

If your child suffers concussion and loses consciousness for a few minutes, place them in the recovery position (see page 284) and monitor breathing. Confusingly, concussion can occur several hours after the head injury, but should only last for a short time and your child will then recover completely. There might be some memory loss and dizziness with nausea.

A straw-coloured liquid leaking from the nose or ears following a head injury, could possibly be a skull fracture which is serious. However, a standard 'bash on the nose' can bring about the same alarming symptoms without the same degree of emergency.

In summary
Healthy bleeding and big bruises are OK. Fear of light and vomiting are not (unless your child suffers from migraine).

You will need to explain or illustrate to your doctor that your child has suffered a blow or sharp knock to the head and describe the severity of the symptoms.

BURNS AND SCALDS

When assessing burns, one of the first rules is 'the more they scream, the less the damage'.

The skin has many layers and the more severe the burn, the deeper the wound goes but the less painful it is, as nerve endings will be obliterated.

In treating you should:

1. Stop the burning by flooding the injured part with cold water for at least ten minutes. This will stop the burning, relieve the pain and prevent further tissue damage. If cold water is not available, any cold, harmless liquid will do, including canned drinks, juice or even milk.

2. Carefully remove the clothing *unless it is sticking to the burn*. Remove watches or jewellery from the burnt area before it starts to swell.

3. Minimise the risk of infection by covering the area, ideally with a sterile, non-porous dressing or any clean, non-fluffy material. The large area of skin damage often involved in burns is extremely susceptible to infection. A freshly laundered cotton sheet, clean plastic bag or cling film make good temporary shields until the wound can be properly dressed.

4. If possible, take your child to a hospital to have the wound cleaned and dressed properly. If you are unsure about changing the dressing, ask for advice. If medical advice is unavailable, see page 262, and keep the injury sterile and dressed as you would with other skin injuries.

5. Give your child plenty of fluids.

If the wound becomes infected, antibiotics will be necessary.

The best relief from pain and swelling is paracetamol syrup (Disprol/Calpol).

DO NOT

1. Break blisters. If you do, you will invite infection.

2. Apply ointments or creams, even those marketed and sold as 'burn creams'. They are rarely effective and often damaging.

The fats or oils in the ointments hold the heat into the skin and so exacerbate the damaging process.

Paris's scalding

Simon was on the telephone and I was in the kitchen. In between us darted our forever busy little Paris. Suddenly, howls of surprise, then pain caused Simon to drop the phone and me to scream. Paris was gripping an upside-down, empty mug that he could barely have reached. His body was bright pink and still steaming as the coffee ran down him. His eyelids, cheeks, chest and tummy were burned.

He was wearing a nappy when he grabbed my coffee off the kitchen table and poured it down himself. It had channelled directly into his nappy and bathed his groin in scalding fluid. As a result his 'beep beep' (as Paris calls it) was scorched. Paris was howling in agony.

I tried 'burn' cream but realised, immediately, that it was useless and would not limit the damage. Instead, Simon and I raced up to the shower and began to douse Paris in cold water. Despite his protests, instinct told us that this was the best way. It was worth it. He had two blisters and no scars. The pain is, of course, forgotten.

ELECTRIC SHOCKS

Low standards of health and safety in many parts of the world result in unsafe electrics. Loose wires, frayed flexes and absent fuses can lead to electric shock.

Children should be taught as soon as possible that electricity and water are a fatal combination.

In mild cases, the patient can suffer mild burns but, in severe cases, a child might lose consciousness and his heart might stop.

What to do

The most important point is to separate your child from the source of electricity before touching them. If not, you may be shocked too, and thereby unable to help them.

If possible, unplug the source or separate your child from the electricity supply using wood (branch, broom etc.), plastic or newspaper, or anything non-conductive that will protect you. If you have no choice, grab a child by its clothing and drag him away. Once the contact has been broken, check for burns. Limit burn damage with cold water and sterile dressing. If a child is suffering from shock you may need to resuscitate him. If a child is breathing but unconscious, place him in the recovery position (see page 284).

BLEEDING AND TRAUMA

Abrasions, grazes and minor cuts are rarely serious, provided that nothing remains embedded in the skin and your child is up to date with his tetanus vaccinations. Even pinpricks can spread tetanus.

All mammalian animal bites and scratches which draw blood should be taken very seriously. Even if the wound is superficial, rabies could have been transmitted and so thorough cleaning and hospital treatment is necessary (see page 254).

Deeper cuts and lacerations, especially those to the scalp, often appear worse than they are, but don't panic, and act quickly to limit the bleeding.

Treatment of severe external bleeding

1. Apply pressure to the wound. Use a pad if possible, otherwise use your bare hands. If there is something stuck in the wound, such as piece of glass, do not attempt to remove it, as this may cause more damage and make the bleeding worse. Instead, apply pressure to either side of the wound to compress the ends of the damaged blood vessels.
2. Elevate the injury above the level of the heart to stem the flow of blood to the area. This can be made easier by lying the child down on the floor.
3. Apply a pad or bandage if available. Alternatively, continue to grip the wound and apply pressure to the wound with your hands.
4. If bleeding is severe you might need to treat your child for shock (see below).
5. Call for medical help.

Internal bleeding

Your child may present with the following symptoms after a trauma or accidental ingestion:

- Pallor
- Cold, clammy skin

- Fast, weak pulse
- Pain
- Thirst
- Restlessness and confusion
- Bleeding from orifices

If you suspect internal bleeding:

1. Lie the child down and, if possible, raise the legs.
2. Call for an ambulance or medical assistance.
3. Insulate from the cold.
4. Loosen constricting clothing.
5. Check and, if possible, record pulse, respiration, and levels of response every ten minutes.
6. Treat for shock (see below).

SHOCK

Shock occurs if the blood pressure drops, or if there is a reduction in the amount of circulating body fluid as a result of severe bleeding, leakage of fluid from burns and vomiting with diarrhoea.

Symptoms

Initial signs are a rapid and pale, cold, clammy skin.

Further signs:

- Weakness and dizziness
- Nausea, possibly with vomiting
- Thirst
- Rapid shallow breathing
- A fast, weak pulse

As the oxygen supply to the brain dwindles, the child will become restless and anxious, and might yawn or gasp for air, eventually becoming unconscious.

Treatment

1. First remove or treat the cause.
2. Lie the child down keeping the head down.
3. Raise the legs.
4. Loosen tight clothing.
5. Insulate from the cold.
6. Check and record breathing, pulse and response levels.

DO NOT allow the child to move.

DO NOT allow the child to eat or drink.

Reassure them constantly and stay by their side.

If bleeding is under control and there is no danger of shock developing, you must then concentrate on minimising the risk of infection (see page 262).

FRACTURES

Not all fractures are immediately obvious. Some, known as Greenstick fractures, which are common in children, are splits in young bone and can be missed by a doctor and even on an x-ray.

The extent of the pain and the difficulty in moving a part of the body indicate that a fracture could have occurred. The pain will not abate and your child might cry ceaselessly for hours if untreated. They will refuse to let you touch the limb.

There can be signs of shock if a thigh, rib or pelvis is fractured.

Treatment

1. Urge your child to keep still.
2. Support the injured limb.
3. Immobilise the site of the fracture by splintage or with your hands. Use anything available for a splint, such as a branch, a thick, rolled-up newspaper, or adjacent leg.
4. Use a bandage, if available, or strips of cloth to bind the fracture, but check that it is not tight enough to interfere with circulation.
5. Treat for shock (see above).
6. If possible, raise the injured limb and check the circulation beyond the bandaging every ten minutes.
7. If the fracture is open and bleeding, there is a great risk of infection in the bone, which can fester long after the fracture has healed and is notoriously difficult to clear up. You need to ensure that your child is treated with high doses of fairly aggressive antibiotics and be absolutely religious about administering them.

EYE INJURIES

If a foreign body or chemical gets into the eye, lie your child down and try to stop him rubbing it. A foreign body may scratch the surface of the eyeball and cause intense pain and/or infection later.

Hold the eye open and flush it with plenty of water, preferably under a running tap. Unless there is something embedded in the eyeball, you should be able to flush the foreign body into the corner of the eye then remove it with the corner of a tissue. Objects embedded in the eye should not be touched and it is imperative that the child is prevented from rubbing. Medical attention is needed.

If your child's eye still feels gritty and painful once the object has been removed, there could be some superficial damage to the surface of the eye that might lead to infection. Place a sterile pad over the eye and keep in place until the eye settles. Keep a check on it and if it becomes red and weepy, your child will need antibiotics. If you do not have any antibiotic eye ointments or drops, oral antibiotics will work, but could take a little longer. Occasionally, sensitivity to antibiotics applied directly to the eye will cause swelling that will necessitate discontinuation of their use.

After trauma or injury, the eye might be cut or bloodshot. Cuts to the eye need protection with a sterile pad and medical attention. A bloodshot eye often looks worse than it is.

POISONING

Despite the assumption that most poisons have a specific antidote, most do not.

Treatment after acute poisoning involves a basic set of rules which help the patient to recover. These include:

1. Monitoring the casualty's consciousness, breathing and heart rate and resuscitating if necessary.
2. Placing them in the recovery position (see page 284) and, if they will not lie still, holding them on their side or facing downwards so as to prevent inhalation of any vomit.
3. Seeking medical help.
4. Trying to identify the causative agent which could help the doctor to decide whether to pump the stomach, induce vomiting or administer an oral absorbent/neutraliser, for example, activated charcoal.

DO NOT induce vomiting yourself. You might cause further

harm if the substance ingested was caustic. In addition, vomiting may cause some of the substance to be transferred to the lungs, resulting in further serious complications and inflammation. (The exception would be drug poisoning – see below.)

DO NOT give a concentrated salt solution to induce vomiting. It is toxic in its own right.

If, once you reach medical help, the doctor decides that your child should be made to vomit, they are most likely to administer a medicine called Ipecacuana which is safe and effective.

Poisonous plants

In the UK there are few poisonous plants and you will doubtless recognise them through instruction you had as a child.

In tropical countries, plants containing poisonous substances are more common and so is the incidence of toxicity. The greatest risks are always to children, who need lower amounts to be fatal, yet are also more likely to be the inquisitive victims.

Even plants normally eaten by the locals can be toxic if collected and prepared by the inexperienced tourist. Cassava, plantain, ackee, yam and cycads are all potentially lethal.

Treatment
See above, steps 1–4.

Household poisons

These are very dangerous, but it is relatively rare for children to drink them in any quantity. Many are more dangerous due to the corrosive effects on the mouth, oesophagus and stomach than they are if absorbed into the blood stream. You should never make a child vomit as you could do more damage, especially if the substance gets into the lungs. If your child will not stay in the recovery position, hold them on the side or face down so that they will not inhale if they do vomit.

The burning caused by oil-based fuels and corrosive substances such as paraffin/kerosene, petrol, bleach, weed killers and disinfectant can be eased by drinking milk or water. Pesticides and herbicides need careful and specific management. You must seek hospital treatment and take the bottle of substance with you to aid the diagnosis.

Drug poisoning

Some of the drugs you might be carrying are highly poisonous, for example, paracetamol. If you are more than four hours away from medical help, your child is more likely to survive if they vomit. Never use salt water; use the gag reflex – a normal reflex elicited by touching the soft palate in the back of the throat, which induces retching and vomiting. This reflex is best evoked, very basically, by putting your fingers into your child's mouth and touching the back of the throat until they vomit.

Alcohol poisoning

Alcohol is extremely dangerous to children. Inhalation and choking on vomit is a real risk. Hypothermia can be a complication. There can also be dehydration with a dangerous lowering of blood sugar levels. Position your child so that they will not inhale their vomit, wrap them up and give them plenty of sweet drinks.

DROWNING

If, having been under water, your child is unconscious but still breathing, place them in the recovery position (see page 284) and continuously check on their breathing.

Replace wet clothing and protect the child from cold. Submersion in cold water can cause hypothermia. If necessary, give resuscitation and don't give up, especially if the child has been under cold water. The cold slows down the metabolism and children can still be revived after over 30 minutes under water.

15 First Aid Treatment

The aim of first aid is to limit the damage of a condition, aid recovery and preserve life.

ACTION IN AN EMERGENCY:
ARTIFICIAL RESPIRATION

1. Assess the situation.

   In an emergency, you will first need to carefully assess the situation and ensure that there is no further danger to your child or yourself. Don't panic. If you remain calm and logical and act quickly, you will be able to help and could save your child's life.

2. Carry your child to a safe place, depending on the type of emergency. Act appropriately (see above) to limit the damage and minimise the risk of infection.

3. Assess the casualty.

   Shake the child by the shoulders, ask a question and establish whether the child is:

   (a) **Responding and fully conscious**

   Action: treat the injury, calm the child and place them in the recovery position (see page 284).

   (b) **Unconscious but breathing, with pulse present**

   Action:

   • Treat any life-threatening injury.

   • Check that there is no obstruction to the airway. If necessary, tilt the child's head well back to open the airway (see Figure 8).

   • Place in recovery position and call for help.

   (c) **Not breathing but has a pulse**

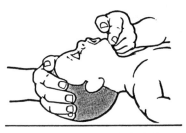

Figure 8. How to position the head of a baby or young child when opening the airway.

Look, listen and feel for breathing for five seconds before judging that breathing has stopped. Look for chest movement. Listen for breathing sounds and feel for breath against your cheek.

Action required for babies and young children:
You must help babies and children under seven years old to breathe by giving artificial respiration for one minute.
- Lay the baby or child flat on his back.
- Open the airway by placing one hand on his forehead and two fingers of your other hand under the point of the chin (place just one finger under a baby's chin), lift the jaw and then tilt the head back gently (see Figure 8).
- Check for, and remove, any obvious obstruction to breathing, by sweeping one finger around inside the casualty's mouth.
- Seal your lips tightly around the nose and mouth of a baby. In small children, pinch the nose firmly to prevent air escaping and seal your lips over the mouth. Keep your fingers positioned under the jaw and the head tilted back.
- Breathe into the lungs until the chest rises. Repeat this five times.
- Check the pulse and look for signs of recovery. If the pulse is absent, begin cardio-pulmonary resuscitation (see below).
- If the pulse is present, continue artificial respiration for one minute.
- Get medical assistance.

Action required for children over eight years old and adults:
- Place the casualty flat on his back.
- Open the airway by placing one hand on the forehead and two fingers under the point of the chin, lift the jaw and then gently tilt the head well back (see Figure 9).
- Check for, and remove, any obvious obstruction to breathing by sweeping one finger around inside the casualty's mouth.
- Using your thumb and index finger, pinch the casualty's nose firmly so that the nostrils are closed. This will prevent the air that you breath into the airways from escaping.
- Take a deep breath then seal your mouth firmly over the casualty's. Blow until the chest rises and continue to blow for a couple of seconds to ensure that the lungs are fully inflated.
- Keep your hands in position, but remove your lips and allow the lungs time to deflate fully by noting the fall of the chest.
- Repeat mouth-to-mouth resuscitation. Give ten breaths of artificial respiration, call for medical assistance, then continue artificial respiration at a rate of ten per minute. Check for a pulse every ten breaths and watch for signs of recovery until help arrives.
- If breathing begins again, place the casualty in the recovery position (see page 284).

If breathing has stopped, you will need to begin artificial respiration immediately. Any delay will starve the brain of oxygen and, after eight minutes, your child will be unlikely to make a full recovery. Artificial respiration will keep a supply of oxygenated blood flowing to the brain, and will ensure that your child should be able to regain consciousness and recover completely.

(d) **Not breathing and pulse is absent**
- Continue to check for a pulse for five seconds before deciding that it is absent. This is best done in babies by using two of your fingers to feel for a pulse in the neck or the groin. In children and adults, check for a pulse in the neck. Slide your fingers between the Adam's apple and the large muscle alongside it.

Figure 9. Failure to maintain a proper airway, as indicated in the left-hand picture, is a common cause of avoidable death in unconscious patients. The right-hand picture shows how the airway becomes unblocked once the head is tilted back.

- Call for medical assistance then begin cardio-pulmonary resuscitation (CPR) by alternate chest compressions and mouth-to-mouth ventilation.
- Chest compressions massage the heart so that it is able to pump a supply of blood around the body and should be carried out as follows:

In babies:

- Place your index and middle fingers one finger's width beneath the nipple line and press down to approximately one third the depth of the chest.
- Do this five times in about three seconds
- Give one breath of ventilation, then repeat the five chest compressions.
- Alternate one breath to five compressions until help arrives. Constantly check for signs of recovery.

In children aged 1–7 years:

- Position the heel of one hand over the lower portion of the breastbone and press down sharply to approximately one third the depth of the chest.
- Do this five times in about three seconds then give one breath of ventilation.
- Repeatedly alternate one breath to five compressions until help arrives. Constantly check for signs of recovery.

In children aged 8 years old and over (and adults):

- Interlock the fingers of each of your hands over the casualty's breastbone using the heels of your hands to compress the chest.
- Lean well over the casualty with your arms straight. Press down vertically to depress the breastbone by approximately two inches.

- Do this fifteen times in approximately nine seconds then give two breaths of ventilation.

Repeatedly alternate fifteen compressions to two ventilations until help arrives or there are signs of recovery.

NB: It is important that you are firm and put your weight behind heart massage. Most beginners are likely to be too gentle. Remember that you have to push the breast bone down, pumping blood out of the heart underneath, to keep the brain alive.

SUMMARY

After assessing the casualty, remember 'ABC'
A = Airways: open the airway by tilting the head back.
B = Breathing: check the breathing.
C = Circulation: check the pulse.

RECOVERY POSITION

For babies under 1:
- Cradle your baby on his side, in your arms.
- Keep the head tilted downwards to prevent the inhalation of vomit or choking on the tongue.

For all children over the age of 1 year and adults:
- Lie the casualty on the back and extend the limbs.
- Open the airway by placing two fingers under the point of the chin and one hand on the forehead, lifting the jaw and tilting the head well back.
- Position the arm nearest to yourself flat on the floor and bent at a right angle to the body.
- Reach across the casualty and bring the furthest arm across the chest, placing the back of the hand against the cheek. At the same time, bend the casualty's far leg.

- Roll the child towards you on to the hand against his cheek and on to his side.
- Ensure that the airway is open.
- Bend the casualty's knee so that it is at right angles to the body.
- Call for medical assistance if it is available.
- Monitor and, if possible, record the breathing and pulse every ten minutes.

NB: If you suspect that the neck is injured, it should be supported as the casualty is placed into the recovery position.

16 Epilogue: Returning Home

- You must complete your course of malaria tablets for four weeks after your return home.
- Any persistent signs of illness should be discussed with your doctor. You must explain where you travelled to and which illnesses you may have been exposed to.

Fever

When high fever presents up to a year after travel to a malarial region, malaria is a possible cause and should be tested for.

Most doctors in the UK will never have seen a case of malaria, and if you neglect to mention to your doctor that you have been abroad they could diagnose the symptoms as flu. Malaria is considered to be the most commonly misdiagnosed illness in the UK. The disease is a good mimic of many other illnesses in its early stages and it is urgent that your children undergo a blood test to exclude it as the cause of high temperature following their return from a malarial region, even if the full course of recommended anti-malarial drugs has been completed.

Pneumonia (including Legionnaire's disease and other atypical pneumonias), hepatitis and schistosomiasis may otherwise be the cause.

Diarrhoea

Diarrhoea associated with travel usually occurs while away or shortly after returning home. Most will be bacterial or viral and short lived. Persistent diarrhoea after tropical travel is most likely to be amoebic dysentery, giardiasis or cyclospora. Intestinal worms should also be considered.

Diseases such as amoebiasis are so rare in the UK that doctors are unlikely to diagnose persistent diarrhoea as a tropical disease unless you mention to your doctor that your child might have been exposed to infection. Discuss where you have been, the exact symptoms and the duration of the diarrhoea to help your doctor, who may then suggest that a stool sample is tested for parasites.

If you neglect to mention that your child may have picked up the infection abroad, your doctor may look for other explanations, such as irritable bowel syndrome or gluten sensitivity.

If you have been to a malarial region mention it. Malaria can disguise itself as a diarrhoeal illness.

Hepatitis

The incubation period for hepatitis is 3–5 weeks, and so symptoms are likely to develop after returning from your trip abroad (see page 135). If you have travelled into a region where your child could have been exposed to hepatitis A without having been immunised, you must mention this to your doctor who will then be able to screen for and treat the disease more quickly.

Rabies

Rabies can take a few years to develop. If your child has been bitten abroad you should have travelled home immediately to receive treatment or been treated there and then. However, in the unlikely event of your child presenting with any of the symptoms of rabies (see page 146) in the future always mention this to your doctor.

Schistosomiasis

Schistosomiasis symptoms can develop weeks or months after exposure. Even if your children are symptom free but have been at risk of exposure at any time during their trip abroad you should visit your doctor on your return home and request a blood test. The timing of the blood test is important, as it may not be positive until three months after initial infection.

Those at most risk of having picked up the infection are those who have been wading or swimming in African lakes, rivers or in other areas where the disease is common (see page 252).

* * *

Tropical disease can be picked up and, although a carrier can remain symptomless for years, there may be an impact on health in future life. If you have any concerns or suspect that your child might have picked up any illnesses, or if your child fell ill abroad and appeared perfectly healthy by the time you returned home, it is still important to discuss it with your doctor. Most are happy to support and screen for anything that is of concern to you.

One week after we returned from the Seychelles with Paris he developed a rash. While abroad we had been in casualty with him following an accident where he had gashed his wrist deeply and needed stitches. The casualty department had been crammed full with sick children, and although we were rushed straight through into a treatment room and although after being treated Paris was taken outside in the fresh air while I collected the prescription, I am certain this is where he picked something up.

The rash was initially quite faint, but seemed worse after a crying fit. I called the doctor out, but by the time he arrived the rash didn't look as red and he was clearly deeply irritated with me. When I told him I was very worried because we had been in a casualty department abroad he dismissed the information as if I was being quite alarmist. However, two days later the rash suddenly erupted and we took Paris to hospital. The hospital treated the information so seriously we were put into isolation immediately and although Paris was pink and miserable rather than being gravely ill, we were kept in for observation and Paris was monitored throughout the night.

The next morning Paris was bright as a button although the rash was still in evidence. We were sent home with the diagnosis as measles (although he had already had his MMR) or a similar virus.

The best doctors listen to a parent's instincts and should never make you feel paranoid. A doctor should always talk things through with you, even if you then decide between you that everything is fine and no screening is necessary.